A Walk in the Spring Rain
and
The Orchard Children

Rachel Maddux

A Walk in the Spring Rain
and
The Orchard Children

*Edited, with an introduction,
by Nancy A. Walker*

THE RACHEL MADDUX SERIES
VOLUME 3

The University of Tennessee Press / Knoxville

Lines from "Long Black Veil" by Marijohn Wilkin and Danny Dill. Copyright © 1959, Cedarwood
Publishing Co., Inc. Reprinted by permission. Lines from "Going to Memphis" (O! Berta), words
and music by Holly Dew. Collected, adapted, and arranged by Alan Lomax. New words and music arranged by Johnny Cash. Copyright © 1959, 1960, Ludlow Music, Inc.—Johnny Cash Music,
Inc., New York, New York. Reprinted by permission.

The paper in this book meets the minimum requirements of the
American National Standard for Permanence of Paper for Printed
Library Materials. ∞   The binding materials have been chosen
for strength and durability.

Library of Congress Cataloging in Publication Data
Maddux, Rachel, 1913–1983.
    [Walk in the spring rain]
    A walk in the spring rain, and The orchard children / Rachel Maddus: edited, with an
introduction, by Nancy Walker.
        p.   cm.
    ISBN 0–87049–757–X (cloth: alk. paper)
    1. Maddux, Rachel, 1913-1983—Homes and haunts—Tennessee—Houston
County. 2. Novelists, American—20th century—Biography. 3. Farm life—
Tennessee—Houston County. 4. Nubian goats.   I. Walker, Nancy A., 1942-
II. Maddux, Rachel, 1913-1983. Orchard children. 1993 III. Title.
PS3563.A3395W35   1993
813'.54—dc20   92-4980   CIP

Contents

Introduction

The two works by Rachel Maddux reprinted in this volume could be called her "Tennessee" books. Both were written after Maddux and her husband, King Baker, moved to Houston County, Tennessee, in 1960, and both draw upon her experiences with and perceptions of life in that area in the 1960s and 1970s. *A Walk in the Spring Rain* is a novel, and *The Orchard Children* is nonfiction, but both books deal with discovery, love, and loss—themes that transcend a specific place.

Rachel Maddux loved cats, and if it is true that cats have nine lives, I think she would be pleased that this is the fifth life her remarkably moving novel *A Walk in the Spring Rain* has had. First published in 1966 by Doubleday, it was reissued in paperback by Avon in 1978. A film version of the novel, starring Ingrid Bergman and Anthony Quinn, premiered in 1970, and the text of the novel was included in the book *Fiction into Film*, published by the University of Tennessee Press later that year. *Fiction into Film* also includes the film script and an account of the process by which the novel was adapted for the screen. And now, cat-like, *A Walk in the Spring Rain* makes its fifth appearance.

What makes this short novel so compelling? It is a love story—the most popular theme in human narrative. But this is no ordinary love story. It does not have a "happily ever after" ending, with the lovers united; it begins and ends in separation and memories. Yet neither is the story tragic or sentimental, despite the comparison with Edith Wharton's *Ethan Frome* on the original dust jacket. Indeed, it affirms the power and possibility of human love, at any age and in any circumstances. As the reviewer for *Harper's* wrote upon the initial publication in 1966, "It is good to find a book written with such economy which seems to lack none of life's dimensions."

Further, Libby Meredith and Will Workman are an unlikely couple. Libby is the forty-nine-year-old wife of a college professor—an educated, sophisticated woman who likes the music of Bartók and is vice-president of the League of Women Voters in her California community. Will is a handyman in the hills of West Virginia, where Libby and her husband, Roger, spend several months while Roger is on sabbatical. "You'll never meet nobody like me," Will tells Libby, and his statement takes on a resonance beyond a simple comment on cultural differences as Libby realizes that she has never met—and will never meet—anyone else with Will's capacity for love: a love that makes no demands, imposes no restrictions.

The delicacy and fluidity of Maddux's style in this novel derive in large measure from her imagining Libby Meredith accompanied by a musical score that represents her emotional state. Maddux told friends that she frequently heard the "music" of a work of fiction before she wrote it; and, in *A Walk in the Spring Rain*, she makes this explicit by introducing Libby against the background of her music, a "pleasant enough melody" with an undercurrent of anguish—a bassoon or a cello—that builds until it overwhelms the melody, just as the love of Will Workman is overwhelming and unforgettable. The novel also owes its intensity to its theme of discovery, not only the discovery of a capacity for love in middle age that transforms Libby, but also discovery of place. Although the novel is set in West Virginia, it owes much of its specific sense of locale to Rachel Maddux's experience of Houston County, Tennessee.

In 1958, Katherine and George Brown bought five hundred acres of land in rural Houston County and named it "Green Kingdom Acres"—a name inspired by the title of Maddux's first novel, *The Green Kingdom*, published the year before. Katherine Brown, a painter, and Rachel Maddux had been friends since 1938, when they met in Kansas City, and the Browns' enthusiasm for their acres of rolling, tree-covered hills lured Maddux and her husband first for a visit in 1959 and subsequently to purchase part of the Browns' land and move to Tennessee in 1960. Baker's ambition was to start an apple orchard, which he did; Maddux set out to learn as much as she could about the natural surroundings of her new home and soon began to write *A Walk in the Spring Rain*. The novel was completed in a short time; Maddux chose deliberately to write a work of novella length after spending nearly twenty years on *The Green Kingdom*.

Some of Libby Meredith's discoveries in the novel, then, are Rachel Maddux's discoveries. The scene in which Will Workman shows Libby watercress growing in the "branch," for example, is quite similar to an experience that Maddux described to her friend Savington Crampton in a letter dated February 28, 1960; like Libby, Maddux was distressed that the only fresh vegetable available in the local market was cabbage, so she was pleased to find "unbelieveably green watercress" in a stream on the Browns' property, and reports "washing a carload of it free from pieces of oak leaves caught in the roots in order to get one small salad bowl full."

Another discovery that the novel draws from Maddux's life in Tennessee is Nubian goats, which she began to raise soon after the move to Houston County. In her 1977 nonfiction work *The Orchard Children*, Maddux describes purchasing and raising two baby Nubians, which she valued as much for their beauty and gentleness as for the milk they eventually produced. Friends in Houston County remember Maddux offering goat's milk at the county fair and hitching the goats to a small cart to participate in the St. Patrick's Day parade in nearby Erin, Tennessee. In the novel, Maddux uses the goats to awaken in Libby a tenderness she had forgotten how to feel—a tenderness that Will Workman needs in his affection-starved life. The love that develops between these two has less to do with grand passion than with nurturance—a reaching out to another person to soothe what hurts, to supply what is lacking.

Ironically, it is this nurturance in another form that ends the relationship between Libby and Will, when the needs of her family require that she and her husband return to California before their year in the country is over. (One reason why the film version of *A Walk in the Spring Rain* is less satisfying than the novel is that their reason for leaving has to do not with compelling family necessity but instead with Roger's desire to go home, so that Libby must choose between her husband and Will. The change has the effect of making the story more conventional, removing much of its power.) Yet in an important way the relationship does not end at all. Not only does Will's direct and necessary love live on in Libby's imagination, but the watercress, the goats, and the sudden glory of an early-spring red-bud tree in bloom have altered the fundamental rhythms of her life.

A Walk in the Spring Rain might be compared with Kate Chopin's *The Awakening*. In both novels, a woman is jolted from her familiar domestic routine by a man who represents a different set of cultural realities. In Chopin's novel, Robert LeBrun embodies the sensuousness of the French Creoles, in contrast to Edna's Kentucky Presbyterian background. But the essential difference is that whereas Chopin insists on the exceptional nature of her central character—culminating in her isolated death by drowning—Maddux instead creates in Libby Meredith a sort of Everywoman, who buys lamb chops while the music of longing and loss fills her heart. The universality of this small, perfect story is best expressed by Ingrid Bergman, who played Libby Meredith in the film. Writing to Rachel Maddux after the film was released, Bergman commented, "There are so many 'Libbys' in the world."

The Orchard Children, first published in 1977, is the account of Maddux and Baker's unsuccessful attempt to adopt two foster children. In its emphasis on the importance of childhood, *The Orchard Children* has affinities with Maddux's only other autobiographical work, *Communication*, written in 1941 when she was twenty-eight and published in 1991 by the University of Tennessee Press. Just as one of the central themes of *Communication* is the need to take children seriously on their own terms—to pay attention to their requirements for honesty and affection—so the message of *The Orchard Children* is that the legal system, which determines who will raise abused or abandoned children, seems often to ignore the best interests of the children themselves.

Even a nonfiction work is shaped by its author, and Maddux sets the story of the children she calls Marilyn and Robbie in a larger context of nurturing, of helping young things to grow. The initial chapters of the book describe the beginnings of King Baker's orchard, and of Rachel Maddux's raising of the Nubian goats that also figure prominently in *A Walk in the Spring Rain*. Young goats and young apple trees thus anticipate the arrival of five-year-old Marilyn and three-year-old Robbie, whose parents have abandoned them to the care of their grandmother. Fittingly, too, the book concludes with an account of the orchard's yield of apples and peaches, measured against the growth of Melissa, the girl whom Maddux and Baker did later adopt.

In between is the story of Maddux and Baker, a childless, middle-aged couple recently transplanted to Tennessee from California, having their lives transformed by their efforts to provide stability for and instill trust in two children who have known little besides rootlessness and dishonesty. Their success in providing a home for the children makes all the more painful the custody battle that ensues when the children's parents are reunited and return to claim the children for whom they have shown so little responsibility. Maddux is most upset because no one seems concerned to find out who the children themselves prefer to be raised by; and when the natural parents are awarded custody, her greatest concern is that the children will feel abandoned by her just as they have been previously by their own parents.

The final irony is that, after moving with their parents first to Chicago and then to Detroit, Marilyn and Robbie end up back with their grandmother in Houston County when the parents are again—this time permanently—separated. The children's father was heard to remark that it was "too bad" that they had not left Marilyn and Robbie with Maddux and Baker.

It took Rachel Maddux a long time to write *The Orchard Children*. The court case that blocked the adoption of Marilyn and Robbie was concluded shortly before the assassination of President John F. Kennedy in the fall of 1963, and the book was not published until 1977. During the intervening years, Maddux and her husband were busy raising Melissa, whom they had adopted as an infant, and the pain of the loss of Marilyn and Robbie had to be put into perspective. But there are clues in *The Orchard Children* to another reason for the delay.

Maddux told friends that the most difficult part of writing *The Orchard Children* was deciding what to leave out, and much of what she chose to downplay in the book had to do with the way in which she and her husband were considered outsiders in this rural Tennessee community. She writes in *The Orchard Children* of the extended kinship networks that unite people in the rural South, and hints at the cycles of poverty and lack of education that perpetuate one another, but she does not mention that a college-educated couple with liberal social and political convictions were bound to be the targets of resentment in such a community in the early 1960s. Whether their position as outsiders, as "different," had any bearing on the judge's decision about Marilyn and Robbie is impossible to say at this distance, but Maddux was careful to present the outcome as the result of a system rather than the attitudes of a community.

Maddux's universalizing of her story resulted, as with *A Walk in the Spring Rain*, in a wider audience for *The Orchard Children*. The book inspired a CBS television documentary, titled "Who Will Save the Children?" and starring Shirley Jones and Len Cariou, which was aired in December of 1978.

Nancy A. Walker
Vanderbilt University
December 1991

A Walk in the Spring Rain

My thanks to Mr. J. D. Lewis, County Agent, Houston County, Tennessee, and his West Virginia colleagues for checking and verifying the flora and fauna which are the background of this story.

—Rachel Maddux

Being the thoughts of
Mrs. Roger Meredith on her way home
from market . . .

Libby Meredith was in the market buying lamb chops for her
grandchild's dinner when one of those quick, California showers
came up. The butcher liked Mrs. Meredith. Most people did. She had
a friendly, pleasant manner.

The good, close family in which she had been reared, the dental
and medical care they had given her, the good schooling, the twenty-
five years of marriage to Roger Meredith, now professor of law at the
university, the beautiful daughter Ellen, the lovely grandson Bucky—
they had all marked her, these things. The sweet smile, the keen
mind, the passion for justice, the good humor, they were all obvious,
there for the butcher or anyone else to see while Libby waited for the
shower to be over. Of course, if you had known her well, you would
have seen the lines of strain, new there since Ellen's illness. When the
shower ended, Libby left the market and began walking to Ellen's
house, where she and Roger were staying temporarily. Mark, Ellen's
husband, had asked them to, mostly because of Bucky, Libby supposed, and it seemed the best thing for the present.

Libby waited for the red light at the boulevard, stepping down
from the curb as the light turned green. A car driven by a drunken,

half-crazy boy came within inches of killing her and, instinctively, she made an agile leap to safety. A few blocks further on, she met Molly Devon, widow of her husband's friend and colleague. Molly, on the arm of her young lover, teetering on heels too high, straining to hold her posture in a dress too tight, said all the tactless things about Ellen and had no realization that Libby, responding correctly and mechanically, heard not a word she said.

Nor did Libby hear the ambulance siren a few blocks later, or notice that new people were moving into the Evans' apartment.

How is it the woman threaded her way in and out of drunken drivers, ambulance sirens, Molly Devon's chatter, completely unaware? How did it happen that she arrived at the house where Ellen lay dying, the lamb chops still in her hand, and had no memory of the journey? She remembered coming out of the market and smelling the fresh, after-shower air. She remembered seeing, in a puddle, the reflection of blue sky and white clouds and of being seized by a terrible anguish.

If you were to set her to music, now, on this walk to Ellen's house (of which she had no memory), why you would have a pleasant enough melody to begin with. It would need a showing of musical competence and sophistication, moving in a brisk, healthy tempo, with perhaps a faint suggestion of ambulance sirens and the drunk boy's screaming brakes (which Libby only dimly heard). There would be that quite conventional interlude with Molly Devon, too.

But somehow there would begin to intrude, beneath the pleasant melody, the quite incongruous note of a bassoon (or, really, wasn't it more like a cello?) that would almost, at first, be buried. Yet somehow, insinuatingly, it would prevail and endure and gradually increase until it had swallowed everything else. So that by the time Libby reached Ellen's driveway (where the leaves lay, accusingly, still unraked) the bassoon, or perhaps it was really more like a cello, would have drowned or devoured every other sound and become the true sound, a human being's desperate cry for help.

For if she remembered nothing of the walk at all (and it frightened her that she didn't) she remembered the rain puddle with clear, blue sky and the white clouds mirrored in it. She remembered the moment of anguish.

What was it really like to her, that moment (a bassoon, a cello, a piece of jagged glass)? Where was Libby, if she couldn't remember where she had been?

I

While I was in the market buying lamb chops for my grandson's dinner, one of those brief California showers came up. I waited for it to be over and then walked out into the lovely fresh after-shower smell. There were still very interesting clouds in the sky and, as I saw them reflected so vividly in a clear sidewalk puddle, I was suddenly filled with anguish as sharp as one feels anguish at twenty. Why do people think that it will or it should be different at fifty? It is exactly the same.

But no, it is not the same, for I did not drop the lamb chops in the puddle, and at twenty I should have. I go about like this all the time with a pelvis laden and leaden with the longing for love of Will Workman and yet no one notices. It is well corseted, this terrible longing, and for our present circumstances, quite expensively so.

I should, I suppose, see Olga Marshall, our family obstetrician, about it. She took care of Ellen when Bucky was born. But after all, how can I? Olga and I are old friends. We have served on so many committees together and learned to expect reason-

able behavior of each other—how can I make myself out such a
fool before her? Not that she would laugh, I don't mean that.
She is, first of all a doctor and a good one and, as a patient, I
know I could count on her sympathy and understanding and
good advice, particularly now that she knows about Ellen. No, I
needn't fear Olga's opinion. After all, no one's could match my
own for disparagement, for in my bitter moments I can see it
perfectly as a very ordinary and well-documented manifestation
of middle age. Even I see myself as ridiculous, lapping up compliments like a schoolgirl in that last, desperate effort to prove
myself sexually attractive.

There are perhaps new hormone shots or tranquilizers that
would make the whole thing disappear and put my mind clear
and unconfused upon the very formidable future facing Roger
and Mark and Bucky and me. But I don't *want* it to disappear. I
don't want it to be as nothing. I don't even want to see it in
perspective. I cling even to this terrible anguish, this awful
longing, for the memories it brings me of being, however ridicu-
lously, *alive*.

Will never seems ridiculous to me, never any way but
beautiful and tragically alive.

Oh, in the beginning, I laughed at him, yes. The West
Virginia hill country speech is so startling when one has never
heard it before. The imitations one hears on television and
believes to be exaggerated for comic effect are, on the contrary,
quite pale beside the real thing. Of course one doesn't say
"hillbilly" there; that is rather an insult. "And don't call it
hillbilly music," Mary Evans said to me when they first talked
about letting us have their place for Roger's year of leave, "the
way I did. Remember, they call it *country* music."

Country music. To think that I, a Bartók fan, when I can

get someone to sit with Bucky, sometimes steal away now for an hour or so, like a person with a secret, shameful vice, to hunt out those awful small cafes where they have the tunes on jukeboxes. I sit drinking reheated coffee, or sometimes beer, and pump dimes into the neon monstrosities. Not that the tunes sound good to me. They are dull and, in fact, they all seem to be the same tune, or rather, as Roger said, there are two tunes—the sad and the fast one. The lyrics are ludicrously sentimental.

But they evoke. They evoke something of Will Workman for me because he liked them. Sometimes I can still find *Far, Far Away* on a jukebox and then I remember Will's saying, "Oh, you listen to that one now. It's awful pretty, and the words are laid out just right."

Why don't I have the records at home and play them on my own player? Because I simply couldn't face their laughter at home. They would think I had gone mad and, as I say, I don't even like them. And then, of course, with Ellen in this terrible condition, such raucous sounds would set everyone's nerves on edge.

It was less than a year ago Mary Evans said that to me about country music. It seems impossible that in so little time our lives could have changed so drastically that now we can never return to the time when things looked the way they did then.

"Why don't you take it?" Evans said to Roger. "You could rent your house for a year, and you wouldn't pay any rent there. The place is just sitting empty. I always think I'll go back to it someday. The land isn't good enough to farm profitably. Nobody would bother you. It's isolated, but there's a really good library, when you need one, only about seventy miles away."

"Oh, no," Roger said. "You don't catch me in that trap again. Once, when I was in college, I went to a friend's summer

place to work on a term paper. The front door fell off, the
plumbing broke down, termites swarmed. I never worked so
hard in all my life and I got nothing done on the term paper."

"Oh, of course," Evans said. "Things do break down. You'd
need a handy man. Will Workman will find you one, with no
trouble. Good Lord, man, you don't realize. It's a different world
there. You can get someone to keep the weeds down around the
house and chop the wood for two dollars a day, and Will Workman himself can fix anything. He's the only one around there I
trust absolutely. But stay away from his moonshine."

"Does he make it?" Roger said.

"No, he doesn't make it," Evans said. "He just drinks it, a
little all the time. Never drunk, though. But the taste of the
stuff. I think they put gasoline in it."

"It's a dry county, you know," Mary said. "You have to go
across the line to get anything to drink."

Roger was to be on half salary for the year and when we had
a really handsome offer for our house, furnished, the idea began
to sound better to him. Of course Ellen was in grand health
then; we hadn't an inkling of anything wrong. Yes, it looked
better and better for Roger but, as Mary said, "It'll be fine for
Roger, yes, but what in the world will you do, Libby, for a whole
year? There isn't a thing. Nothing but the most violent, hide-
bound religion that pervades everything."

Oh I wish Mary Evans were there now and I could have
letters from her with mention of Will. But Evans got a fellow-
ship that he'd long wanted and they're in Italy for a year.
Though, God knows, if Mary were there, with her sense of tact,
she would probably never mention Will, for fear of bringing up
unpleasant memories, to add to everything we have now.

"And you watch for Will Workman," she said, jokingly, as

we were about to leave. "He's reputed to be a devil with the ladies."

"What they call a courtin' man," Evans said.

"He's some hunk of man, anyhow," Mary said. "I could almost go for that myself."

"Mary's chicken," Evans said. "She's scared of his shrew of a wife."

"You bet I am," Mary said. "Meanest woman I ever saw. But *what* a cook."

"Oh, right," Evans said. "Light bread such as you never tasted anywhere else. And *pies*."

"Not a bit better than yours," Mary said.

They were, though. Never anywhere have I tasted such pastry. There was a wild blackberry pie that first night. We arrived in a snowstorm and stopped at the Workman farm for directions. Will insisted we must wait at his house until he had started fires in the Evans place. It was bitterly cold, yet Will went out in his shirt-sleeves. He never wore a coat in any weather. Nor hat, either.

And yes, there it was immediately, in those first few moments—the outrageous, obvious, old-fashioned flirting, so that, tired as I was from the long drive, hungry and half-frozen, I was shaken out of my stupor and hard put to avoid those piercing black eyes. Such alive eyes they were. I remember wanting very much to giggle when he actually winked at me and I thought he could hardly have been more obvious unless his eyelids had been adorned with alternately flashing neon signs saying, *available, available*. I remember I wrote to Mary about it, saying that at my age it was so rare to get it at all that I hardly minded its being so automatic, would in fact have taken it from an automatic machine dispenser if there were such. It is rather a shame

that there isn't such a thing, something like a cigarette dispens-
ing machine, where for a dime one could have a few moments
of feeling desirable and beautiful and highly exciting. For so I
felt, even though I was laughing inside, and I remember the
shock of standing before the bedroom mirror that night and
seeing what an absolute wreck I actually looked. And then I saw
Will's face above mine, the white streak so startling in his
black, curly hair.

"I thought you'd sleep in here," he said, "so I laid this fire
with sweet gum wood." He went over to the stove and lifted the
lid. The fire was roaring now and the warmth penetrated the
room. He closed down the lid and adjusted the drafts. "It makes
a sweet smell, that wood does," he said. Indeed it does. I can
smell it yet.

How cold it was that winter. (What do I mean, *that winter?*
It was only last winter.) It snowed almost continuously and at
the crossroads store there was talk of little else. Some farmers
had animals frozen to death. There were many days when we
could not have made it even to the crossroads without Will's
Jeep, for we did not have chains on the car.

And always, when we reached for firewood, it was stacked
high. The electric pump purred, the washing machine worked at
last, and when the car would not start, Will Workman was
always there with his marvelous genius for any machine. But the
handy man we had requested him to find never materialized.

"We're quite hopelessly dependent on you," Roger said to
him. "We never intended to ask all these things of you."

"Roger," he said (I never quite got accustomed to the use of
first names which was customary there. I was "Mrs. Roger"), "I
would do any *thing* for any*body* if they would just let me."

How many times I heard him say that. But that first time it

struck both Roger and me as odd, for this was a quite successful man and half the countryside was dependent on him to keep farming equipment running. Why did he need to seek approval? It was, in a way, like his flirting, which would have been under-standable in an ugly man, or an old, fat man, in anyone who feared himself to be a clown. But this was one of the handsom-est men I have ever seen and an arrogant manner would have fitted him better. Yet behind the flirting and the quick laughter, I was getting glimpses of naked hunger for the simplest gesture of approval.

"Besides," Will said, "you can't get anybody to work in weather like this. I'm not busy. Nobody's doin nothin. Come spring, there'll be a string of em after me to get their stuff runnin, but right now I might as well be doin this."

"Well, tell us what we owe you, then," Roger said, "for all the repairs and everything."

"I bought a part for that washing machine," he said. "Two dollars."

Later, after Roger had gone back to his work (we had made a quite pleasant workroom for him in the dining room and we took our meals in the kitchen) I again protested Will's not being paid. We were having coffee at the kitchen table.

"No," he said. "I'm happy just sittin here drinkin coffee with you. I'm happy when I see your light go on in the morning. I stand on that hill up there in the dark and wait for it."

It was a strange feeling, waking in the dark, so long before my usual time, and knowing that he stood out there on that hill. When the snow was very deep, he sometimes rode over on horseback. I would get up quietly so as not to disturb Roger and go in and wash my face and dress in the cold air. Then I would turn on the kitchen light and build up the fire. Soon in the cold stillness I would hear Will whistling. He had a beautiful, pure whistle and would whistle the country music tunes as he walked or worked. I think he was unaware of it most of the time.

By the time the coffee was ready he would be at the door and, "Whoo-ee," he would say, "it's cold out there." He would go over and squat down by the stove, luxuriating in the heat. He could squat for an endless time in comfort and would turn himself back and forth, rotating on the ball of one foot, lapping up the warmth of the fire like a beautiful animal. When he slept, I don't know, for he often mentioned being awake in the night and was always up at four. Yet he never appeared tired, his posture was always erect and his movements those of a dancer. And, as Roger said, he would have had to have an extraordinary constitution to be able to handle the steady drinking of moonshine year after year without appearing drunk.

There would be a drawn look to his face, though, sometimes and, if I questioned, he would sigh and shake his head. "Oh, me," he would say then, "sometimes I am just outdone." And then would come forth what The Wife had done. The catalogue of meanness was endless—the precious, delicate tools senselessly destroyed, the moonshine discovered in its hiding place and poured on the ground, the doors hooked and locked in his face, tempting him to break them down with his bare hands, which he could easily do.

His hands. My God, his hands. They were in such perfect proportion it was weeks before I noticed they were twice the size of any hands I had ever seen. It was that way with his whole body, all in such proportion that one didn't notice the tremendous size of the man—the width across the shoulders for example—until measuring it against something else.

"I caint understand," he would say. "I've told her and told her I would love her if she would just let me. Why, how I could love a woman! There's no one could love more than me. Why, I could love a woman so that the roof just come off the house from the happiness inside. Why would a woman not want to be loved, can you tell me?"

"Oh, no," I said. "It must be very complicated. I suppose in her mind she must have grievances?"

"She says what she wants is just to go off some place where there ain't nobody she ever knowed and I said to her, 'That's right. That's where you belong. Where there ain't nobody and no thing alive.'"

"I should think you might have gone away yourself if it has been so bad," I said.

"I been away," he said. "I worked in Detroit. I been in the Army. I like to of died away from here. Why, in Detroit, I couldn't see the sky hardly, and I had to ask someone, some *stranger*, how to find my room. Come fall one year, I thought about squirrel huntin in the woods and walkin over the leaves. I wanted to rip that pavement up. I like to of went crazy. Work all day and never see no kin. Never hear your name. Why I was *born* here. My papa was born here. Papa he always come back, too. Said he couldn't quench his thirst all the time he was gone. If you always drank from a spring, that other water with them chemicals they put in it . . . it just never tastes like *water* to you."

Will was progressively more "outdone" as The Wife's tantrums and threats increased. Bickering made him sick, he said. The Wife threatened constantly to leave. "But this time," Will said, "I want an end to it. I want it to be over. She's gone so many times, and always come back. I caint keep goin through it over and over. The Boy's grown now. Ain't no need."

"It's awfully sad," I said.

"Talk about sad?" he said. "Sad ain't no name. All I know is,

in thirty-two years she never once met me at the door when I
come home and she never once put her arms around me lessn I
coaxed her."

The awful dreariness of it depressed me. Though for all I
knew, she had good reason for her hatred and perhaps he had
done some dreadful thing long ago, still why didn't she have an
end to it?

"She don't want me," he said, "and she don't want no one
else to have me, and that's about the story of it. And yet, I
loved her. I loved that woman. We was barefoot kids together.
And I worked. I worked hard all my life. I worked in the Depression for forty cents a day. I wasn't never on WPA. I always
worked. I worked in steel mills, I worked all over. Anything
except the mines. I never worked in no hole in the ground. I
could work all day and night and I still could. She helped me to
save, I will say that. She did. But then, about four years ago, the
last time she come back and it didn't mean nothin again, the
heart just went out of me for savin. The Boy, he gets everything
I save anyway."

"I wish there was something I could do," I said.

"You kin," he said. "You kin wear that little ole green dress
with the round neck you had on that first night, and git out of
them ole britches."

Why didn't I, then? Why didn't I wear the green dress if it
would have given him pleasure? Well, I tried. I was so touched
at his having remembered it. He could only have seen it once,
for a short while, on the night of our arrival, and it has been
more years than I can remember since any man noticed what I
wore. Not that I'm a slob, or dowdy. But I'm not Lollobrigida,
either. To tell the truth, I never did have them whistling in the
streets, even in youth. Mary Evans and Ellen always notice
when I get something new, and that's about it. So I got out the

green dress and tried it on and Roger found me in hysterics on the bed.

"What's all that funny?" he said.

"I forgot about the long underwear," I said. "I was tired of blue jeans and thought I'd put on a dress and I forgot about the underwear." Both Roger and I had nearly frozen to death the first few days, and one of our earliest purchases at the crossroads general store had been long underwear for both of us. I had worn blue jeans or slacks ever since, with stout, flat-soled shoes. The green dress pointed up the tremendous change in our lives. Without high heels it was ludicrous, and in any case it was highly impractical.

"I think you're a little stir crazy," Roger said." You've been shut up here too long. I have to go into the city soon to put in a day at the library. Why don't you come with me?"

But it wasn't the city I wanted. It was to have more of the country. As Mary Evans had said, what would I do here? What I wanted to do was not to miss this marvelous, and perhaps only, chance we might ever have to live in the country. I wanted a vegetable garden and I wanted some animals. I didn't want a dog or a cat; I wanted animals one can't have in a city. It seemed such a shame to be on a farm and not have any animals about. Yet, having only a year, what could I do? I spoke to Will about it.

"It don't matter about the time," he said. "You can always sell them off when you leave. Cattle now, would be expensive. You've got no feed; you'd have to buy it. Pigs is nice. You got plenty of time to raise little pigs to sell or butcher. And you'd only have to buy corn."

"But I don't like pigs," I said. "You know, I've always wanted to have a couple of goats. Little ones."

"Milk goats?"

"I guess so. I don't really know anything about them." What I knew was from having read *Heidi* to Ellen when she was little, and having had it read to me by my mother.

"There's a man not too far from here, which he has milk goats," Will said. "I'll take you and Roger over there and we'll see. Goats would be good, all right, for here. You won't have to buy much food. Except we'll have to keep them up or fix the fences. Evans ain't got much on this place, but one thing he's got and that's a few fine fruit trees. Your goats would kill them in no time."

Ah, my precious babies, where are you now? Did Will keep you?

"When can we go?" I said.

"Any time," he said. "I'll find out first has he got some. But why you still in them ole britches? I thought you'd have a dress on today."

"Oh, hell," I said. "I did get it out and try it on and . . . I can't."

"Why not?"

"Well, it's not practical here. Everything's too rough. If I stepped outdoors in any shoes but these I'd turn my ankle and fall flat on my face. And, besides, I got too self-conscious about it."

"But I want to see you in a dress," he said.

"Well, that's just it. If I put on a dress you'd make too much out of it. I'd be trying to please you. Oh, for God's sake, I feel like a simpering old fool, standing in front of a mirror trying on dresses just because, for the first time in years, a man noticed what I had on. Listen, I'm forty-nine years old. I have a grand-child."

"Gal," he said, "don't talk like that about yourself. There's a lot of woman left in you. Just a *lot*."

"Yes, there is," I said. "There is indeed. But it's woman and not, I hope, an adolescent girl."

He moved over quietly and took hold of my shoulders. "What you so all-fired upset about?" he said. "Why don't you just straighten yourself? Ain't nothin to get so mad about, just puttin on a dress sometime. You got a lovely shape."

I backed away from his touch and tried to control the laughter rising in me, for the thing that had come into my mind was an old cartoon: *My good man, you mustn't speak to me like that: I'm vice-president of the League of Women Voters,* which Mary Evans had given me when I *was* elected vice-president of our League.

"Oh, well, the truth is," I said, "it's the long underwear, if you want to know. It's so damned cold and I need the underwear. I can't wear a dress with long underwear."

"Well, the spring, then," he said. "Spring comes, you'll wear a dress?"

"All right. When spring comes. But is it ever coming?"

"Now I got another reason," he said. "I'm about crazy for it to come already. I don't never remember winter to hold on this way."

I was in a rage for spring myself, mostly because of a terrible hunger for fresh vegetables. "Doesn't the crossroads store *ever* have any vegetable except cabbage?" I said to Will.

"Well, there's cress in the branch right now," he said. He pronounced it brainch, as everyone did there. No one ever said brook or rill, and the term creek was reserved for larger streams. "You like cress?"

It takes my breath away even now to remember that scene— the trees all bare and gray, the icicles hanging from the huge stones over the branch, and the branch itself blue against the deep snow that covered everything. It was rough going, plodding through the snow, and many places the banks of the branch were so overgrown with tree roots that we had to go into the branch itself and make our way from stone to stone. Will's hand was always there ahead of me as I took precarious steps and then, as we made a sudden turn, there in that pure whiteness was the spot of bright green watercress like an emerald on a white tablecloth. As much watercress as I have bought in my life, I had never seen it growing before, and I was carried away with excitement, so that for a while, pulling it out of the icy water, I forgot how terribly cold I was. I was laughing with pleasure and I looked up at Will. His cheeks were very red and he was smiling. "There's just gaboodles of it," he said. "Gaboodles of cress."

We filled my basket and started back to the house. After I had slipped twice, Will put the basket down on the bank. "I'll come back for it," he said. Then he picked me up in his arms and carried me, stepping surely over the icy stones. Inside me somewhere I could hear the tiny voice of the League's vice-president protesting, but I turned by head against Will's chest and closed my eyes. I was suddenly filled with a sweet bliss to be carried like a child. After all, I weigh one hundred and twenty-five pounds, and this sort of thing doesn't happen to me often. His chest was so wonderfully warm to my frozen cheek. Then I became aware of his heart pounding furiously.

"I'm heavy," I said.

"Oh, I could go on this way for hours," he said, and he tightened his arms about me and held me closer to him.

Was it then? Was it the day of the watercress that I was caught and held fast in this waiting that never ends? No, I think not. Not yet. No, it was later, after I had the goats.

II

Talk about pretty? Pretty ain't no name, I thought, when we had chosen two from the herd. *Oh, my darlings, there was never a question; you were so much the most beautiful.* "Now, their mother was mixed Toggenburg and Nubian," the old man (which, he has goats) said, "but the buck, he's pure Nubian."

Neither Roger nor I had known about their eyes with the horizontal pupils, which gave them a look of being truly different creatures. "But it's very pleasant here," Roger said. "I thought goats were supposed to be such smelly creatures."

"Oh, no," Will said. "That's the billies. Only the billies smell. The nannies are sweet. Look yonder." He pointed to a distant hill where, in solitary splendor, the black Nubian buck stood alone in a pen. "That's all he's got to do, Roger. Just stand there till he's wanted." And the two of them laughed.

"How soon will they be weaned?" I asked innocently.

"Weaned?" the old man said. "Just take them. Take them. They'll eat when they get good and hungry. I need the milk. I thought you'd be here before this." It was a harsh land with brutal ways, and not only for the animals. *How panicky and frightened you were, my pretties, and I no less so to hear your cries, so like a human baby's.* Will tied a piece of rope ("Not rope," he said. "That's sea grass") around their necks and held them in his arms in the back seat of the car while Roger drove. "They'll be all right," he said.

And they were. Startled and frantic, they leaped about in the calf's stall in the barn while I sat quietly in a corner on an old milking stool watching Will make them a tiny hideaway out of a cardboard carton. *His beautiful knife with which he cut the door in one side. How slender and delicate it was.*

I carry a knife myself now, very like it, just for the feel of it, and for the memories it brings. I see the razor-sharp blade in his beautiful huge hand. I see him cutting redbud blossoms from a tree. I see him squatting in the garden, deliberately and slowly scraping the dirt from the first icicle radish that I might eat one then and there. When Roger comes to me now for the scissors to cut open his packages of books I think with impatience, Why doesn't he carry a knife?

"There now," Will said, moving very quietly into the stall and placing the cardboard hideaway in one corner. "We'll put some hay inside it and they'll keep each other warm there." In they went, away from the dreadful, strange people, and at last their frantic movements stopped. Will squatted down beside me and we sat silently waiting. When the two beautiful heads, somehow looking like toy camels in spite of the long ears, poked out of the tiny door and stared at us, without panic, we looked at each other and smiled.

On the way back to the house he said, "By the time they smash the box, it'll be warm enough they won't need it. Don't worry over them so. Tonight or tomorrow they'll eat some of the hay and they've got water. They'll be all right."

But I did worry. In the night I woke and thought how wonderful now it seemed that European peasants kept their animals in or next to the house. How I would have loved to reach out and touch the goats to see if they were warm, even if Will had said that he has seen twin babies dropped in the snow and live. I stayed in the house that first night, but in the morning their water was frozen and the next night it snowed again. I dressed warmly and went out into the howling, icy wind, fighting my way to the barn, my hand growing numb around the flashlight. The wind covered the sound of my entrance and I could hear Will whistling and knew he was with the goats. I stopped just inside the door to wipe my nose and then I lit a cigarette and went through the barn to the far corner where the goats were. I leaned over the inner wall of the stall and saw him there, sitting on the milking stool, the babies safe in their cardboard box. He looked up at me. "Honey," he said, "don't never smoke in a barn."

The next day the goats ate corn out of my hands. Will showed me how to shell an ear of corn and I sat on the milking stool, holding the grains of corn in the palm of my hand, and the goats came timidly, their soft lips exploring, sucking up the corn like tiny vacuum cleaners. Less timid, greedily, they pressed until they were leaning against me, impatient, impatient to eat.

"Now you got them," Will said. "Now they'll be yours." By the next day I could reach out with one hand and touch their silken heads while they ate corn out of my other hand. Progressively they grew tamer so that I could pick them up one at a time and hold them on my lap and stroke them. How like little deer they seemed, with their tiny hooves, their stick-brittle legs, the sweet woodsy smell of their fur. The inside of their long ears was silken smooth, marked with parallel ridges.

The days grew warmer and a great happiness would come on me sitting there with the goats, watching them leap onto the roof of their hideaway or come dancing to me for corn. I would stroke their lovely warm heads while they leaned against my thighs and hours would go by. Time would stop. I suppose I had not been so happy since Ellen was a baby. Often while I sat so Will would come quietly into the stall to watch or sit in the open doorway to their enclosure. Sometimes a strange, hungry look would come into his eyes.

"You got a soft hand for them," he said.

"Oh, they are lovely," I said. "I can't remember when any-thing has been so satisfying." And in a rush of love I gathered the brown one to me and kissed it.

"I suppose you got a word for that," he said.

"For what?"

"For the way you love them goats," he said. "For the soft hand."

"Oh, tenderness, I suppose," I said, feeling my eyes suddenly burn with the excess I know myself to have of it, so that I would pour it out on strangers if it were not that I know they would call the police or turn from me in fear. It has grown so much greater in me in the last years, this awful flood. In railway stations it's the worst, I think. People look so tired there, so lost sometimes. Oh, isn't it sad that in our world it is so hard to give it? God knows people need it. The faces of young men so often show, I think, how terribly they want it. Yet, alas, they all want it from Marilyn Monroe.

"It's a purty word," Will said.

The little brown goat moved from under my stroking hand and leaped away suddenly to join the blue one. I looked up at Will and caught his face in a look of tiredness, which was very rare. "Tenderness," he said. "That's what I always been so godalmighty short of."

It was then that those strange, sweet days of languor de-scended on me so that I understand how it is some people can quite slip away, over the edge, from reality. It was as though I too, like the earth, lay supine, waiting for spring to come. The melting snow swelled the branch until the water frothed over the footbridge and the sound of it could be heard in the house. What did I do? I don't remember. I was happy. I watched the goats growing. The days went by. When Roger went again to the city I saw with surprise that the library books he had brought me the last time were untouched. I, who lived always with a book in my hand, I who will read anything, even the wrapper around the toothpaste and every word on the scouring powder label while I stand at the sink, I had not even opened one of those books. Then the frantic letter came from Ellen *oh Ellen, Ellen*, worrying that I had not written for three weeks.

I was shocked at myself and drove in immediately to the crossroads store where there was a phone to call Ellen. *How you laughed, dear Ellen.* But I did not make myself go into the city with Roger.

"Now don't go completely native on me," he said. "Remember we have to go back when the year's up."

I planned to give myself a good shaking up and to go over the recent mail and answer letters. I did get them all out, I know. I had them spread on the kitchen table with the pad of writing paper all ready, and then when I looked out the window I saw in the distance a hint of green on the hill. So faint it was, that it disappeared while I stared at it. Yet when I looked away and back again, it was there for a moment. I saw Will coming across the yard and went to open the door for him. He came into the kitchen and checked the fire in the stove as he always did. Then he sat down in a chair across the table from me and sighed.

"Well, The Wife, she taken off," he said. "Gone to Kentucky to her sister's. Says she's not comin back. I hope it's true this time. This argument all the time, it's about got me sick."

"I'm sorry," I said, "that it is like that."

"Yes, she taken off," he said. "I caint understand. Why would she want to do what she did? She taken everthing off the sideboard, which there's a big one in the dining room, like it would be over there on that wall. Well, she usually keeps some dishes there and photographs of The Boy and a teapot belong to my mother, and all things like that. Well, she packed all that away, so that it's bare, and she put out the picture of the dead baby. Now, why? It just hurt me so to walk in there and see that."

"Oh, dear," I said, "It's awfully sad to lose a child. Was it recent?"

"No," he said. "Twelve years ago the little boy died. We carried him clear up to Chicago. He lived to be a year. First he seemed all right and then, well The Wife, she thought he was blind. So the doctor here he had us to go up to Chicago and they said there he didn't have no covering over his little brain. The doctor he said to me, "Well, I'll tell you this way. You got a field here that won't grow anything and down yonder there's a good field, just grow everthing. Well, what you do is work on that good field and let the othern go.'"

"Perhaps it was merciful," I said. "Don't you think so?" *Merciful I said, my dear Ellen. Oh, mercy, mercy.*

"Yeah," he said, "It was, I guess. He had the purtiest skin, though, you ever saw. White? White as that sheet of paper there. I held him. I held him in my arms. . . . "

Quietly he slipped out of his chair and came around the table to me. He squatted down beside me and perhaps a too acute awareness of his body so close to my side made me move away slightly. He closed his eyes and bent his head, but he did not touch me.

"Listen," he said, "I don't mean no harm against Roger. I like Roger. But put your hand on me, the same as you would one of your little goats, or some wild thing you found out in the woods. Put your hand on me and just don't push me away." And he stayed there with his eyes closed, waiting, waiting as though for a blessing, so that in the silence of the room I felt I could push him away and splinter the man into a thousand fragments.

I put my arm around him and bent my head over his. I moved my hand over his shoulder and my tears dropped onto him. For wasn't it eloquent, the way that he said the cry one hears everywhere, shouted into silence or mouthed unheard into noise? Oh, it was no more nor less than a statement of the human condition, not rare, not unusual; it was just that in Will Workman, the condition was raw.

"Don't pity me," he whispered. "Don't pity me."

That was the moment. That was the time when I became hopelessly entangled with the man. Any moment up to then I could have withdrawn. I could have been safe from this waiting that never ends.

"There is green on the hill over there, Will," I said.

He stood up then, effortlessly, smiling. (*He* was not crying. *He* looked radiant.)

"Right," he said, "and I kin show you a redbud tree in bloom."

III

Indeed there was a redbud tree in full bloom and two days later there were three more, so vivid against the bare gray branches of the other trees, themselves festooned with cardinals that seemed like scarlet fruits. After the redbuds came the swollen leaf buds of the hickory trees, and, startling as rouge on the cheek of a gray mule, was the soft, subtle red of the swamp maples. Both banks of the branch were sharply outlined by the first flat leaves, two by two, of the touch-me-not.

Then the dogwoods blossomed and pseudopodia of green crept over the hills, spreading almost while I watched. The frogs set up a frantic screaming in all the swampy places and suddenly there were wild blackberry bushes knee high. Then the green went uncontrolled, as the pace of spring accelerated, and climbed the huge trees to the sky. And the blackberry bushes were up to my waist. The wild plum and the sarvis trees burst into white clouds of bloom.

And the sound of the whippoorwill began on the dot of dusk.

The strange, soporific days of my languor were gone. I had become two eyes searching for the sight of Will Workman, two ears listening for his whistle. So that I was a strained and wait-ing thing drawn to the window, pulled to the door, until he would come into the house. Then I could rest. His presence rested me. I would sink into a chair and half listen to what he said. It did not matter to me what it was. I had no desire to speak. I would savor the sweet rest of his presence and feel my eyelids turn to weighted satin until, if he left the house alone, I would become again a window, a door, a waiting thing.

For distraction I would run to the goats, who were full of play now, frolicking in their butting games and leaping sideways down the road as we walked. I was not timid with them any more; I knew now they would stay by me, would, if I were out of sight for a moment, bawl like angry babies. *Oh, my darlings, my darlings, how you must have cried!* I did not need a rope or any kind of restraint upon them and I would take them into the woods to feast upon the elms, the wild sassafras, the cedars. Oh how they ate. Always hungry now, insatiable they were. And why was it—I never understood—that the terrible thorns of the wild blackberries did not rip their tender lips to ribbons? Even yet, even here, I sometimes see the landscape through goat's eyes, as primarily edible, and I remember their delicate lower jaws sliding sideways back and forth and seem to hear their steady crunching. *How they played! If only for a moment now I could witness their playing.*

But this is not right. I am confusing the way it is *now* with that time. That time was not all of such intensity. There were many days when I was relaxed and natural with Will. There were the days when Roger joined us in making the spring garden (*What became of it all? Were all the lovely lettuces choked by weeds?*) and I knew in his presence I was safe from indiscretion. There were the highly exciting electrical storms when the power would fail and Roger and I would sit talking by lamplight. Oh, there were plenty of times when I had control of things and Will and I spoke naturally together and laughed—the new kittens he brought from his place, the baby chipmunk, the tiny wild squirrel that he found, its mother having been shot, and which he carried about with him inside his shirt. And there was that delicious day I had said to him, "Oh, you're a wonder, you are" (But what had I said it about?) and he answered so seriously.

"There ain't nobody like me. You'll never meet nobody like me. Leastways, I never did." And, like a mother who protects her child against the knowledge of evil, I knew I would not tell him that everyone believes himself to be unique and, if necessary, will prove it, if only by being what he believes to be uniquely ill. But Will, of course, was under no compulsion to prove it, never having been in doubt. To him it was sweet certainty.

"Though I'd like to," he said. "I'd like to meet someone just like me."

"What would you do?" I said.

Then, with that vivid visualization which was synonymous

with imagination for him (like the sideboard would be over there on that wall), he looked over my head with this curious smile and I knew that he *saw* him over there, the man just like himself.

"Why, watch him," he said. "Stand back and watch him to see what he's goin to do."

How wonderfully young, I thought, to think, in the fifties, of one's own behavior as full of possible surprises. Not to believe that one knew almost exactly what one would be doing every day for all the rest of one's time.

Oh, of course there were many delicious, relaxed days. There was the first day we picked the tender pokeweed shoots (just gaboodles of it, we found) and I learned to make poke sallet. (The pokeweed pickles I made, are they on that high shelf yet, all lined up in their neat row?) And the wild elderberry blossom wine that Will and I started. (Is the huge crock sitting still in the cool spring where we left it, or has it been dashed against the rocks by rain swellings?) And there were the night fires we had, the three of us, eating our meals outside and delighting in the show of lightning bugs, until Roger began to go around singing, "How'm I gonna keep her down in the city, after she's seen the farm?"

Oh, it was glorious, that spring, the most wonderful I ever had in my life. Yet, just as the beauty of it had for undertone the knowledge of rattlesnakes and copperheads reported about, so did we see, at last, in the general store, Will's son, "The Boy." He was unmistakably Will's son at first glance, yet it was a resemblance seen in a distorting mirror, a Will gone sour or caricatured, so that instinctively I recoiled from him. The neat black cap of Will's hair was, on The Boy, a bushy mop, unkempt, with exaggerated sideburns. The chiseled lips were gone blubbery and swollen, the wonderful muscular body gone flabby.

But most horribly, the beautiful dark eyes, so alive and trusting, were in the son mean and calculating. He was no boy; he was thirty years old, had wife and children of his own, and had but recently returned again, with Will's financial help, from some "trouble" in Detroit.

News of "the trouble" carried as far as Kentucky via relatives ("The Wife's related to half the people in the county, which I'm related to the other half," Will said) and The Wife had returned.

"She's afraid I'll give him money," Will said. "And she's right. I have already, and I'll probably do it again. I always say it's the last time, but how can it ever be the last time, so long as they live, and they're your own?" *So long as they live, dear Will.*

"Ah, me," he said, "the cars wrecked and turned over, the drunk arrests, the trouble, trouble. And him with never a scratch. I seen a car he turned clear over, and he walked away from it. And the fights—the way he fights. I say to him, 'It's enough to fight with your fists. You don't have to stomp somebody to death, no matter what he done.' The calls, I don't know how many, that come in the night. Seem like he can't call except at two o'clock in the morning, which I finally had the phone taken out. 'Daddy, kin I have two hundred dollars? Dad, kin you send it right away?' I sold all my guns finally. I had me some fine guns, but The Wife all the time sayin 'Hide the guns, hide the guns,' until I just got rid of them. Of course that don't keep him from gettin one of his own, but he ain't walkin around mad with one of mine anyhow."

My heart ached for Will (he was whistling "Blacksheep Boy" these days), for, though Ellen had never given us a moment's trouble, still we used to worry when she was out with inexperienced drivers, or when she ran a fever. One can't raise a child without tasting a special anxiety.

The Boy got a job in a local sawmill but had a fight with the foreman. Soon he was in more serious trouble which threatened a prison term. I never knew the charges exactly, except that there was a girl involved and Will had to sell a piece of property, but whether this was for bail or to satisfy someone bringing charges, I don't know. At any rate, The Boy was out with a trial date ahead of him.

"Seem like," Will said, "everthing just all monkeyed up."

"Was he always difficult?" I said. "Even as a child?"

"No," Will said, "seem like he come home from the Navy just mad at everthing. But when he was a teensy boy, he was always laughin. And purty? The purtiest little ole boy you ever did see. I taken him everwhere, just everwhere with me. I always had his hair cut just like mine, then. I never did hold with having them look like girls. And, when he left here to go to the Navy, there was nine girls on that little station platform to see him go. Of course there was about half of them which it would be better he never spoke to at all. I told him so then, and he said, 'Daddy, how come you know so much about little girls?' I remember it left a nasty taste in my mouth. I don't have nothin to do with little girls and he knows it. It's just I know the people they come from. Everbody knows."

"I'm sorry you have this new trouble," I said.

"Yes, it's pretty bad. And I caint understand it at all. His wife loves him. And she's such a pretty little thing. She lets him drink at home. He don't have to go out to drink. She put up and put up with him. 'Boy,' I said to him this last time, 'I don't know. I tried and tried. I caint tell you nothin. Seem like nobody caint tell you nothin.' 'Well, Daddy,' he said to me, 'caint nobody tell you nothin, either.' 'That's true,' I said, and I guess maybe it is, 'but I kin keep out of trouble.'

"I don't know what it is. He's smart. He kin get good jobs.

But he keeps comin back. If I had a garage he was goin to be a mechanic or if I was farmin he'd want to farm. Seem like he always wanted whatever I had."

Will sat quiet for a while. "Well," he said, "I got to go. I got to get The Wife to sign her name to a deed so I can sell some ground I own and she's just likely to ask everthing else I got in return for it. I got to have the money for The Boy and she knows it. Yeah, everthing just all monkeyed up. If I didn't have you to talk to, I don't know what I'd do, times like this."

He saw the tears in my eyes. "Now," he said, "don't you worry so about all this. It'll straighten." He walked to the door then and repeated, as if to convince himself, "It'll straighten. It's got to."

Oh, wouldn't it clear the air if I could just once, after the dinner dishes are done, walk into Ellen's living room where Mark and Roger sit in their restrained politeness ("Cigarette, Roger?" "Can I get you a drink, Mark?") and with a sigh just say something *real*, like "Seems like everthing is just all monkeyed up"? But no, of course it would not clear anything. They would be shocked. Even little Bucky can't cry out his trouble to me, but must kneel politely and say his proper Episcopalian prayers each night without any show of emotion. I do try to do everything with Bucky just as Ellen did, though Ellen herself was brought up an agnostic. "But then Bucky faces a different world than I did," Ellen said, "and besides, I had Roger," which surprised me a lot because if ever I saw two men alike, it's Mark and Roger, and I had always thought that Ellen had been attracted to Mark for this very reason. Not that they look alike at all, but in their personalities—and particularly in their inability to show emotion or even witness other people's—they seem so alike to me.

No, I will not throw any such bomb into Ellen's living room.

I will take Ellen's nurse her tray, put Bucky to bed, wash the dishes and then go in to sit with the two of them while all three of us try to read our books and our newspapers and wait until we can decently creep away to our beds and hide in the dark where the walls shout "Ellen! Ellen! Ellen!" and we wait for her death. Well, Mark and I, I think, wait for her death. Roger hasn't begun to accept it yet. He sits for hours in her room, just staring, and of course hasn't made any pretense of working at all. I long for the time when his year's leave is up and he will have to go back to teaching. Now he studies nothing but cancer, cancer, until he must be a world authority on it. But at least I accomplished one thing. *On my knees* I begged him to stop insisting on carting Ellen to any more hospitals or clinics for new treatments and let her poor body rest. *Oh, my baby, the monstrous things they have tried on you.*

Anyhow, Dr. Robinson finally got Roger to take a sedative to sleep and I am grateful to him. I don't know if Mark sleeps or not; his room is on the other side of the house. I sleep in Bucky's room and I do want always to be available to Bucky. I guess that's why I don't take anything to sleep. Or maybe it's because in the nights I have Will close to me in my thoughts without interruption. I often step out into the yard, though, close enough to hear Bucky if he should call, and then I long for Will's presence sometimes with such intensity that it seems to me he must come, *he must come in the next moment,* walking with his long stride down the driveway and without a word simply take me in his arms again and let me have shelter there against that rock of a chest.

IV

His arms. I am ashiver at the beauty of his arms. When the warm days came, he changed out of his wool shirts to blue cotton ones, and the sleeves were rolled up very high, almost to the shoulders. I suppose they were simply the way a man's arms were meant to develop if he had from earliest childhood done everything physically for himself, but I had never seen such.

His muscles were not bulged as professional athletes' are. The upper arm was smoothly tapering to the elbow, but it was twice the girth of any I had seen. I knew then why he never wore a coat. Any free action would have been impossible for him.

I had met him at the kitchen door as usual, just after dawn. Always we stood quietly for a moment inside the door, rejoicing in the presence of each other. Quietly we would let the inch or two of space between us build up its intolerable and unacknowledged pull before I stepped back and moved to the stove to pour the coffee. But this morning at my eye level across the inch of space was the olive skin I had never seen rolling over the muscles of his arm. Just underneath the skin I saw the pencil-sized great vein crawling upward in its outward curve. I was lost on the pathway of that vein and longed to trace it with my finger until the longing burned into a wish to trace it with my lips.

"What?" I said, in complete confusion. "What did you say, Will?"

"Go ahead and touch it if you want," he said.

"I'm afraid to," I whispered, surprised as much by the whisper as at what I had said. But it was true; I felt that beyond the touching of that vein lay a waiting abyss, and I was right. I stepped back quickly out of the range of that magnetic inch of space. And now it was Will who whispered.

"Ah, I love you so," he said.

"No, Will. You must not say that. You must not think that."

"Why?" he said. "Why must I not love you if it makes me happy?"

"Because," I said. "Because you mustn't. There's nothing ahead for you. Because your own marriage is unhappy, you mustn't think that other people's are. I love Roger. Why, we've been married twenty-five years. I wouldn't think of doing anything to jeopardize such a history as we have."

"I ain't askin you not to love Roger," he said.

Now he moved naturally and relaxed, putting an end to the moment's tension, and sat in his usual place, waiting for me to get his coffee. He smiled up at me, his black eyes sparkling. "Why, it just makes me so happy to love you," he said. "It's somethin to think about." Then he looked away from me out the window, releasing me, and I saw his face suddenly age. Almost to himself he said, "It's better than nothin."

I laughed at his frankness; it was so refreshing that he assumed I did not need the realities sugar-coated, but was well aware of the value of what was between us, that it recaptured from youth that complete absorption in the beloved.

"At night I fall asleep thinkin of you," he said, "and in the mornin I wake up thinkin of you, and I wouldn't take nothin for that."

It had never occurred to Will that it is immature and unrealistic to wish to prolong the blissful state of living between memories of the last meeting with the beloved and fantasies of the next. Oh, and who cares what it is called, wasn't he right that that was the best of it all, that time? How sad it is, the way we are made, that in such a short while we are thinking instead, on waking and falling asleep: *What time is it?*

Well, I agreed with him; I wouldn't give anything for it, either, for it made me feel alive, though I would not admit it to him yet. And then, so naked and vulnerable was he, without tricks of self-protection, he let me see straight into the current fantasy, as I was to know and share so many later.

"If you belonged to me," he said, "would let me wash your back when you bathed?"

"But I don't belong to you," I said.

"I know," he said, "but if you did? Would let me give you a bath? Would you let me in the room when you bathed?"

"Oh, Will, I don't think we should talk like this. It's *never* going to happen. Why torture yourself with teasing like this?"

"Well, then would you tell me, do you let Roger wash your back?"

"Oh, well, of course," I said, thinking of the jolly baths Roger and I used to have together in that first old house we rented, but so long, so very long ago.

"That answers me, then," Will said. "You would, if you belonged to me. I knowed you would really. I guess it must be thirty years I've wanted to bathe a woman, and then pat her dry with a big clean towel, and let her be all warm and sleepy in my arms."

"Oh, my God," I said, in protest of this picture of the angry prude that must be The Wife, "it's a simple request. You shouldn't have had it unsatisfied for thirty years."

"Oh, well, I could pay someone to let me, I guess," he said. "I often thought of doin that. But then, it wouldn't be the way I think of it, I know. Someone you gotta pay, I don't want to give a bath to."

"Really it's so sad, Will. I just can't bear it."

"So many's the time," he said, "when I finished eatin before The Wife I would go around the table and pick her up and set her on my lap to finish her meal. And The Wife, she don't think nothin of that."

"I don't understand what you mean, Will, that she didn't think anything of it," I said, for by his expression it was clear he was trying to communicate something important to me.

"Well, she . . . ," and here he raised his huge hands and hit against the air, as The Wife must have hit against him. "She just don't think *nothin* of it."

"Oh," I said.

And I could hear again his intense whisper as he had knelt that earlier day: *The same as your little goats or some wild thing you found in the woods. Just don't push me away.* Yet, parallel to my pity ran my anger at him that he had allowed this to happen to himself, that he had not in his beautiful strength risen up and demanded decent treatment or the freedom to find it elsewhere.

"What in the world is the matter with you," I said, "that you have put up with such treatment for thirty years?"

"Oh," he said, "I kept thinkin that the Good Lord would find some way for us to be together, because I am so *willing.*"

I sighed in exasperation. I still do. "Oh, well," I said, "it certainly is no business of mine."

"Why ain't you in a dress?" he said. "It's not cold now. I know you're not wearin long underwear now. I seen those pretty little pants on the clothesline for weeks. They like to tear me up, they're so sweet."

So at last I began looking at the newspapers again. Not that I paid attention to the news; I was looking at the ads to find some suitable cotton dresses. Oh, dear, that was such a bad time. I hate to remember it. I found a dress, all right. The minute I saw the ad I knew it was a dress Will would like And then, unfortunately, I saw written under it, "Junior Miss Department." It simply threw me. Now I can see that it was a perfectly simple dress, with good lines, suitable to almost any age, really. I even have one similar to it. It isn't as though it had been covered with ruffles or bowknots. But at the time, I couldn't analyze its lines; I was so thrown by that "Junior Miss" label.

I remember I threw down the paper in disgust and went to the bedroom mirror. "You fool, you *fool*," I said to my reflection. "Are you losing your mind completely? What in the world are you drifting into—mooning around here so touched that someone looks at your underwear on the clothesline. 'Junior Miss' indeed. Oh, aren't you cute, though? Aren't you just too *cute?*" I moved the light so it would show up every last wrinkle, every gray hair. What a state I got myself into.

And it would have been the next morning that Will said for the first time in his quaint, old-fashioned way, "Whose baby are you?" So he got the full load of my self-anger turned upon him. I mocked his speech in an exaggerated manner and said in the nastiest way possible, "Whose lil ole baby am I? Why, I ain't nobody's lil ole baby. I'm a lil ole middle-aged fool in a junior miss dress, that's what I am."

He laughed, missing all the meanness in my voice, not hurt by my mimicking his speech. He laughed and bent his face close to mine. "All right," he said, "tell me, then, whose lil ole middle-aged baby are you?"

"Oh, my God," I said.

I could never do it; I could never bring myself to say to him that simple word which meant so much to him in his own stubborn belief of the ways of love. I always saw myself in a posture of coyness, one knee bent, finger in mouth, and it outraged me. Oh, I am sorry, Will. Now I'll say it. Would it help you now if you could hear me? Shall I whisper it? Shall I go out and shout it from the top of Ellen's house? *Yours, yours, yours, yours, yours!*

Oh, no, I must not walk along the streets crying. Indeed when that happens I *will* go to Olga Marshall. I swear it.

Isn't it curious that I didn't know fleeing would make things worse? It seems so obvious to me now, but then I honestly thought that a day or two in the city with Roger would put everything in perspective for me. I had some kind of idea of being with people "of our own kind" and by that I guess I meant people who were similarly educated. Though, now, of course, I no longer know what my kind is.

It was the first time I had been away from the goats and I kept seeing trees and plants of which they were particularly fond. There was one ornamental tree near a dress shop I entered that would have been just the right height for the little brown goat when she stood on her hind legs as she often did, her delicate front legs held bent before her while she stretched her neck for leaves to eat. I thought suddenly how sweet the blue one looked when, attracted by some movement, she would turn her head, a few mitten-shaped sassafras leaves hanging from the side of her mouth. Oh, I wished I had not come, even though I did get some essential shopping done, including a definitely senior cotton dress.

We had dinner at the house of a colleague of Roger's and, though they were pleasant people, I had the greatest difficulty paying attention. They naturally asked about our impressions of the hill country and I found myself constantly wanting to quote Will. It was, after all, from him that I had learned every plant, every recipe, every anecdote. Yet, I felt myself trembling and forced myself to be silent.

The night in the hotel where we stayed was worse. It seemed to me it would never end. I sat by the window looking out at the spring night. Across the street, under the light, stood a man that, against all reason, I instantly assumed to be Will. Had he known how lonely I would be and been drawn to me as I was to him? My heart began to pound inside me until I felt I would smother and, with relief, I saw the man move down the street. How shattering it was to be a the mercy of a man's shape seen under a street light. But how marvelous, really, to find one's heart beating so, to have one's whole being contracted to such an intense focus. That's the way it always was, a kind of horror to find myself so at the mercy of forces within me, and a thrill that they were still, somewhere, there. Not deadened. Not gone. Not even much changed.

I remember I was in such a rage to get back that I resented the necessity to stop for lunch on the way home. *Yes, I thought of it as home.* I found myself eating with outlandish haste and had deliberately to control myself while Roger sat over his coffee and cigarette. Near the end of the trip we ran through a violent spring shower traveling in our direction, so that all the rest of the way the wonderful freshness blew into the car and we drove through washed greenness.

I didn't even stop to hang up my traveling clothes, so unusual for me, but as soon as I had changed, found myself running, actually running, down the road to the barn until, out of breath, I had to stop. Oh, how lovely are those country roads after rain. The gravel in that light is almost orange and on either side of the road the green reaches to the sky.

Hearing my footsteps, the brown goat began her conversation, a low um um um which rapidly changed into her usual ah ah ah ah ah and then, when I came in sight, she began her

impatient and imperious bah-a-a-ah-bah! Both the goats pressed
against the gate to their pen so that I had difficulty getting it
unlatched and then I was laughing with happiness to have them
in my arms, pressing, twisting, nuzzling. I turned them out to
run while I went into their stall to see to their feed and water.

And there stood Will inside the stall, waiting, his arms held
away from his sides so articulately that without question I
moved to him and for the first time I felt myself held against
that rock of a chest and wrapped in his arms. So naturally, so
easily, I took his kiss and let my hands slide over his back, my
fingers gratefully receiving the long-wanted knowledge of the
great muscles over his shoulder blades. It seemed to me that I
could sink through his skin and become part of him. All
through his body I could feel the subtle tremor of change summoning from mine the will-less *answer* of desire so intense and
wild that my nails bit into his back. I was buffeted upon shattering waves and seized by such violent trembling that I would
have fallen if Will had not instantly sensed that I was past
recognizable landmarks. In a second he was changed as though
some chemical had washed all desire from him and transfused
support instead. With the greatest tenderness, I felt myself
slowly enfolded and supported. "I'll hold ye" he said. "I'll hold
ye."

He kissed the top of my head very gently. "I'll hold ye," he
whispered. Then I felt myself lifted up and carried in his arms.
He put me down on the milking stool where I could lean against
a fence post. "Rest a while," he said. "I'll take care of the goats
and bring them back to you. I knowed that you had it in you
strong the very first time I seen you. I felt it. Now that I *know*,
there ain't no limit to my waiting. Don't be afraid. I wouldn't
never hurt you."

V

I tried to deny it, disparage it, destroy it, in the weeks which followed.

"No, no, Will," I would say. "It isn't the real thing. You know, there is a kind of madness that overtakes middle-aged women until they lose all sense of dignity and make absolute fools of themselves. Don't hope for something real; don't build so much on it."

He would let me babble on, watching me with such a patient, almost amused, expression and then he would reach out and touch my breast and hold me to him. Instantly, at his touch, I would be reduced to helpless trembling.

"That ain't real?" he would say. "You tryin to tell me that ain't real?"

Angry at my defeat, my eyes would fill with tears and I would pull away from him.

"Ah, we couldn't help it, could we?" he would say.

"Of course we can help it," I said. *That's what I said.* "Children talk like that. The whole point of being our age is that one *can* help such things. And we must. This is not like me, this kind of furtive behavior. Why don't you *help* me?"

"Why don't it make you happy?" he said. "It makes me *so* happy. You're just so . . . torn up."

"Well, of course I'm torn up," I said.

"Me," he said, "I could stand to be pestered just forever. But it's too hard on you."

"Oh, hard on me," I said. "That's not the point."

I tried to see him as he had looked at first, with his outrageous flirting. I told myself that there must have been many women like myself that he had said the same words to ("Watch out for Will Workman," Mary Evans had said), that he was always alert for the quick opportunity, the furtive, stolen affair. And I thought I would scare him. I would see him crawl back in fear right before my eyes, and that would do it, that would restore me to sanity.

"But you surely don't think that I would love you and continue to live with Roger," I said. "Suppose he had walked in here when you were holding me? Where would you take me, then? Are you prepared for that?"

Now, I thought. Now, I'll see him backtrack, and he'll look a small-time Lothario to me, and then I will be all right.

"You're right," he said, seriously. "We would have to leave. They'd be so nasty to you here; I couldn't stand it for you."

"Where would we go?" I said, hearing my own voice forced into hard meanness.

"Why we'd have to go to Pittsburgh," he said," he said, "to the steel mills, or to Detroit to a motor plant, so I could work. I couldn't get no money loose here in a hurry, without I had The Wife's signature."

And I had thought to see him crawl! Suddenly I had such a vivid picture of this magnificent man transplanted from the hills he loved to an assembly line in some dreary, congested city. I saw him coming out at the end of a work shift, his lunch box in his hand, his body aging. I could remember his saying, "Why, in Detroit, I couldn't see the sky hardly, and I had to ask some stranger how to find my room. Come fall one year, I thought about squirrel huntin in the woods and walkin over the leaves. I wanted to rip that pavement up. Work all day and never see no kin. Never hear your name."

"Oh, forgive me, Will," I said, "forgive me. That was a mean thing to do. I was testing you and it was cruel of me. I've no idea of leaving Roger ever."

But he seemed not to hear me, lost in his vision of how we would live. "Talk about work?" he said. "Why, I can outwork anybody I ever saw. Work ain't nothin. I could work until I had to crawl home, but if you was there waitin for me, why it would all be like nothin in a minute and I could go back and do it all over again."

"Stop, Will," I said. "You must stop. It's never going to be. Everybody my age knows exactly what to do when a thing like this happens. It's very simple and very clear." *Simple, I said.* "I must not see you, that's all."

"I mustn't *see you?*" he said, in such sudden anguish that I said (and of course it didn't matter in the least what I *said*, but I didn't know it then), "Oh, just for two or three days, Will. Let me get hold of myself. Let me have a chance to think."

"Two or three *days?*" he said.

"Oh, Will, it isn't the end of the world," I said. *But wasn't it, though?*

"If that's what you want," he said. "There's a man over at the crossing been after me to put in an electrical system in his house. I've been puttin him off. I could do that in two days if I stuck right at it. What'll you do?"

"I don't know. Maybe I'll put in my garden," I said.

"All right. I'll think of you doin that. I'll get the ground ready for you before I go. I won't see you for two or three days, but you think of me while I'm workin now, will you?"

"I'm going to try not to," I said, "but no doubt I will."

"Listen," he said. "You mustn't believe about me what you hear around here. Oh, I know what they say. The Wife starts most of those stories. I don't know why; it reflects on her. But I never bothered to deny them and maybe that was wrong."

"Oh, Will . . . " I said.

"I know," he said. "You'd think to hear that I went draggin up and down the road takin everthing in sight. But it's not so. I never had nothin that wasn't ready and waitin for me, and nice and clean."

"You don't have to tell me this, Will. It was just some meanness that possessed me when I said that about going away. It will never happen. It will never be."

"Never?" he said. "Nobody knows about *never*. There's three of us now, but there won't always be."

"Why, *Will!*"

"Don't look at me like that," he said. "I ain't thinkin nothin against Roger; I ain't wishin nothin. It's just that at our age, there won't always be three of us. Caint nobody say. Don't nobody know these things."

I had been so horrified at his remark and now that I realized I was mistaken, I laughed suddenly and said, "Why I'll probably die first, and I'll tell you what I'll do. I'll come back and haunt you."

"Yes," he said, "there's a song like that. It's a beautiful song, about a woman in a long black veil. She would walk like on that hill over there and the man that loved her, he'd see her."

It was real to him, the possibility of haunting, and I remembered that I was in the land where the sound of the screech owl (called scrooch owl), foreboding death, causes real fear, and the stories of ghosts and haunts are traded back and forth with belief.

"But now that I think of the song," Will said, "I believe he had harmed the woman or she couldn't have haunted him otherwise. And that wouldn't never happen to us. I wouldn't never harm you."

I heard him whistling it all that morning while he plowed

the garden space and raked it, though I did not recognize it at the time and it was weeks before I got the words:

> *Sometimes at night when the cold wind moans,*
> *In a long black veil she cries o'er my bones.*
>
> *She walks these hills in a long black veil.*
> *She visits my grave when the night winds wail.*
>
> *Nobody knows, nobody says.*
> *Nobody knows but me.*
> *Nobody knows but me.*

Oh, if I had not insisted on those two days, could it have been avoided? Was it the waiting that had me so concentrated on Will that I opened the door, that I let The Boy in? A thousand times before I die I'll live the horrible hours over again. Is there ever a night that I don't go through it all, writhe and twist away from it as I try?

The two days seemed endless and, though I enjoyed planting the seeds for a while (how sweet the earth smelled!) a lassitude came over me, so that I had to go into the house and lie down. But I could not sleep. I could not read. Will's black eyes were constantly between me and the book. I heard him whistling. I remembered each caress. By the end of the second night I was in a state of tautness, fearing that, since I had said two *or three* days, I might have yet another such day to put in. Yet I hoped that there would be some sign that night, that he would drive by the house.

Roger was in his study after dinner and I kept working in the kitchen long after the dishes were done, for it was from the kitchen window that I could best see car lights. I defrosted the refrigerator and cleaned the stove, and still there was no sign.

At last I gave it up and took a hot shower. Yet I still was not sleepy and dreaded going to bed. In my robe and nightgown I went into the living room, planning to sit and read for a while. I remember I had some idea of perhaps writing to Ellen, for being close to Ellen could always lift me into a kind of warm happiness. But I hadn't time to start either a book or a letter for there was the knock and immediately my whole being was filled with joy and I ran to fling open the door. *But wasn't there a moment of wondering why I had heard neither Will's car nor his whistle? Had there been, though, I would have ignored such wondering, so great was my desire that it be Will.*

The Boy had entered the kitchen. He pushed me back so he could close the door before I was hardly aware that he was not Will. He reeked of alcohol and sweat and he was laughing.

"Was you expectin my daddy?" he said. "That why you got on that lil ole bathrobe?" He jerked my robe open and stood looking at my nightgown. "Well, now, ain't that purty, though?" he said.

Why didn't I scream? Why didn't I call Roger? Why was I so obsessed with the idea that I could protect Will from the embarrassment of having Roger see his son in this condition? Or was it my own guilt and fear that The Boy might have been spying on Will and me?

I pulled away from him and fastened my robe. "What do you want?" I said. "Your father's not here."

"Oh, I know he ain't here," he said. "I taken good care to see he ain't." He laughed evilly and moved close to me so that I was sickened by his breath. "What do I want? Why, I want what my daddy's gettin. I want some ass."

"You're drunk," I said. "Get out of here."

"Oh, no," he said. "I ain't gettin lessn I take you with me."

"Now you go," I said. "My husband's in the next room."

"Is that why you're whisprin?" he said. He smiled and drunkenly put his finger up before his lips and then he whispered, "And we don't want him to know, do we?" Then he leaned toward me. "Don't you worry about him. I been watchin him through the window. He's asleep."

"Please go now," I said. "You're completely mistaken." It was the wrong thing to say. I sensed it instantly.

"Oh, no, I ain't mistaken," he said. "I know my daddy. It ain't money brings him here. I seen that ole car you alla drivin. Ain't nobody with money drive a car ten years old. And it ain't a still. I been all over this place. Ain't no still here. So it's gotta be ass. And I'm gonna have me some."

He started toward me and I knew that it was no longer possible to keep this from Roger. I started toward the study but The Boy caught me by the shoulder. Mercifully, I saw Will coming silently through the kitchen door.

"Boy," he said, in a very quiet voice. "Boy, let loose of her."

The Boy turned and looked over his shoulder, but he didn't loosen his grip on me. "Daddy, don't you mess with me now. I'm warnin you. I got me a gun."

"I know you got a gun," Will said, still in that quiet, controlled voice. "I been followin your track for hours. I heard about ever place you've been. Come on now, Boy. You and me's leavin here together."

I was so relieved that Will was there and I still believed that we might keep this ugly scene from Roger. I did not fight The Boy but thought I had only to endure a few moments more and it would all be over. But The Boy turned his back on Will contemptuously and now held me closer.

"Oh, no," he said. "I ain't leavin, Daddy. You think," he said to me, "that my daddy can fix it for you good? You ain't had it fixed at all. You let me show you. I'll fix it for you so it *stay* fixed."

"Boy," Will said, "take your hands off her. I'm warnin you."

I saw his horrible face turn from mine and look back jeeringly over his shoulder. Then Will's fist was there. The Boy let go of me and fell backward. Oh, the sound of his head on that cement floor. I hear it over and over and over.

I stood there feeling sick and utterly befouled for I don't know how long before I realized. Will was squatting by The Boy, looking at him. I wondered why he didn't pick him up and get him into his car while he was unconscious. Then I saw Will lean over and put his ear on The Boy's chest.

Slowly he raised his head. "Lord have mercy," he whispered. "Lord have mercy."

I stood there shaking all over, my teeth chattering and, as in a dream, saw Will slowly rise from The Boy's side, move over to a kitchen chair and sink into it slowly.

"Go get Roger," he said. "Don't hurry about it. I got to think."

Roger had fallen asleep over his work, his head on his crossed arms. I had a difficult time waking him. "Roger," I said, "come into the kitchen. Something terrible has happened."

"Good God," he said, when he saw The Boy. He started to bend down.

"No need, Roger," Will said. "He's dead. Nothin you can do for him. Sit down." Then he looked at me. "You, too," he said.

He was so quietly impressive we both obeyed. I was still shaking terribly and I felt, as though they were running sores, the places where The Boy's hands had been on me. Will looked directly at Roger.

"Roger," he said, "I need you now. And I guess you need me, too. I want you to get out your car and drive me in to the sheriff."

"All right, Will," Roger said. "I'll get the car out right now."

"No. Just wait a minute," Will said. "We got to get somethin straight here. Ten minutes after I talk to the sheriff this'll be all over the county. It'd be better we all say you was in the kitchen when he come in and she was in there. Just change places, that's all you gotta do."

"Oh," Roger said. "Perhaps you're right."

Then Will looked at me. "What was it he wanted when he come in?" he said. "Was it money or liquor?"

I realized then what he was trying to do. "Liquor," I said. "He wanted me to get him a drink and I wouldn't do it. Then he got mad."

Will looked at Roger. "I knew he was drunk and mean. I heard at the crossroads and I been followin his tracks for a couple of hours. I was right behind him. And when I come in he was actin so bad I had to knock him down. He's got a gun."

"Yes, I see he has," Roger said. "All right, then. We were both in the study, say, and I came out to the kitchen to get a drink of water. The kitchen door's unlocked and The Boy came in, demanding a drink. I refused. He got nasty. Then you came in, Will, and knocked him down."

"Right," Will said. "Now we got it all straight. That way we'll leave her out of it. You wouldn't believe how mean and nasty these people can be around here if The Wife got to stirrin them up the way she thinks."

"You all right?" Roger asked me. "Can you stay here alone? I'll stop at the first phone and call an ambulance. How do you call an ambulance here, Will?"

"I'll tell you all that in the car while we're goin," Will said. "If you'd get your car now and come round here I'll be right out."

As soon as Roger was out of the house Will stood up slowly and went over to the sink. He drank a glass of water. The light

over the sink cast a harsh light on his ravaged face. I stood up,
too. Will looked at me. "I said I'd never bring you harm," he
said, "and I mean to keep my word. After we're gone, you go out
to my car. There's a sack full of lilacs in the back seat I was
bringin to you. You taken it out to the branch and dump it. The
sheriff he'll likely go through my car. But don't take a flashlight.
Somebody might see you."

"All right, Will. I'll do it."

"And put on a dress before the sheriff gets here."

"All right."

He went over to The Boy and squatted down by his head.
With terrible tenderness he smoothed the sweat-stuck strands of
hair off The Boy's forehead. "Boy," he said, "this the most
terrible day in my life, you know that. Oh, Boy, Boy, why you
have to do it? Why you have to touch the one thing. . . ."

VI

From our standpoint it was all amazingly uncomplicated. Will
was not even detained. "I know where to find him when I want
him," the sheriff told Roger. "Will Workman ain't goin to run
nowhere. I knowed him all my life." When Roger asked about
an attorney for Will the sheriff said, "He ain't goin to need one,
I don't think. This is a clear accident and the grand jury's goin
to see it that way. There ain't goin to be no true bill. There ain't
goin to be no trial. No sense spendin the county's money. It's
too bad it had to be his own daddy, but Will done this county a
favor. That Boy, he's been mean bad since he was fifteen years
old. I ain't had a easy Saturday night since then, excepting the
time he was in the Navy. Why, even his own mother don't like
him."

For the first time since I had known of him, I had a feeling of sympathy for The Boy when I heard this.

"I think we'd better go to the funeral," Roger said. "It might not look right for Will if we didn't."

Oh, that interminable funeral ("Hep them, Jesus. Hep them"). There were three wasps buzzing around the ceiling of the sad little church. And afterward, at the bleak, hillside graveyard, The Wife stood like a stone by the grave and, when Will took her arm, I am damned if, even here, she didn't push him away with her sharp elbow.

It was exactly as the sheriff had predicted, pronounced an accidental death. There was no trial. We did not see Will for several days and then in the woods, walking with my goats, I came upon him, simply standing alone, staring, and he might have been standing there for days. He looked ghastly.

"Oh, my dear," I said. "You haven't slept at all?"

"No," he said.

I sat on the ground with my back against a tree. "Come lie down," I said. "I will hold you." He lay at right angles to me with his head cradled in my left arm, his mouth on my breast, and instantly fell asleep. The fingers of my left hand began to tingle and slowly the whole arm grew numb and I thought, if Roger should come on us now, I would not move, nor explain. I no longer care. *Agony takes precedence.*

I remember I felt I had discovered some deep philosophical truth with this phrase "Agony takes precedence." To repeat it still gives me a feeling of having touched knowledge of ultimate reality. Though now, of course, it is a question of *whose* agony takes precedence.

The goats left their browsing and came, all curious to sniff around Will's head, blowing the air out of their nostrils in snorts. With my free right hand I pulled their long silken ears to make them go away, but they were determined to stay near and at last lay down, one on either side, and pushed with their warm bodies as close as they could. But they did not disturb Will. He slept on. Now and then one of the goats would rear up on its hind legs, seeking a tempting morsel nearby, and crawl over on its knees, rear elevated, to chew a while, only to return again and lie down as close as possible. It was very curious. They had never acted that way before.

I bent my left knee to help support Will's heavy shoulders and gradually I grew stiff and then numb with his heaviness. Somewhere I could hear the sound of insects like small hammers beating on steel. A bird lighted in the tree next to us and sang out a song of excruciating sweetness.

It occurred to me that it was Thursday, the third Thursday of the month, and I remembered the meeting of the Committee to Recommend Legislation, where ordinarily I spent this day. It seemed the wildest joke to think if they could see me at this moment. The Committee seemed, as it still does, something from another reincarnation or another planet.

In his sleep Will smiled. Then he opened his black eyes suddenly and looked at me.

"Ah," he said, the smile fading, "I dreamed of him when he was a teensy boy, so pretty and laughing."

Isn't it so? I so often dream of Ellen now when she had her first red slippers, or squealing with excitement on the high swing.

When Will was fully awake he was instantly aware and solicitous of my condition. With slow and expert movements he massaged life back into my arms and leg and, one huge hand upon my back, he lifted me carefully to a standing position. There flashed through my mind a picture of Molly Devon at the Carlos' party, Molly, whose lonely widowhood had been transformed by falling in love with a man younger than herself. I could see on her face that night (and I felt it all through my joints) the effort it cost her to get up off the floor cushion without asking help, without holding onto anything.

I can remember it all now, how the picture of Molly flashed through my mind while Will was so easily, so tenderly, rubbing away the numbness and the pain, and I thought how blessed it was to be loved by someone whose small needs have all been distilled away in the heat of a great need—that if only I should be warm-hearted and loving, all other attributes would be accredited me.

"Ah," he said, "you're all I've got now."

I wanted to protest, then, that he did not have me, either, that he must not think so of me, and yet in his grief it seemed such cruelty to speak so. He would not have listened; he would not have heard anyhow. For he was working out in his mind then how he could arrange to open up a shop in a nearby town where there was need of his skill and where the chance of success was greatest. The Boy's widow, he said, now expected him to support his grandchildren and, since The Wife had once again gone off to Kentucky, still refusing to give her signature, he could not sell or transfer any property.

"He left no insurance, then?" I said, assuming that The Boy would have let policies lapse or borrowed on them in one of his times of trouble.

"Oh, yes, there's insurance," Will said. "I saw to that. I always paid the premiums and kept the policies, ever since he's had children."

"Then, why?" I asked.

"Well, The Boy's wife, she says that the insurance money is to take the place of a husband, that she's goin to keep holt of it until she gets another husband, and that it's up to me to take care of the children. And, I guess, from her way of seein things, there's justice in it."

"But my dear," I said, "there's no justice at all. Of course she's upset now, and hardly knows what she's saying, but as time goes by it would be reasonable to expect that she might consider your way of seeing things. Why must you look at it from her way of seeing?"

"Why, don't you *know?*" he said. "I thought you would *know* why it looks that way to her."

I didn't. I should have understood then what he was carrying on his soul, but I didn't understand until that last terrible day.

Every moment we had together became more precious after Will got his shop going. He would travel sixty miles sometimes just that we might be together for ten minutes during the day.

"I was workin on a machine," he would say, "and it's all monkeyed up." He could always find me immediately, no matter whether I was in the woods or the garden or in the house. He always came straight to me. If we were in the woods, he would hold me in his arms, but if I was in the house he would sit across the kitchen table from me, and we would simply be together in our eyes without speaking. Then, in a few moments, he would stand up. "It'll be all right now," he'd say. "It just takes a minute. It just takes patience," and he would go back to work.

He never articulated his grief; he simply wore it like a subtle skin that enveloped him. I remember his face in the firelight so clearly. The three of us ate together almost every evening around a huge fire. It is all with me now as components of my terrible hunger to take his grief into myself—the sound of the whippoorwill as the coals were ready for cooking and then, as darkness came, the lightning bugs starting up everywhere, a little ahead of the stars, and the summer evening throbbing with our longing. And in the firelight, his beloved face.

I often see such a look on Mark's face now and I suppose my own may look like that to someone else. Roger's doesn't. Yet. Perhaps it will after Ellen dies. If only Roger could show naked need. . . .

VII

To be so needed, to believe one's hand has the power to alleviate pain, one's smile to lighten grief, isn't that a large part of it? I thought. Isn't it just that Will has made me feel important, that I am content to slide about on such dangerous ground without facing what is happening? For a curious thing had made me realize that something *was* happening which needed facing.

I had seen the pokeweed plant and it had been a warning sign to me.

I must have had some idea that Will's grief would change things between us, would put us back on safe footing. Yet it changed nothing, unless it was that it made his love more intense. My own, I would not even admit to. I put my mind away from it just as, somehow, I erased, for a time, the ghastly scene in the kitchen. I had never known The Boy, really, and after the initial shock and the relief of finding that Will was free, some trick of the brain simply erased it all from my mind. *I wish it would work now, that trick, that I could get through the nights without reliving it all and hearing that sound of his head on the cement floor.* But then I walked over the very place on the kitchen floor a hundred times a day, my mind never remembering, the sound of my own humming in my ears.

So long as I had the certainty that sometime during each

day I would see Will, I was Libby Meredith, married to Roger, seeing after our needs, and in excellent health. How marvelous I felt then. Never a cold. Never a headache. Here I cannot summon up what it takes to sweep up the leaves in Ellen's driveway. I am ashamed of it day after day. Yet think what I did there: laundry and cleaning that I had for years had done for me, heavy gardening in the ever-growing heat of May and June, and the miles I walked through the woods.

Yes, I was Libby Meredith and Will was our friend and helper who, because of his trouble and grief, now needed our friendship and our support and company. Then in a moment, at sight of Will's actual presence, it would all disappear and I was—who was I? who am I now?—I was a woman on fire, pulled to him, wild for his touch. It was he who controlled things; I can see it now.

Then when he was gone, I would feel this woman leaving me and in her place would come again Libby Meredith, familiar, unquestioning, unthinking. But not the same really.

"I must say the country certainly agrees with you," Roger said. "I've never seen you looking so well." It was true. I hadn't noticed. I looked in the mirror and was shocked. I was radiant, a woman in love. How could Roger see and not know? Why, I thought, this is why you don't think, don't face what's happening. You're *using* Will's love for therapy, and you know it. It isn't for his sake you let him come every evening, and as often as he will. This is not kindness for his grief and his loneliness. You couldn't *bear* to have him take this away from you.

For our love grew more ardent and at every opportunity for privacy we approached closer and closer the time of reckoning. It must have seemed cumulative and progressing to him. How could I have treated each incident as though it were isolated, by itself, a fluke, a moment's loss of control? How could I?

In May there the wild blackberries blossom and in farms like the Evans' where once-cleared land has not been cultivated for many years, the bushes take over everything except the shaded woods and timberlands, so all the level reaches near the house were a sea of white blossoms, and they drifted white and mildly fragrant over the sides of the roads. The goats were mad for them and would get so many ensnarled about their heads while they ate they often looked like dazed brides frightened by the photographer's flashbulbs. The briars tore at my cotton dresses and ripped my arms and legs so that, if it had not been so hot, I would have gone back to the blue jeans Will hated so. I had great bunches of the blossoms in the house, even though they shattered over everything and only lasted a day or so. They looked so cool against the old, dark wood.

When the blackberry blossoms were gone, the white heads of Queen Anne's lace bobbed along the roadsides like long-necked adolescent girls in big hats and then the elderberry bushes shot out their huge umbrellas of delicately scented creamy-white blossoms. And once, clippers in gloved hand, as I reached to cut a heavily laden elder-blossom branch, I saw a whole familiar area of ground taken over by a strong and completely different plant which seemed to have sprung up overnight. Once I had seen it, it seemed to be everywhere, a miniature forest. When I looked carefully at it I saw, from the leaves, that it could not be anything but pokeweed.

But how, I thought, how did they get to be *this* size? For earlier, when Will and I had gathered the tender young shoots for poke sallet, these had been at ground level, and what's more they had been hard to find. But I realized of course that it had not been overnight. It was already late into June.

Why, I thought, half our time here is *over*, and for the first time I realized that Roger and I would be going back. I saw us already transplanted. I saw our life. And the sound that came out of me was a groan. I had dropped my clippers and, bending over to find them, I felt myself bowed down as if by a great weight. How could it be that I dreaded it that much and yet had never been aware of discontent?

I did not gather any blossoms that day. Truly it must be a time for taking stock. Something must be deeply the matter. I walked very slowly in the shimmering heat down to a shaded rock on the edge of the branch where I sometimes bathed. I took off my shoes and sat with my feet in the cold water. I bent over and bathed my face. Time seemed to stand still. How was it my whole being could be in rebellion at the thought of returning to a life nobody had forced on me, a life I thought I had made myself, and one that I had always thought of as very pleasant and fortunate? Or had I? Did I think of it at all when I was living it? I can't remember now whether I did or not. Certainly that day on the rock it seemed to me that I had never before found fault with it.

Then why this overpowering feeling of dread? I thought of the things we liked best, the concerts, going to the theater, having Mary and Evan over to dinner, the League. They all seemed. . . . *They seemed dead.* Quickly I thought of Ellen and Mark and Bucky. No, *they* didn't seem dead, thank God. Only very far away.

But if I really loved the country so much and had only just discovered it, was it not possible to have it? Of course it was. I was not necessarily doomed to live in the city against my will. If it meant so much to me as all this, we could move to the suburbs or, if that seemed too far from Roger's work, we could at least manage a vacation place or a place I could get to on weekends perhaps. There was no tragedy here, no awful doom, I said to myself. If I had lost my taste for the theater, for concerts, for the League, why I could stop going. People change. If I had changed, well then I would change things. If it was so important to me to have long idle days to walk in the woods, to look at plants, instead of busy days with many people, well then I would *have* long idle days. Why not? Even goats. If I needed goats, I would get goats. Why not?

Really, I thought, if I found myself living a life I didn't like because it no longer suited me, whose fault could it possibly be but my own? I knew myself to be most fortunately free of responsibilities and serious financial worries and if my happiness required even violent changes in my life, they didn't have to be dismissed as hopeless or impossible. They could certainly be discussed and planned for, and quite possibly attained.

Why, certainly, I said defiantly to the minnows in the branch, and to the crawdad now poking his orange toenails cautiously out of his pebble cavern. And I saw those other woods, not so vast of course, not so wild, and perhaps even those other goats. And with them I saw that other me. And I, too, like the concerts and the theater and the League—I too seemed *dead*.

For it was Will, and being loved, that made me alive. And these . . . these did not transplant.

I saw it then, not too sadly, the late Indian summer of Mrs. Roger Meredith, the last flaring of the sparks before the embers die. You can't make it out of woods and goats and idle days. You can't make it *alone*.

"Well, well, well, Libby," I said to myself, "all this philosophizing out of the humble pokeweed plant?" For the pokeweed is already quite loaded down with significance, standing as a symbol of poverty. To have been "brought up on poke sallet" is not only to have had nothing all one's life, but to have come from people who had nothing. So strong a symbol is it that

there are many who boast they have never tasted it, though its
flavor is much superior to and more delicate than that of spinach, and this boast is sometimes made by people who eat turnip
greens, which are much stronger. But turnips and spinach must
be planted. Some effort must be made to grow them, while the
pokeweed is wild and free for the picking, a gift to the poor.

There is even a song (I suppose there are many) of poverty,
despair and defeat that has the lines:

> *Poke sallet is my bread and meat*
> *And it will be till I'm dead.*

And now I, too, was seeing a powerful symbol in it, for I remembered Will's having said, "Oh, it will grow big as a tree and turn
blood red, and then it is poison. Then you mustn't eat it." It is
so. I have seen color prints of it since, a fantastic tree shape,
blood red in color, with red purple berries hanging in clusters.

The early tendernesses, the innocent caresses, the days of
the watercress and the goats' hideaway, like the tender green
pokeweed shoots hidden among the grasses, had somehow
grown to formidable size. This huge hunger between Will and
me had already strewn a dead boy on my kitchen floor. Would I,
then, let it continue until it was big as a tree, blood red and
poison?

How could I bring myself to send him away not for "two or
three days," but for good, when every fiber of me cried out to
cling to this *life* for the few months remaining? In the back of
my mind hadn't I known all the time that we would be leaving
in a year, that there was safety for me?

"Oh, Will, Will, Will," I cried, and was dumfounded to find
myself sobbing uncontrollably. I, who never sob, and rarely cry
at all. Did I really, then, love him so much?

"I would give everthing I got," he had said to me only the

day before, "just to have you wrapped all around me for one night, just to make love to you all the ways I could. How I could love you, Libby."

And I? Would I give everything? For the first time I considered it. It was mad to think of leaving, of going off with this man, behind us strewn mates, children, grandchildren. It was mad, yes, but it wasn't new in the world. It had happened before. Of a sudden I remembered, now with sympathy, the people of whom I had been so contemptuous, who had done just that.

"Oh, between a man and a woman," Will said, "when it is right. That's the grandest thing of all. Everthing else good is just part of it. Ain't nothin—not makin a livin, not takin care of children—nothin means what that does."

I saw the two of us and the minute we moved out of the woods, we were. . . . Yes, we were ludicrous. And not alone because, in middle age, we should have given such importance to passion. No, just in our essential personalities, we were a ludicrous combination. Ludicrous, and very sad.

"Why, Libby!" I heard Roger saying. "What's the matter? Did something frighten you?"

"Oh, Roger," I said. "Did you want something?"

He sat down on the rock beside me. "Why, no, Libby. It's just that you were gone such a long time from the house and when Will isn't with you, I worry about the snakes. You don't take precautions, you know. You walk everywhere. . . ."

Suddenly I turned to him wildly. "Oh, Roger," I cried, "love me, love me," for in my heart there was a terrible fear. If I was so vulnerable, all unknowing, what was to keep it from being, when we returned, the laundryman, the milkman, anyone at all who could summon up a certain tone of voice, who could pay me a few compliments? What indeed was to prevent my utter destruction?

I was wrong, thank God, about that. It is never anyone but Will.

"Why, Libby," Roger said, "you know I love you." And how could there be such blindness in a well-intentioned person, that he didn't touch me?

"Oh, I know it," I said. "Come, give me your handkerchief and sit with me awhile. Put your feet in the branch. I guess I must be having middle-aged lady troubles. Probably I need hormones or something."

He stuck his hand down in the water. "In that?" he said. "It's too cold. Why, it's freezing. Look at your feet. They're like lobsters."

"So they are," I said. When I lifted them out of the branch they began to tingle. I dried them on Roger's handkerchief and put on my shoes. Roger gave me his hand.

"Come on in the house," he said. "I'll make you a drink. We'll go out to dinner, shall we? We could drive to that place on the river. It might be good. And, anyhow, it's air-conditioned."

"All right," I said, and as we walked back to the house together there was a mad little jingle racing round and round in my head:

> *Feed the baby when it cries.*
> *Give it a drink, give it flies.*
> *Give it anything, anything except*
> *That for which its soul dies.*

VIII

Oh, the revelations I have had in public places! Somehow, I suppose such places serve as a guarantee to Roger that a certain decorum will be kept, a certain limit will not be passed. He was right about the restaurant for me, all right; it did distract me from my sorrow. I did respond to getting dressed, to the long drive, to the restaurant which was on a national highway and catered to tourists. The food was good. The air-conditioning was very pleasant. It was a world away from the farm.

"I just realized today that half our year is over," I said. "Hasn't it gone fast?"

"Oh, I don't know," Roger said. "In some ways."

"How about your work?" I said. "Will you be able to finish it in a year? Are you nearly halfway through?"

"Well, anyway," Roger said, "it's been good for you, hasn't it? You've really enjoyed it."

"It's been wonderful, Roger. The most glorious spring I ever saw."

"Well then, it's not a total loss," he said.

"Loss? Why, Roger, what's wrong? Don't you like it here? Is it wrong for you?"

Roger was buttering a roll, very deliberately. "Oh, it isn't the place, Libby. I suppose the same thing would have been illuminated for me any place."

"There's something wrong with the work, isn't there?" I said. "What is it? You've waited so long to have this opportunity—"

"That's the way I should have kept it, I guess. All those years I didn't have time to do it, I could always imagine it would be brilliant and original. People are amazing, aren't they? Imagine going on half salary for the privilege of finding out one is quite mediocre, really, when one could have stayed on full salary and maintained the illusion of brilliance."

"Oh, I don't think it's an illusion at all, Roger. You've never spoken this way before about your work. I think you're just off your feed. Take a day or two away from it. Come play in the woods with me. You've been pressing too steadily. When you go back to it, you'll see—"

"No, Libby, it's not the mood of a day, really. I suppose I've had a growing suspicion for years. After all, if it had been truly original, I would have done it long ago. I would have made the time somehow. A lack of time doesn't really stop anyone."

"But why does your disappointment come out just now, Roger, if there isn't some—"

"Oh, it's natural I wouldn't have run myself down to you Libby. After all, your good opinion is very important to me. The heat just broke down my defenses today, I suppose. Now don't make too much out of my complaining. It's not *bad* work. It's adequate. It's scholarly. It will help toward promotion. It'll serve its purpose, all right. It's just that it's not what I'd hoped."

"I'm sorry you feel that way, Roger. And I'm sure you're wrong. You'll see. Mayn't I read it soon?"

"Not just yet, Libby. It's . . . it's not in order. Oh, well," he said, "let's not ruin our dinner over it. Your steak's getting cold."

"That's not important, Roger. It's much more—"

"I don't agree. The older I get the more I come to believe there's nothing so important as getting through the present moment with some . . . grace."

How different my life would be right now, I thought, if once in some present moment I could see him *not get* through with grace. *Now there may be such, at last. But I wouldn't have wished it on him at such a price.*

"Perhaps you're not alone with your middle-age troubles.

Maybe I'm experiencing that 'time of discontent,'" Roger said. "I understand men do."

"Of course they do," I said, "and it can be quite formidable. We shall have to take very good care of each other."

"We'll do that," he said. "But I do hope yours isn't formidable, Libby. I always count on your good nature, so—your good cheer."

"Oh, you can count on it, Roger. If it runs short on me I'll run down to see Olga Marshall. I believe she has it in big bottles."

"The coffee's good, don't you think?" he said. "Shall we have some more?"

The moon was rising as we came out of the restaurant and we took the river road home. The night air was alive and shimmering and there was a delicious breeze off the water. How is it, I thought, it seems such a long time since I have actively sought happiness, as though it were of no importance? Oh, I didn't mean happiness as a permanent state, which sounds so very childish when one hears an adult prating about it; I meant the momentary thing, the flood of pleasurable aliveness which can dwindle so imperceptibly in a busy life that one forgets even to examine its absence.

Yet if it could so marvelously have been restored to me so that I remembered its great importance, could I not restore its memory for Roger? For it was not as though we had never had it. We had. We had been lovers, truly. And was it not just now, at the time when he faced this crucial disappointment in his work, that I should focus every resource I might possess in his direction? How was it I could feel so unknowing, so helpless, to do in life what I had only to die to accomplish automatically? It had struck me forcibly several times in the last few years concerning our friends, and particularly when Molly Devon's husband died, how immediately on death, in the eyes of the mate, one became transformed into, and mourned as, a lover. Was longing an absolutely essential ingredient? Everything in me rebelled against such finality.

"Oh, it's too beautiful to go in, Roger," I said when we reached home. "Let's build a fire and stay out awhile." And I thought surely, lying on blankets under the moonlight beside a fire I can beat through the wall of politeness between us and we can be real to each other in our needs.

"Oh, I thought I'd turn in early, Libby," he said. "I feel sort of dull. Do you know if we have any aspirin?"

"I'll get it for you," I said. "I didn't know you had a headache. Why didn't you tell me?"

"I don't really," he said. "It's just threatening. It's probably that damned tooth again."

"I *am* sorry," I said.

I remember that night in every detail. Never have I felt so awake, so alive. Not to disturb Roger, I went out onto the porch and stood with the moonlight full on me. The hot stickiness of the day was gone and the warm summer night was just right for a light negligee, so that I needed no wrap. I heard the sad whimper of a screech owl and felt the excitement of gooseflesh on my arms.

Ah, come now, Libby, I said to myself. You're not going to crucify this man because he has a headache, surely? Is there not tomorrow and tomorrow and tomorrow?

Why couldn't I banish the headache, though? Why couldn't I make him alive and aware of the moonlight, excited at the screech owl's call? Why couldn't I do for him what Will had done for me? Wasn't it possible? I could hear Will's voice saying, "Oh, you are soft, Libby, all soft. So soft."

Well, no, I couldn't use that line to Roger. Nor was it

possible to think of saying to him, as Will had said to me the day before, "How is it I only have to look at you and I'm ready, just *ready*, Libby? Why, I don't even have to touch you. Isn't that wonderful?"

The humor of what I was trying to do, standing there in the moonlight, a middle-aged woman alone in the summer night, struck me as so ridiculous, I could feel laughter mounting up in me, bubbling right up to where my eyes, surprisingly, were smarting with tears.

Oh, what crime, what crime had Roger and I committed against each other? What had we done? What was our guilt? Nothing. Nothing, indeed, except that we knew each other too well. We knew each other so well that, in a time of change, we didn't know each other at all.

Oh, we would see each other through, Roger and I, somehow summoning whatever "grace for the present moment" we could. Yes, we could be counted on to do that to the end of our days. But we would surely have to be beaten and utterly smashed, even if then, before we could utter a simple cry from the naked heart.

How long, how long, had he been disappointed in his work without my knowing or even guessing? And no amount of love would ever compensate for that in this man. It was useless to try. I was beaten before ever I started. I shivered in the summer night and went inside.

Yet, the very next day, when I went in to tell him that lunch was ready, I saw on his face exactly such as a look as I would have wished. From the papers on his desk he looked up at me with a radiant smile of happiness.

"I came to tell you lunch is ready," I said, "but you look as though you shouldn't be interrupted now. Lunch will keep. I'll just put it back in the refrigerator."

Today is another day, I thought, and yesterday was only a temporary mood. How silly I had been to make such a tragedy of it.

"Oh, no," Roger said, standing up from his desk. "I'll come right along. I was just writing a letter to Ellen. I can finish it later."

IX

It was on one of Will's quick trips during the day that he brought us the message that Mark was trying to reach Roger by long-distance phone at the crossroads store. I thought first: *Bucky! Something has happened to Bucky.* For I knew that Mark was aware of our circumstances from our letters and would not try to reach us by phone if it were not some kind of emergency. I never once thought of anything being wrong with Ellen somehow. Will stayed at the house while Roger and I drove in. It was an agony waiting in the car while Roger tried to reach Mark. Finally I went into the store to wait. There was no phone booth, just the instrument hanging on the wall. Everybody in the store knew of the call by now and, like me, they all stared at Roger and saw him take the news, heard him question Mark about which doctor was in charge. Then abruptly he said, "We'll be home as soon as possible, Mark. We'll leave tonight."

I knew he would not tell me in front of the people in the store and I walked ahead of him out to the car. "It's Ellen," he said. "Mark says she has cancer. She's in St. Luke's and they've had only one doctor. Mark hasn't asked for a consultation yet."

"Cancer? Ellen! But she's so young . . ." I said, even though I knew really that many young people do have it.

"Of the brain," Mark said. "It's a mistake in diagnosis. It's got to be a mistake. How long will it take you to pack?"

After Roger had explained to Will what had happened and asked him to stay after us and close up the place properly, Will came into the house. It seemed to me that he was following me around aimlessly and the sight of his helplessness made me wild.

"There's not a drink in the house," I said. "Not a drop of anything." We had been out of liquor for days and neither of us had cared enough to go after any. Now I wanted a drink, a blow on the head, anything that would clear my mind enough to organize the packing. I kept thinking stupidly that there were clothes on the line that would have to be packed damp in something. But in what?

"Here," Will said, handing me the flat pint of moonshine he seemed always to carry on him somewhere. "Should I go to the kitchen and get you a glass?"

"Never mind," I said. I took a taste of it from the bottle and a wave of nausea came out of my burning throat. I fought it down and breathed deeply, taking in the sick-sweet smell of wild honeysuckle that will always be synonymous with disaster for me now. We were standing in front of the living-room window, and outside, on the horizontal roof beam, I saw a lizard doing push-ups to the rhythm of my heart.

"What must I do, Libby?" Will said.

"I don't know," I said. "I don't know what you mean."

"Where will you be?" he said.

"I suppose we'll go to our daughter's home, Will. Our house is leased and besides, there's no one to care for Bucky, Ellen's little boy. It would be less. . . ." (I had started to say "traumatic" and realized by this simple word that I was already back in the old life.) "Less hard on the child not to have to change houses."

I turned away from the lizard which seemed to be making me breathe faster and faster. Then I saw Will, standing there helplessly, holding the bottle of moonshine in one hand.

"You're leaving me?" he said.

"Why, Will," I said, "Ellen's our *child*."

"I kilt mine for you," he said.

"*What?* Will, you mustn't say that. It was an accident. You know it was. Everyone knows it was. I *saw* it." And suddenly it dawned on me why he thought there was "justice" in his having to support his grandchildren, and I felt the terrible gulf between us, like the word *traumatic*, that made it impossible to explain to him that what would be very good for his grandchildren would not even be adequate for Bucky. At the same time I was raging with impatience at him that he had pulled this on me *now*, when I had to pack. I felt the moments going by, pressing, pressing.

He took a long drink from his bottle and fumblingly screwed the top on it and put it in his pocket. Then he stood looking down at his right arm, his fist clenched.

"Why did I hit him then?" he said to his arm. "I never hit him before. I stopped him from stompin a man to death. I stopped him from shootin a man. All I ever did was put my arms around him and pin his arms and squeeze like that until he went weak and give up. That's all I had to do. Why did I hit him, then?"

"Oh, no, Will, " I said. "No, no." I couldn't say, *I have to pack now.* I began to back away toward the door. What must I say? I thought. What must I do? He was oblivious to me, staring at his arm, held out before him. I kept backing toward the door, wanting to scream, "Not now, Will. Not now. Help *me*, now. Help me."

I stood there, holding onto the casing, unable to leave Will, sick with nausea and fear, those damned clothes on the line looming as an impossible obstacle. Somewhere very close a whippoorwill started its urgent cry. Though in the early spring, and at a distance, it is such a pleasant sound, once in a while one will get so close and cry so insistently that the call seems to the listener to be inside his own head, accelerating, accelerating.

I have to make Will move, I thought, before I can do the packing. I must break him out of that trance. I have to go to him and touch him. But just then he lowered his arm and sighed deeply. He was unaware of my presence and he took a step nearer the window.

"Right," he said to the whippoorwill. "Whip him, whip him. *Whip him till he dies.*"

X

I have arrived back at Ellen's house once again, with not the faintest memory of how I got here. It is a wonder I do not get run over in the streets. And here are the lamb chops safe in my hand, not seriously damaged with the print of my fingernails which have left crescents in the butcher paper. How many people did I pass, I wonder, carrying about with them comparable loads of confusion and wild rebellion against the facts of their lives? Is it not amazing that we go about more or less in outer order, our hair not wildly unkempt, our garments not awry, while our inner fists, bleeding and unmanicured, beat upon the walls of our traps?

There are those damned leaves in the driveway, still. I must get them swept up today. Why is it so hard for me to do these simple things?

Well, I must go in now, put the lamb chops in the refrigerator, and relieve Ellen's nurse so she can have her walk. Then, if there's time before Bucky comes home from kindergarten, I'll have a nap.

I think often of writing to Will, but I never do it. Have I not, after all, done him enough harm? I have no way of knowing whether or not The Wife might not have returned to receive my letter before Will saw it. Besides, the postmistress is related to her; the postmark alone would be enough. And there is no way I can telephone him without alerting everyone in the crossroads store.

So often now I think of the time, shattered and shaking with passion, I pushed back from his arms. "Why do you do it?" I said to him. "Why do you get mixed up with such a complicated person, Will? I shall always be too destroyed by guilt to love you furtively, too cowardly to love you openly, and without the guts to send you away. Why don't you find someone who can really love you? Believe me, you'd have no trouble finding, surely. Why do you stay around me?"

"Why, because," he said, "you're just like me. And that's hard to find."

Oh, no, Will, you were right in the beginning when I thought you so naïve. We never find anyone exactly like ourselves. We are all unique. In a horrible way, we really are.

I see Roger's car is gone from the garage. It would be easier for Roger, surely, if we went back into our own house after. . . . He'll miss his own study more when he begins teaching again. But then, what about Bucky? What about Mark? Well, when the time comes, we'll see which would be best.

Oh, Will, my little goats. Did you keep them? Did you sell them? I didn't even see them that day. There was no time after the packing. Roger had his papers and books all ready and I knew if I held the goats in my arms, it would be real to me about Ellen, and I should break to pieces. The goats must be big now, ready to have babies of their own. . . .

Talk about sad? Sad ain't no name.

After my nap I'll shower and change clothes and play a game of checkers with Bucky while dinner's in the oven. Maybe he'd like to help me gather up the leaves. Yes, that would be better. He can work off some of his energy that way and, if he's with me, I'll get it done.

Does the doctor come today? Yes, it's today. Roger will be home early then, to talk with the doctor. Perhaps the doctor will stay for cocktails with us.

From the window near the table where I set the cocktail glasses ready I can see the front walk and part of the street. So often I stand there with the shaker in my hand, watching for Mark to come home, and seeing the evening light settle down on the street like skillfully measured stage lighting.

We do not have the whippoorwill here.

I am grateful for that.

The Orchard Children

To Debbie and Danny and Melissa

More and more people are seeing the need for a children's advocate. Foster parents and biological parents are represented in court, but nobody is representing the children and they are still being considered as property in a very archaic sense.

—Miss Christopher

. . . abandonment in law would have taken place by the time the parents' absence has caused the child to feel no longer wanted by them. It would be that time when the child, having felt helpless and abandoned, has reached out to establish a new relationship with an adult who is to become or has become his psychological parent.

—*Beyond the Best Interests of the Child*
(Joseph Goldstein, Anna Freud, and Albert J. Solnit)

1

Walking through the orchard, our reason for being here in Tennessee, I stumbled on a ravaged rabbit's nest (a dog? fox?) and, before I thought, picked up the lone, abandoned baby rabbit and started toward the house. Its warm, furry body nestled in my hand. Its ears were folded one over the other tightly against its head and its eyes weren't open yet.

What am I doing? I thought. Rabbits were supposed to be our enemies, now that we had an orchard. Hadn't I, last fall, moved from tree to tree with King, tearing off squares of aluminum foil while the cold wind beat upon the foil like a Chavez percussion work? And hadn't he, on his knees, carefully wrapped the trunks of three hundred trees against the destruction of these very creatures? A rabbit can easily girdle and kill a number of apple trees in one night.

Obviously the thing to do was to bash the little creature's brains out on the nearest rock. If only the dog or fox or whatever it was had destroyed the whole family. If only I had walked by another path. A few hours without food would have settled the matter. Or if only I hadn't seen.

But I *had* seen.

How simple now seemed the "complicated" life we had left in Los Angeles, where one's enemies stayed enemies and didn't turn into warm and hungry balls of fur in one's hand.

In the house I heated goat's milk and could find nothing except an old ear syringe, once used for the cat, to substitute for a feeding bottle. The ear syringe was all right with the rabbit, though. It was too hard to suck on, so he beat his little teeth on it in a starvation tattoo and took each drop as I pressed it out. He caught on very quickly. Wrapped in a white face towel to catch the dribbles, he swallowed the syringeful of milk and fell asleep, blind, trusting and warm. I put him in a shoebox punched with air holes and set him on the mantel, out of the cat's reach. He would die, I knew. Behind me there was a lifetime of eyedroppering abandoned birds. They always died. Why did I feel obligated to draw the process out as long as possible?

Other things, too, were complicated, I remembered, as I looked in the mirror while washing my hands. My hair, for instance. Living beyond the range of any telephone wires, it had seemed too difficult to make appointments at the nearest beauty shop and I had decided to let my hair grow. Theoretically, it is at least always possible to keep long hair neat.

I remembered Joseph, who had cut my hair in Los Angeles. He cut hair exactly as I wrote books. He "felt his way," he said, and didn't know when he started how it would turn out. But when he was finished with it, all you had to do was run a brush through it. Every hair fell in place and it stayed that way for a month. Joseph was fascinated about King's dream of an apple orchard in Tennessee.

"Is he really going to do it?" he would ask each time I came into his shop. "No, he's not really going to do it. Is he?"

"I don't know, Joseph," I'd say. "He's talking about it. He's awfully sick of driving thirty-five miles bumper-to-bumper to work with the sun in his eyes and thirty-five miles home with the sun in his eyes again. If we don't move to Tennessee, we'll have to move closer to his work."

"It's murder," he said, "those freeways. I complain all the time. You know, I'm always talking about getting out of this rat race, too. Going back to the Middle West and getting a nice little farm."

"*You*, Joseph?"

"Sure, me," he said. "Why not? But to tell you the truth

with your husband and me, I don't think it's really the freeways so much; it's just our age. Your husband ever farm before?"

"No."

He laughed. "Me neither," he said. "I guess that's why we think it would be so great."

"That's why he's being so cautious about deciding," I said.

"Well, anyhow," he said, "it just excites me to talk about it, to hear about somebody who *might* really do it. But you? You think you'd like to live on a farm, Mrs. Baker?"

"Oh, I don't care, Joseph. I don't care where I live. I'd just like to live with a happier man."

"Just like my wife," he said. " 'Whatever you want,' she always says. 'Whatever you want, Joseph, do it. It's all right with me.' That way, it's all on my head, you see. If she'd say *no* or *yes*, either way, maybe I could do it."

Haircut by haircut we got closer to going to Tennessee, and Joseph always greeted me with, "Well, what about Tennessee? Is he really going?"

"He's using his vacation to go see about the land," I told him. "He wrote me the county agent brought out a soil expert and a horticulturist. You have to have a certain kind of slope and it's there, all right. The University of Tennessee will super-vise the whole thing. It's nice to be where they *want* new people to come in. And anyhow, we could never afford a hundred acres in California."

"A slope?" he said. "You mean you raise apple trees on a hill?"

"It sounds like it," I said.

"So?" Joseph said. "He's made up his mind?"

"He's going to come back and talk it over with the people he works for and see if they'll give him a leave of absence. His vacation wasn't long enough."

"I don't know if I can stand it or not," Joseph said. "I want him to do it so bad. I want *somebody* to do it and not be sorry."

"It's a real pleasure to talk to you, Joseph. You're the only one. Everybody else thinks it's madness. I ran into King's doctor on the street and he thinks that after twenty years in Southern California, King will die of a heart attack in the first snowstorm."

"Oh, my," Joseph said, "snow. In Ohio it snows. Man, we used to have fun. And the seasons. I like the seasons changing. God," he said, "I wish I was going."

"Well," I said, "what's keeping you?"

"Aw, listen, Mrs. Baker," he said. "Who am I kidding? That phone stops ringing for five minutes, I'd worry my head off. But your husband—he wants to do it, I hope he does it."

"So do I."

When King, the next winter, actually did get a leave of absence and returned to Tennessee, Joseph's excitement was terrible. I was pretty excited myself. It might even be my last haircut from Joseph.

"I'll tell you the truth," he said. "You're lucky. He's gone back again; this time he'll do it. There really is something wrong with this place, you know. Just for instance. In Ohio, when I was getting started, my wife and I, we saved up our money and we bought this couch, see? Well, it was nice, but nothing colossal. So we invited our friends in to see it. They sat on it, they looked at it, they admired it. They were really glad for us. I can remember it. They were really glad. Well, so we moved to California. I had a pretty nice shop. It wasn't big enough. So I got this place. The house wasn't big enough, so we got a bigger house. Last week they delivered a new couch for the new house. It's ten times the old one. So last night we had some friends over and you know, first thing, what one of them said?

'How much it cost you?' Nothing about it's nice or they're glad for us. Just 'How much it cost you?' Well I don't care who knows; it's paid for. So I told him. 'You idiot,' he said, 'I could have got it for you wholesale.'

"It's just," Joseph said, holding the comb and studying my head in the mirror, "it's just *impossible* for a man to get a sense of satisfaction in this town. No matter *what* you've got, somebody's got ten times better. No matter you keep building little by little, it *never* looks big to you. You get a swimming pool, the guy across the street has two swimming pools. Because his aren't paid for. Nobody makes any difference between what's paid for and what's not paid for."

He gave my hair a good stiff brushing, removed the protective garment with a flourish and studied my image in the mirror, his head on one side. "All right, Mrs. Baker?" he said.

"Fine."

"But I talked all the time," Joseph said, "and I didn't get to hear about Tennessee. What's the news?"

"I had a letter yesterday, Joseph. I think we're really going. He's got two hundred apple trees in the ground. You know anybody wants to buy a house?"

I couldn't help laughing at Joseph's open mouth. I guess he truly *hadn't* believed it all along.

"Why, for two cents," he said, "for *two cents* I'd go with you."

Alas, poor Joseph. The leaves were not fully out on those apple trees before he had died of a heart attack. Would it have come sooner or later if he had had his little farm in Ohio? I wonder. Would anything have helped? This sadness was one more in the list of casualties among our friends and acquaintances succumbing to failing hearts, alcohol, tranquilizers and the spreading gray blanket of eroding depression.

Not to mention the marriages strewn over the landscape.

When a marriage that has withstood the vicissitudes of twenty years can't stand twenty years and a day, and when not only the bystander can't understand what happened, but the people to whom it is happening can't explain it—yes, Virginia, there really *is* a scary time, and its name is middle age. *Run, run, run like a rabbit; try a different way.*

The rabbit. He did not languish and die, as he was supposed to. He grew by the hour. His eyes opened. His ears unfolded and stood straight up. On his next trip to town King bought a doll's bottle and nipple from the dime store and this was more like it, man. I transferred the rabbit to King in order to take care of a pan that was boiling over. From the kitchen I watched, fascinated. In one hand King held the baby rabbit, wrapped in its white towel. In the other hand he held the doll's bottle. It was a picture, all right, but not of a farmer.

The rabbit outgrew his shoebox. We borrowed a birdcage from a neighbor and in this the rabbit stood on his hind legs, rattling the bars for his bottle to be brought.

"When are they old enough to start eating solid food?" King asked.

"I don't know," I said. "I've been through all our books and I can't find anything." We had books on wasps, beetles, birds, cats, dogs, goats. But nothing on the diet of baby rabbits. "I could make a request at the library. . . ."

King began to laugh. "And by the time it came he'd be as big as Harvey, sitting at the table, yelling for his bottle."

It wasn't Miss Emma's fault. Tuesdays, Thursdays and Saturday afternoons Miss Emma opened the little room in the basement of the courthouse (people said if I thought that was small, I should have seen it before the new courthouse was built). She made a careful list of my requests, and next time the bookmobile came to town (if the bridges weren't washed out and if it didn't snow) she handed over the list. Months later she would greet me with books left on a subsequent bookmobile visit. If I could remember the books by then, chances were I had forgotten why I had requested them.

To one accustomed to the Los Angeles public library system, where, for the price of a postcard, sent from even the most remote suburb, a skilled professional librarian will do the most painstaking research for you better and more thoroughly than you can do it yourself—well, it was one of the bigger adjustments. And to one who had always consulted a book for every problem, it was difficult to learn that there are other ways. Finally I just walked out the door and picked a handful of lespedeza and dropped it in the rabbit's cage. When he was ready he ate it. I put away the doll's bottle and began picking lespedeza.

"This rabbit won't die," I said to King.

"You'd counted on losing?" he said.

"Yes, I had. I couldn't walk by and leave the thing on the ground, blind and waiting. And I didn't have the guts to bash his brains out. But to feed him while he slowly died of natural causes, *that* I could do and, I knew from experience, that in time I could forget."

Yes, I had counted on losing. Ever since Joe McCarthy, hadn't we? Even before. Right through Jerry Voorhis, Helen Gahagan Douglas, Dean McHenry, Adlai Stevenson. . . .

"Well that's got to stop," King said. "You can't raise apples that way."

And raising apples was why we were here. Or was it? An awful lot of people asked us that, as before they had asked why we were coming, until we asked it, in privacy, of ourselves, hoping for a revelation. "But won't you miss . . . ?" people had asked me. They listed the comforts of civilization, friends,

intellectual stimulation, concerts, theater, even California itself.
I said I didn't care where I lived; I only wanted to live with a
happy man. That's what I had said. Had I meant it?

And King? Was it simply apples for themselves? He was not
that simple a person. "Well," he said once, "I want to make a
monument." And another time, the first time we heard Anna
Maria Alberghetti sing "Mira," his eyes had misted over at the
line: "Everybody knew my name." "That's it," he said. "That's
why we're really here, I guess. That's what I really wanted."

We said that we wanted to have a try at fighting nature
instead of our fellow man, a battle for which we were both ill
suited, and so equally that it had to be recognized our coming
together had been no accident. It was the fact that our new
neighbors were competing with nature instead of one another,
King said, that explained a quality of innocence they seemed to
have. "They're up against a different enemy," he said. "It's a
different game."

Or was it only that they seemed innocent to me because I
was constantly reminded of my childhood in Kansas? I heard
words I had not heard in forty years: *infidel* and *Robert Ingersoll*
and *afflicted child*. It was all somehow like going back in time
half a century. Yet, often, the charming innocence seemed only
a universal childishness. To meet middle-aged men called Billy
Joe and Dickie Bo, to hear men in their sixties talking about
"my daddy," and never, never to meet anyone who had spent
twenty-four hours alone—these things sometimes gave us the
illusion of being in a kindergarten for giants. There seemed to
be an endless supply of kin for everyone. Responsibility for
decisions could be referred back and back and back until it got
lost.

Well, we were here, without any kin, and we had thrown
ourselves into a strange environment with only the county

agent and the Extension Division of the University of Tennessee to guide us, and we, for a change, had decided to quit fighting it (whatever *it* was) and "let life happen to us."

It was pretty scary and, even to us, it often seemed foolhardy. But it was exciting and it was alive.

The first apple trees were planted in what had been a cornfield. There were 120 Lodi and ten Jonathan (necessary to pollinate the Lodi), forty Summer Champions and forty Golden Delicious. The field was surrounded on three sides by timber land and on one by a road. The trees were planted on contour, the rows forty feet apart to allow a tractor to go between them, the trees in the rows thirty feet apart. They cost sixty cents apiece. In order not to lose a growing season, King put them in in December and January, digging each hole by hand in the frozen ground. The sowing of the orchard grass, which would make a firm turf for the tractor, the liming of the soil and the clearing out of the old cornstalks, stumps, briers and scrub tree growth would have to wait until spring.

In between the apple trees, for three rows, King planted twenty Red Haven peaches as an experiment. There was considerable doubt that the peaches could withstand the freezes which often came at blossoming time and, since peach trees were shorter-lived than apples, he expected to cut them out later.

They were so tiny, the trees, just little bare sticks among the old cornstalks. King tied red rags on them to keep them from being lost. In contoured lines they waved, the red rags. It seemed a wild dream that there could ever possibly be apples there.

The natives said not. Corn they grew, and tobacco. Hogs and beef cattle. But not fruit. We were shown old fruit trees that had never borne fruit and some that had small fruit which fell off the trees before it was ripe. "Well, you see," the state horti-

culturist said, "they've only had electricity here since TVA,
only about eight years in some places. The houses were all built
on the low ground, near the water, close to the streams. They
planted their fruit trees around the houses to have the fruit
handy. The roots are all sitting in mud. They're waterlogged.
You have to go up, up. Someday people will realize that every
one of these ridges and hills is a potential orchard. Besides, it's
ten degrees colder in the lowland."

We couldn't raise fruit, the natives said. Except for the
Swedes, nobody ever had. They could all remember the Swedes.
Fifty years ago a group of them had come. They kept to themselves and raised apples. Good apples. The people could remember when there had been so many apples that carloads of them
had been shipped out. But the climate must have changed since
then. And even the Swedes were all gone; nobody knew where
or why they'd gone. It was as though the Swedes had had some
special quality that had now gone out of the world.

The secondhand Ford tractor cost five hundred dollars. The
land was twenty dollars an acre. When these were paid for and
the trees were in the ground, it was clear that King would have
to find work. There was only one industry at that time, a factory
manufacturing gages. They didn't care that King was over forty;
he had knowledge of mathematics, a rare possession. He worked
a forty-five-hour week and often it was fifty. The pay was less
than half what he had made in California, but he was fifteen
minutes from home and it meant we could hold on for the
present. While we were waiting for the time when we could
build our home among the apple trees, we lived in the house of
friends who had gone to Nashville to work. With the house
went a horse named Dan and a cow named Huldah.

That cow. I was determined to learn to milk that cow. Most
of the neighbors considered it hopeless and advised a quick sale

before the milk dried up from my mishandling. They spoke as though milking were similar to ballet, something one simply had to have mastered in childhood. There was one, though, Luther Biggers, who had a great fund of patience and more time than most, and he stuck with me.

How utterly inadequate language is to convey directions for, or impressions of, motor activity. I was told and told how to do it and I thought I understood, but nothing happened. No milk came out of the cow. Sweat came out of me, buckets of it, despite the snow and ice all over the ground. For at least a hundred times nothing happened and then suddenly, one day, there it was—a stream of milk. *Then* I understood the directions.

Getting the milk to come out of the cow, that's only part of it. You've got to get it in the bucket. Not in your eye, not on the ground, not on the stall wall, not all over your shoes, but *in the bucket.* Huldah, all through this, was amazingly patient. Generally she stood still and only occasionally whacked me across the face with her wet tail, but very often she looked back over her shoulder and sighed at me with an expression of great contempt. She grew very fat because I had to feed her all the time I milked in order to keep her still, and the corn in the bin began to decrease alarmingly. It took me an hour to milk her (it took Luther Biggers five minutes), 465 pulls on the right rear teat, 350 on the front right, 300 front left and 450 rear left. The barn had once been a tobacco barn and was extremely lofty. The huge beams on which the tobacco had been hung to cure were still there. Some light came in through the ventilating spaces high in the top of the barn and its pattern through the cobwebs I memorized while I rested my arms from their excruciating pain.

I would carry the milk back to the house, strain it and put it in sterilized jars in the refrigerator, and nothing has ever given me such a feeling of being rich as to see all that milk I had milked myself. But I couldn't bear to drink it; it was just too valuable to swallow. I saw people in the grocery casually lifting cartons of milk out of the dairy case, and it horrified me. They hadn't any reverence at all. I suppose that is the way a coal miner must feel, to see somebody throwing coal on a fire, *just burning it up*, thoughtlessly, as though it had been made out of air by a machine.

The horse, Dan, was a bay with black mane and tail, about twenty years old. Neither King nor I rode (I'd been on a horse only once). Not only could I not ride; I couldn't even lift the saddle. Dan simply grazed about on four hundred acres for whatever he could find and came down to the barn at night for a few ears of corn and some hay. I took him an apple whenever we had one. For several nights he failed to show up. We could not find him anywhere. Then one night, driven by hunger, he came. I heard a great commotion and looked up to see this huge animal floundering about wildly. He weighed, I suppose, 1,800 pounds, and I barely missed being crushed against a wooden fence by all of it. Something seemed wrong with one back foot or leg. It was then, in that moment of panic, that I learned a horse can't get along on three legs the way a dog can. I managed to get in front of Dan and with some corn enticed him into a stall of the barn and got the door shut on him.

I went around inside the barn to the other side of the stall, where I could watch him. Confined to the smaller space, his attention on the corn, he became quieter and could hold his foot up. When King came home he went into the stall and looked at the foot. There was a huge spike sticking in it. King got hold of the spike and pulled. Out shot a stream of pus with great force. Then Dan set down the wounded foot right in a pile of manure.

Well, what were we going to do? It was somebody else's animal and we were responsible for it. On my desk in California I had always kept the vet's phone number beside the telephone, along with our physician's, the ambulance's, the police and fire departments'. Here there was not only no vet; there was no phone. There were not even wires or poles within miles. (There was no fire department for the county, either.)

I stood in the barn, watching Dan and shivering with the cold. Had there really been such a place as Dr. McCrary's Small Animal Clinic in Los Angeles, where I had sat with a cat on my lap? The doctor's receptionist in her white uniform would ask each person in turn, "Name, please?" and invariably the concerned owner would answer, "Bibi" or "Bobo" or "Spot" or "Rex," and the receptionist would say, "No, I mean *your* name," because, of course, while the pet owner was thinking only of the sick pet, the receptionist was thinking of whom to send the bill to.

Here there was no vet in the whole county. To call one from Clarksville was a thirty-five-dollar minimum charge, it was rumored. Should we, or should we not? There were, though, recognized local experts and their advice, as it always was for any injury, was to soak it in kerosene "to take the pain out." We heard so many tales of the miraculous healing powers of kerosene used on human beings that it got to be one of my nightmares that the AMA would someday come out in headlines with the news that, after all, they had discovered kerosene *was* the best treatment for ax wounds, knife cuts, burns, infections, and that I would have to go about the county taking back my words against it. I did, though, begin to understand how it had achieved its great reputation. In the old days, when there were few roads and no cars and no electricity, kerosene had always been there. Rather than stand by helpless, as I would have done, a mother with an injured child had been expected *to do something*, if only to take away the panic. So she had reached out, and kerosene was there. Soap was there, too, probably, but it had seemed too common, not enough like "medicine." Some people survive, even if nothing is done. In their survival the memory of the pain lessened and the seriousness of the wound became often exaggerated, I suppose. What they remembered was that their mothers *had done something*.

I was damned if I would give in and soak Dan's foot in kerosene, even if I could have got him to stand still for it. In the county seat there was a well-educated pharmacist who ran a modern pharmacy and I had heard that he knew a right smart about veterinary medicine. To him we went for advice. He had on hand anti-tetanus serum for large animals, animal penicillin, cheap disposable plastic hypodermic syringes and veterinary needles of the right size. I was tremendously relieved and impressed. I told him of the neighbor's advice to use kerosene. He smiled. "Well," he said, "don't quote me, but if it was my horse, I would put my faith in penicillin."

Leaving the pharmacy, I suddenly visualized myself giving those injections and I turned back. "Where do you shoot a horse?" I asked, because I knew that Dan was not going to lie down on a bed while I hunted around for the upper outer quadrant of his buttocks.

The pharmacist elevated his chin. "In the big neck muscle," he said.

It all sounded fine until we got out to the barn and I had the alcohol, cotton and syringes on a clean tray, and suddenly King and I realized we'd seen too many movies of enraged stallions who stood on their hind feet and kicked the bad man to death. Fortunately, we had Luther Biggers to help us. He and King each held ends of a rope which encircled Dan's neck.

"What do you think the horse will do when she sticks that needle in him?" King asked Luther.

"I don't know," Luther said. "My horses, I always soaked their wounds in kerosene to take the soreness out."

It certainly is a big muscle, that one on the side of a horse's neck. I'd never really looked at one before. I walked up to it with a false air of competence and swabbed a spot with alcohol. Then I went back to my tray and picked up the syringe with the anti-tetanus shot. If he broke loose and made a second injection impossible, at least he wouldn't have to go through the agony of tetanus. This is no time to be timid, I thought. *Do it.*

"Now, Dan," I said, "you hold still." I hit the muscle with all the force I had. He never made a move. I injected the anti-tetanus serum, withdrew the syringe, swabbed the hole with alcohol, stepped back and exhaled. He stood like a lamb and waited for a repetition of the whole thing with the penicillin shot. King and Luther let loose the rope and we all laughed. There was nothing to it.

By the third day Dan could walk without so much floundering, though he favored the sore foot. Gradually he began putting his weight on it and in a few weeks I saw him running on a hill against the winter sky. All alone there in that vast landscape, I let out a cheer.

And I had a great sadness for all city children who never have the opportunity to experience this kind of confidence. There is always an authority to call for everything. A vet for the kitty cat, a plumber for the leaking tap, a heating engineer for the furnace—the list is endless. Amateurs shouldn't presume, it is believed. The world comes to be a few authorities ministering to a vast number of helpless people who don't know and who are intimidated even to try. I had been one of that vast number.

Not that I intended to go overboard and eschew doctors, veterinarians, engineers, or to try the "natural, self-sufficient life." On me, it would have been particularly ridiculous. I was still recovering from an insidious, slowly progressing paralysis, now fortunately arrested. In order to do such a simple thing as grasp the handle of a toothbrush while at the same time rotating it sufficiently to clean my own teeth, I was absolutely dependent on injections of chemicals I couldn't manufacture myself. No, definitely, I was the wrong candidate to be a "nature" fanatic. The next time I needed a veterinarian I would call one if I had the money, but if I didn't have the money I would do the best I could. I would not stand helplessly in panic. And I would *not*, by God, soak whatever it was in kerosene.

It was a great moment, seeing the horse silhouetted, running, against the sky. I walked back to the house, took off my coat and cap, made fresh coffee, replenished the firewood in the stoves and managed the dampers in what I felt was a masterful manner. Well, now, yes, maybe I could have some animals of my own. I had been scared of the responsibility before. What if they got out? I was unable to chase them. What if they were caught in a fence? What if they got sick and died? Well, they might. They might. I would risk it.

To be honest, this risk I was contemplating—it wasn't a herd of wild buffalo or a pride of lions. What I wanted and had been timid about trying was two tiny baby goats. I had U.S. Department of Agriculture Farmers Bulletin No. 920, "Milk Goats" (10¢), to study and I subscribed to the *Dairy Goat Journal*. Also, I enrolled in a correspondence course from Pennsylvania State University on Dairy Goats ($2.00). If the goats didn't grow too fast, I hoped to keep ahead of their problems. The only milk goats nearby were owned by Preacher Gafford.

There was a sudden thaw in March and we waded around in the mud watching Gafford's goats in the sunlight. They were grade Nubians with long, hound-dog ears. A "grade" Nubian is the offspring of a purebred Nubian parent mated to another of inferior breeding. I had already read, and it was one of the things that interested me particularly about them, that goats suffer loneliness in a degree different from other domestic animals, and will sometimes even die of it, so I knew I must get at least two. Finally the choice was made: a black one and a brown one. They cost $7.50 apiece and cried just like human babies all the way home. They weighed about five pounds each and I could hold them both in my lap. They were four weeks old.

In the stall we had fixed for them, they hid in the darkest corner, trembling with fear. They would not eat or drink. They had not been weaned, but Preacher Gafford said they would learn to eat when they got hungry enough. In the short interval after I left them with a bucket of fresh water and before it had time to freeze solid, I suppose they must have drunk some water, and they may have nibbled a little hay, but they didn't eat anything else that I saw for two days. I sat by them in the stall, shelling corn on my lap (I was so proud of learning how to do it that I wore a blister on my thumb, which was finally replaced by a callus). At last their curiosity and hunger overcame their fear and they inched closer. I had ample time to study their strange and beautiful eyes while I sat motionless, my hand extended full of corn, waiting for them to try the first nibble. The three white plumes of our breath ascending in the freezing air made the only movement.

At last the suspense was over. They ate, and pawed the ground impatiently for more corn when I was too slow with shelling it. They pressed against me with their warm bodies (goats have a normal body temperature of 104 degrees) and at last I held them, warm and contented, on my lap. How fast their hearts beat, how sweet their shiny coats smelled. I had not realized how clean they would be, compared to cows. Their excrement was neat dry pellets and their tails were immaculate. They squatted in a most ladylike way to urinate. They were in all respects quite like deer, a fact which came to be frightening in hunting season. They had eight tiny white teeth on the lower jaw and were, I found out later, quite efficient at shelling their own corn.

My books said that goats can manufacture their own vitamin B_{12} from hay in the presence of sunlight, so as soon as the sun came out I moved my stool outside the stall into the small yard that was the only place we had stoutly fenced. Dan, the horse, jealous of all the corn the goats were getting, used to stretch his head over the fence and watch. The brown goat would stand on her hind legs, reaching up to him. Once she licked him on the nose.

Sometimes Dan yawned. It was something I had never thought of, a horse yawning. It certainly was a thorough, impressive yawn. I suppose animals do get bored sometimes. What a marvelous TV program it would make for insomniacs, after the late-late show: all kinds of animals yawning. The yawn of a hippopotamus must be wonderful to see.

Perhaps Dan was simply tired of the snow. To King and me, the first snowfall, after California, had been such a thrill. No mud, no slush, no car tracks. We made snow angels in it and ate it and threw snowballs and made snow ice cream, and did all the things we hadn't done since childhood. The second snow was great, too. And the third, fourth, fifth, sixth, seventh. But about the twelfth or thirteenth, it began to pall and we began to wish for spring. Finally there was just too much snow and ice. There was even a blizzard in April that first year and everyone kept telling us it was an unusual winter.

Oak slab wood from a nearby sawmill cost two dollars a load and each load we bought we thought would be the last, but it was necessary to keep the fires going all night in order to prevent the pipes from freezing and so the pile of slab wood dwindled alarmingly. The woods were full of dead timber and we knew for next year we should be cutting our own wood, for which King needed a chain saw. They cost about two hundred dollars new and we were very alert to any mention of them. Once as we were leaving a restaurant on the lake, the proprietor indicated two punch boards near the cash register.

"You want a chain saw or a turkey?" we thought she said.

"I don't want a turkey," King said, "but I sure am interested in a chain saw. Which board is for it?"

"They're both for turkeys," she said. "One's twenty-five cents and the other's a dollar."

"I thought you said one was for a chain saw," he said.

"I don't know why you keep talkin about a chain saw," she said. "All I ast you was, 'You wanna *chaince* on a turkey?'"

We had other troubles understanding the local speech, though I have the impression that we didn't have as much trouble understanding them as they did us. Not that they said so, directly, but things just often had a way of not turning out as we had expected. One child asked me if I had come from a foreign land over the water and another asked if I was a Jew. He had never seen a Jew, he said, but he'd heard that they talked funny. What amazed me most was that national television seemed to have no impact whatever on their speech. Somehow their speech was very infectious for me, though. I had been there only a few months when I heard myself saying I wanted a new milk bucket with a li-yud on it.

Our hay supply was dwindling, too. We were trying to make it last for the cow until there should be some green pasture, and so it was best to take the goats to the woods, where, even in winter, they could find food. There were ferns that stayed green all winter and also a wild bamboo plant. Here and there in sheltered spots there would be green honeysuckle which hadn't frozen. Of course they ate bark (particularly the pungent sassafras), the evergreen cedars and the fine powdery dust in old stumps. Also, when the snow was not covering them, they ate the old oak leaves off the ground.

At first I had been reluctant to venture out of the small yard for fear the goats would run away and I would be unable to catch them. On the first short journeys out I carried pocketfuls of corn with me. But in two or three days I realized I couldn't have lost them if I had wanted to. They would dash ahead of me, they would dance in circles around me, but if I turned a corner on the road so that I was out of sight for a moment, their cries would begin and their little hoofs would beat frantically on the road until they reached me. I grew very confident that they would stay with me and follow me home and I began to leave the road to explore inviting paths in the woods.

I stayed on the paths that were on level ground because that was what I could negotiate, but kept going a little farther than I had intended each time. The goats were such clowns. They put on such wonderful shows. I would be laughing at them before I realized how far we had gone. On the way home I would stop and sit on old log stumps and rest, but often I was too cold, too hungry for hot coffee. The goats knew they would be fed when they got to the stall, so they went homeward at a faster pace.

Somehow, when you are very cold, you do make it back to the fire. Pain just didn't hurt as much in the woods watching goats play as it did on a suburban city street, and I didn't really care whether it made any sense or not; that's the way it was.

To be alone on five hundred acres of land—it was the greatest blessing to the ear. To the spirit. To be rid of busyness, which to me is the essential curse of our civilization. It was as though not just one's lungs were meant to breathe, but one's whole body, one's hair, eyebrows, toenails, and I was just finding it out. I was sorry for everybody who had to live in a city.

Without realizing it, I had grown careless and overconfident in the woods. The goats and I explored farther and farther afield. Once I got really lost and finally gave up trying. I decided simply to follow the goats, even when the direction seemed absolutely wrong to me. We ended up at the barn. Another time we came suddenly onto a steep slope, at the bottom of which was a spring I had not known about. I stopped, but the goats went leaping down over the tumbling rocks. The black one slipped, fell in the water, struggled against an old log, which suddenly rolled in a position to pin her down. She was caught and helpless. I went stumbling and falling down the steep ravine to her, thinking: All the world talks about "sure-footed as a goat," and I have to get a clumsy one. She kept fighting and getting herself wedged in tighter and tighter and then she began to cry in real panic. I got to her and got the log moved, freeing her without getting too deeply into the icy water myself, and then I realized where I was.

I was at the bottom of a ravine, and I couldn't make it up the inclined ramp of the Los Angeles railroad station without the help of the handrail. No handrail in the ravine, sure enough. It would be many, many hours before King came home from work and, even then, how long it would be before he could

locate this ravine I couldn't say. A goat is not a dog. You can't
send one for help or get one to bark until someone hears. The
goats, in fact, the wet one shivering and miserable, had gotten
the hell out of the ravine in about two seconds and watched me
curiously from above.

Well, I did not suppose that I would freeze to death there,
really, even though an icy wind was blowing up yet a new
blizzard and the sky looked very dark and threatening. Eventually, even in the dark, King *would* find me. Still, I didn't want to
stay there all day. I started climbing. I made about ten feet
before both legs simply gave out and I fell flat. I reached above
me to a tree root and pulled and, to my surprise, I actually
moved a little. Over sharp rocks which were cutting my clothes
to pieces, but I moved. I suppose it was the milking that had put
some power in the arm muscles; something certainly was different. I reached for a further root and rested, inched up, rested
again and reached again. It took about an hour, I guess, but I
made it to the top of the ravine. I made it.

Before the summer was over I could walk uphill without
holding on to the trees. I suppose I could have done the same
thing in Vic Tanny's gym in Los Angeles, or, with enough
discipline and endless dull hours of exercise, in my own living
room. But I hadn't done it. I didn't do it. And I hadn't even
known I could.

The progress was very slow, but it was steady. And I had the
goats to watch and laugh at and learn about while it was taking
place. If you are trying to recover from paralysis, my advice to
you is to get two baby goats. Laugh your head off while you're
following them to the woods and crawl back home any way you
can.

It wasn't very long until I had the coming of spring to watch.

2

King says he remembers that first spring as one continuous maddening frustration over breaking and broken-down machinery. All week, at the factory, he would wait impatiently for Saturday to be able to work in the orchard by daylight, only to have each piece of equipment he needed lose bolts, foul spark-plugs, develop carburetor trouble, rupture hoses or, in general, tear up the patchwork repair job he had done on the previous Saturday. It didn't help any to see a documentary on TV proving that a small farmer, in order to make an annual income of two thousand dollars, needed thirty-five thousand dollars' worth of equipment.

The pH of the orchard soil tested 5.6 and the recommended pH was 6.5, so it was urgent that lime be put on the soil. The commercial lime truck weighed ten tons, loaded, and the operator was afraid of getting bogged down because the late snows in April kept the ground soggy. Finally the ground did dry out enough that he would risk it, and if a ten-ton truck can be said to go on tiptoes, his did. The little red rags on the trees had survived and carefully the operator guided the truck between the rows without knocking any trees down. It cost thirty-eight dollars to lime the orchard.

But I remember that first spring as one long glorious drunk. I was drunk on spring. I thought I remembered the coming of spring from childhood in Kansas, but spring must be, like pain, impossible to remember accurately.

First, in the swampy places, smudges of pale red were blurred into the gray from the buds and seeds of the swamp maples. Then the edges of the branch were suddenly delineated in green by the flat pairs of touch-me-not leaves. In the swamp the stiff thick blades of calamus shot up to the sound of the frogs' croaking and Luther Biggers said it was time to go frog-hunting. He wore rubber boots and a warm coat, held a flashlight along the barrel of his .22 rifle, and shot the frogs between the eyes. He brought in one the size of a puppy dog. The nicest part of all was that he cleaned them, too, and soaked them in salt water. All I had to do was cook the legs. It was a change of diet.

Soon the redbud trees burst into bloom while everything else around them was still gray and bare. Next came the white sarvis blossoms. That first Easter we had redbud and watercress salad to celebrate and always, after that, we had it for Easter dinner, the colors glistening and brilliant with olive oil, which I had at last discovered in the local grocery on the shelf with the medicines.

I'm glad we got here in time to see the grocery before they "improved" it. It was a real general store, the *only* store, in fact, at that time. Work clothes and shoes were found in the back, grain for animals and chickens on one side. The men's caps and hats were never over size seven, so King was never able to get one on his head. The dairy feed came in bags of printed material and the women would go in and choose. I came to know the designs by heart and the next summer recognized many of them in skirts and blouses on the street. It gave me a feeling of companionship with the people as nothing else ever did.

Whole nutmegs were sold in bulk, two cents apiece. That first year there were old wooden drawers or bins that held dried beans of many varieties in bulk, black-eyed peas and onion sets, other seeds in bulk, and one drawer labeled, simply, "Junk." I couldn't resist looking. It *was* junk. When "progress" came later and baskets and other self-service features were initiated, the old wooden drawers were torn out to make space. I missed them.

At the meat counter there was hamburger and sometimes

rib steaks, many varieties of sausage, pork liver (never beef, never calf), chicken and smoked hog jowl (pronounced "jole"), which was called, laughingly, in memory of the depression, "Hoover ham." There was never any lamb or veal. There were country eggs and homemade butter, labeled with the maker's name and the date made, the good yellow pounds topped with designs from ancient butter molds.

On the side of the store opposite the animal feeds was the post office, and on one wall hung the only telephone for many miles. The store was the real news center, the place to get warm, the place where all freight was delivered (including our apple trees), the place where one learned of broken bridges, flooded roads, fires, ambulance calls, and of course deaths.

The dogwoods began to bloom, usually white, but now and then there was a rare wild pink one. Walking in the woods with the goats, I came upon a sea of white violets half-buried in the old oak leaves. Each day after that was one exciting discovery after another. The swollen buds of the hickory trees began to unfurl and the folded umbrellas of May apple strode up the bare sides of the gullies. Blackberry vines leaped out and the subtle chartreuse of witch hazel. Luther Biggers said it was time for the first poke sallet.

The best place to look for poke is around the foundations of old houses. There had once been eleven tenant houses on this land before it was worn out, and the piles of stones that had been at the corners were still to be located among old leaves and weeds. Here, sure enough, were the tiny green shoots of poke. According to Luther's grandmother's recipe, one had to boil the leaves three times and discard the water to "take the poison out." My edible wild plants book said the root was truly poisonous, but just what would happen if one didn't boil the leaves I never did find out. Once was enough for me, though.

That "three times" sounded very familiar and magical to me. The local witch who stanches blood says the words three times over the wound and the one "who takes the fah out of burns" blows on them three times. Anyhow, however many times boiled and the water discarded, the tender green leaves are chopped and added to scrambled eggs.

There is *no* taste like it. The first fresh asparagus in the spring is very good, yes. But poke sallet is even better. Why it is not in city markets I'll never know.

It was time to plant corn if we were going to. One long, narrow field adjoining a spring branch looked black and fertile. A bottom plow had been included in the tractor deal, so King plowed the field. He had never used a plow before and he made a few terrible scars in the earth before he got onto the fact that it was necessary to be going the same direction on adjacent rows. This left the field in great clods. An investment in a disk harrow was not justified to raise three acres of corn, so we hired Izora Haneline's boy to disk the field for us. Then King set our plow so that only the point went in the earth and he dug long furrows. Then we walked down the furrows putting in fertilizer. The fertilizer cost $6.25.

People who raised large amounts of corn had mechanical corn-planters, but this was not practical for us. As a matter of fact, on that soil, it was doubtful that one even saved money by planting corn. One might come out ahead buying corn for the small amount of livestock we had, putting the land in the corn bank and getting paid for *not* growing corn. But we wanted to plant corn once, at least. Corn is the very fabric of rural farm life. So we were going to plant it by hand. King said there should certainly be a photographer from *Life*, to record what was probably the last field of corn planted by hand in America.

The hybrid seed cost $6.10 and was treated with a fungicide which turned our hands purple. We walked along the furrows dropping the seed and then we walked back along the furrows kicking the dirt into the furrows to cover the seed. I can remember we stood at the end of the last furrow, our purple hands hanging down tiredly, streaks of purple on our faces from wiping off sweat, and I couldn't believe there would ever really be corn there.

Yet in a few weeks there they were, in pretty straight rows, the little green corn plants. We had planted corn; I don't know what else I had expected. But still, when there actually *was* corn in row after row, I was almost hysterical with excitement. Luther Biggers said we should plant pumpkins in part of the field "to climb up the cornstalks" so we could have frahd green pumpkin to eat later.

The cornstalks grew and there was enough rain so that they flourished and were green and tall. But would it "make" was the question, meaning would ears of corn form? It made. The ears of corn appeared. They grew. To step out of blazing heat into the shaded corridor made by green cornstalks growing over one's head in a field one has planted oneself is really as great a thrill as I had imagined from reading Llewellyn's *How Green Was My Valley*. We saw the ears of corn forming and touched the red-dish-golden silk and I remembered that this had been my mother's "dolly" when she was a child—an ear of corn wrapped in a cloth, with the silk for hair.

Yes, the corn made. The news was out. And squirrels appeared. They perched in the tall stalks, they tore off the ears. They sat and looked us straight in the eye and ate our corn. The *knew* we couldn't kill them.

The Jersey cow had been bred to an Angus bull and the

little bull calf was all black. He looked like a toy bear.

"Get away, little bear," I said to him, "so I can milk your mother."

"Not *my* mother," he said. "No."

I asked Izora Haneline how to get the calf away so I could milk the mother. "Why, just push him out of the way," she said. "Shut him up in a stall till you get through."

Izora can hold a milk bucket between her knees and *squat* down to milk. No milking stool. Well, I tried. I pushed the toy bear. It was about like pushing a house aside if it gets in your way. I decided to wean the calf to a bottle.

I wonder if the bleach manufacturers realize what sadness their conversion to plastic containers in fancy shapes brought to farmers. Those wonderful old brown glass bleach bottles—how tough they were. You could scrub them, boil them, scald them, drop them, and best of all, a calf nipple would exactly fit on the necks of them. It wasn't easy to switch the black calf to the bottle, but once he really got onto it, he would come running at the sight. I kept him on the bottle longer than it was really necessary, because it made him so easy to manage. He would follow that Clorox bottle right into a stall or through a gate or anyplace else I wanted him to go.

Unfortunately, what they call "hunching" is part of drinking from a nipple, and since the bottle was held by me, it was me he "hunched." One day he hunched me right off my feet and I realized he had somehow changed from a toy bear into a two-hundred-pound calf. We cut a hole in his stall and I held his bottle with a wall between us after that. The wall was made of one-inch-thick oak boards and could stand a lot of hunching. As long as the calf didn't actually get hold of the bottle, I could still lead him around with ease, but the wear and tear on calf nipples was great. His big tough teeth tore right through them and every time I went to the county seat I bought more calf nipples from the Purina dealer.

About this time I heard from my nephew that he was interested in bonsai trees and I thought horn weights would be an interesting birthday present for him, to use in shaping the growth of the branches, because the weights were graduated. Though most people who raised beef cattle in the area now had polled herds, I had seen in one house I visited a set of horn weights from the old days when Herefords' horns had been trained to curl downward. I thought the weights quite pretty in themselves and certainly they would be a great novelty to my nephew. So, from the Purina dealer, I ordered a set of graduated horn weights of the smallest sizes. Of course I was thinking of delicate branches of bonsai trees, and he was thinking of how long I had been buying calf nipples.

"Well, how old did you say this calf was?" he said, in puzzlement.

"Oh, they're not for the calf," I said. "He's hornless. They're for my nephew."

"Your *nephew?*"

Before I could explain about the bonsai trees I could see it all going through his mind, those old stories that Yankees really had horns. . . .

We got it all straightened out and through his relieved laughter I heard one of his customers saying, "I drove by there and saw her once. It's something to see, her leadin that big steer around with that bottle like he was a puppy dog. It's a sight."

"You'd better send him to market if you aim to sell him," the dealer said. "He must be about right now. One of these days you're gonna forget and think he's a puppy dog and *he's* gonna *remember* who he is."

The dealer was right. The market was right. It was time to

sell. I sent word to the man who hauled small lots of cattle to auction for farmers. I saw my toy bear loaded on his truck and I turned my back and went into the house. I never wanted to be in the cattle business, I knew that. And I had a great surge of sympathy for Pleasant Amick.

Pleasant Amick was a retired businessman from Chicago. For years he had dreamed of living on a farm, eating out of his own garden, drinking from his own spring, owning a smokehouse full of country hams. The first thing he bought was a giant freezer. The next thing he bought was a feeder pig. Then he put his garden in. He fed that pig personally and scratched it behind the ears. He talked a lot about how fine it was going to be to have that pig in his freezer and his smokehouse. But time came to butcher it and Pleasant Amick postponed the butchering. The weather was right, the sign in the almanac was right. Neighbors offered to help Pleasant butcher and his wife warned him the hog was going to fat. It was clear to everybody that the prime time to butcher the hog was gone. Still Pleasant Amick postponed the butchering with one excuse and another. At last he went out and bought him a strange hog, had it butchered and delivered, and he called for a truck to take his hog off to auction and sell it. Before the truck came he left the house and that day he spent in a bar in Clarksville. I talked to a man who saw him there. He said Pleasant Amick just sat alone, drinking quietly and waiting for the day to be over. Once he said to the man, "Listen, you may not believe me and I don't give a goddamn if you believe me or not, but that pig laughed at my jokes."

I believe you, Pleasant. I *believe* you.

The summer heat was ghastly. Hot, close and humid, the air one breathed seemed to sit in the lungs like old, wet lint. The branch was spring-fed and icy, too cold for swimming, but the creek nearby was a lifesaver. We cooked the evening meal outdoors, not to add the heat of the stove to the house, and then, as evening came, the night breeze would lift, sung in by the whippoorwills, and one could live again. There was a kind of fierce pride in having made it through one more day alive. The stars, like great gobs of shiny ornaments, were there for the reaching and the scent of wild honeysuckle came in waves. Often the summer storms broke suddenly and violently with glorious displays of lightning and deep, rich rolls of thunder. The wild blackberries were plentiful and big that year, though the heat and the thorns made them difficult to get.

For ten dollars we bought an ancient mower designed to be pulled by a mule. Pulled by a tractor, it took two to operate. One had to sit on the mower and operate the lever by hand. A Pitman bar necessary to make the teeth work cost eight dollars. To have the hay baled was far too expensive. Modern hay-baling equipment is too wide for the roads and has to be disassembled and loaded onto huge trucks for moving. People who bale hay usually charge a share of the crop and the amount of hay we had was too small to make it worthwhile, so we hauled the hay in a wagon after it had dried sufficiently. Oh, the anxious days while the hay lies out drying. There is no experience in city life that compares to how one holds one's breath against the threat of rain while the hay is drying. Here for the first time I heard the local pronunciation of *ruin*—ruhrn—and terrible stories of entire years' supplies of hay, cut and lying in the fields, absolutely ruhrned by sudden rains. Along with these, too, were stories of barns burned down when hay was stored insufficiently dried so that bacterial action deep within the hay started fires. Altogether it was a tricky business. We stacked ours loose in the barn and, luckily, had dry weather.

I had so long waded through a sea of mud in the barnyard

because of the May rains that to have the yard dried up at last and the barn full of sweet-smelling hay inspired me to clean the goats' stall and their yard. Then I kept on working to put the barn in order and tidy up the feed room. The barn, in fact, was in so much better order than the house that I told King I wished we could sleep there.

"Well, why not?" he said.

I had long wanted to know what the animals do all night. We filled one of the stalls about two feet deep with loose hay, put blankets over it, took a flashlight and settled in. We took the old cat with us to inhibit, we hoped, the mice from running over our faces. About the snakes who came to eat the mice— well, we just put them out of our minds. There was a full moon.

So we found what the animals do all night. They eat. Chomp, chomp, chomp, sigh and chomp. Sleep a little and eat some more. The cow lay down to sleep. The horse slept standing up. The goats lay curved against each other, the black one's head across the brown one's neck. The full moon splashed its light through the tops of the stall doors, the cracks in the walls, the ventilating spaces near the roof. The frogs in the swamp kept up their singing. Somewhere a dog barked. Miles away on the Tennessee River a tugboat sounded its whistle. At dawn the birds began to call.

Late in July the elderberries ripen. In the evenings we would drive along the roadsides hunting the huge bushes, in clumps of two or three. We would cut off the umbrella-shaped clusters of berries, load them in baskets and bring them back to the branch, where I could sit with my feet in the icy water, slipping the berries loose from their stems, my hands turning blue from the juice. The purple, lacy framework of the umbrella after the berries have all been peeled off the stems is one of the most delicately beautiful structures I have ever seen. I would make the jelly late at night after King was asleep, when the house had finally cooled off. The kitchen shelves were becoming quite beautiful with promise for the winter: pokeweed pickles, blackberry jam, elderberry jelly.

By the end of August the dominant whites of the landscape begin to give way to lavenders and purples. The tall ironweed comes into its vivid purple bloom and huge wild lavender thistles are adorned with blue-and-yellow butterflies and fat black-and-yellow bumblebees.

School starts in late August, even though in the classrooms it is unmercifully hot. Summer seems to go on forever. But suddenly one seems to be running out of time too fast in the day. Darkness caught me at the barn with chores unfinished several nights in a row before I could realize that real changes were happening. A coolness came into the nights, chill enough to have a fire. One morning a light frost showed up on the car windshield and that meant it was time to gather wild persimmons for pudding and wild grapes and, near the river, in certain years, the wild muscadines. Muscadines smell like the hot tar machines used in mending asphalt pavement that we used to follow as children in the summertime. Inside the tough purple skins of the muscadines there is an incomparable flavor.

And it was time to harvest our corn. Luther Biggers snapped off an ear, peeled down the husk, stuck his fingernail in a grain of corn and said the corn was ready. There is quite a technique to be mastered before the ears snap down and off, and by the time I had learned it, my hands were bleeding all over the husks. Luther had not thought to tell us to wear gloves, since he had a pair made of calluses always with him.

Twist, bend down, snap and toss the ear onto the wagon. It is a four-movement dance. When the wagon moves on ahead of you, you hear the sound of the dry ears hitting against one another. Distant thunder is called locally "corn wagon rollin." I never hear distant thunder but what I imagine that gigantic and heavenly mule pulling a corn wagon through the furrows of a distant sky, the golden ears rolling and settling. Of course mechanical corn-pickers are used on large farms now and in later years we did not find it profitable, really, to grow small amounts of corn, but still there was a grand thrill in having done it all once by hand, from the planting to the harvesting, and the next winter, feeding this corn to the goats, I held history in my hands.

Corn was still lifeblood to some small farms around, the way it had once been to all of them. Cash money was for medicine, for clothing, for funerals and for seed. Otherwise, if you had corn, you could make out. Everything ate it: the chickens that laid the eggs, the pigs that provided the winter's meat, the cows that provided the milk. The people ate cornbread three times a day. Izora Haneline on the next farm still made cornbread three times a day on a wood-burning stove right through the heat of August, because she always had. Even in these days of improved packaged feeds, still there was the old feeling of terrible insecurity to have an empty corncrib with winter coming on. And in the depression, when no one would pay for their children's labor or for teachers to teach them, or a decent price for their cattle or their crops, the moonshiners had bought their corn. There is a kind of hard, solid, golden reality about corn. Children who came to visit us were always fascinated by a barrel of shelled corn, content to run it through their hands over and over again.

Since I always carried some in my pockets when I walked with the goats in case I needed it to get them to turn homeward, I gradually came to have a couple of grains of corn in everything I owned. Washed from pockets, a few grains were always in the washing machine drain. It was such an integral part of life that somehow it just worked its way into everything. Even far away in a distant city where I went to bury my mother, I found a grain of corn inside one shoe, and thought longingly of the farm.

All through the previous early spring King had spread ammonium nitrate in white circles around the trees in the orchard, so that the weeds grew green and taller than the trees in the summer. It was a constant job digging out weed-free bowls around the trees. Not only do the weeds rob the trees of the fertilizer, but they make encouraging cover for field mice to nest in. It is a terrible sight to see a tree one has invested two or three years in standing at an angle and to find that one can push it around at will because of the damage mice have done to the roots. Because of the old cat we feared to use Endrin on the grass to kill the mice.

There was also need to spray, mainly Malathion, against the aphids and other insects who damaged the leaves and made them curl and die. King had only a hand sprayer then, attached to a tank strapped over one shoulder. In his pocket he carried one of my hairpins and a needle for cleaning out the nozzle, which was constantly getting plugged up. From ads in *The American Fruit Grower* he sent for spray-equipment literature to study for the future when we might have enough money or enough credit to buy it. It seemed, though, that we would never have any money because of the tires (pronounced "tahs" here). Tires, tires, tires—everything needed tires. The car, the old truck, the trailer, the tractor (one rear tractor tire cost seventy dollars)—they would have casualties in waves, like influenza among office workers. And they all ate gasoline like gluttonous monsters. In vain do you tell yourself that orchards existed before tires were invented. That was then. *Now* you have a secondhand tractor, and it follows from that that you will somehow find yourself working to support an animated junkyard. There were days when it seemed that all the world was held together with miles of old wire, a world in which an apple tree could not possibly exist.

Suddenly the autumn colors burst upon us. The red maples point to the yellow beeches, shouting, "You think that's good? Watch this!" Sourwood turns scarlet first, then sumac. The goats found red buckberries to eat as we rattled through the fallen oak leaves. They loved the rich green leaves on the bamboo bramble, but never touched its deep-blue berries.

One after another the local schools had their harvest festivals and we longed for the autumn when we would have apples to enter in the fair. Along the country lanes a flower called hearts-abustin-with-love bloomed forth and if I hadn't seen it with my own eyes I would never have believed it. What we used to call in Kansas something "just really too gaudy," these flowers are orange and purple. Well, later, when I found them in a wildflower guide, I found out these aren't flowers at all. They're purple seed pods which burst open to reveal orange-red seeds. The real flower happens earlier and is so inconspicuous I hadn't noticed it.

Fall is the time for the county fair, which I wanted to study to find out how I could show my goats the following year. It was time, too, to get wood stacked ahead for the winter fires and water pipes insulated and winter underwear unpacked. And it was time to find a mate for the goats.

Nothing in the goat literature had given me any hint of how difficult this might prove to be. The literature advised the owner of grade goats always to breed to a thoroughbred buck so as to improve his stock constantly, but such was the prejudice against goats in the area, and the ignorance concerning milk goats, that no one took my search seriously. I was directed to seek out distant scrub goats or nonexistent goats. One, located after a long trip, we learned had been "clamped" (castrated) only the day before. If we had been in the dairy-goat business, it would not have been an inordinate amount of time spent, perhaps, but we were in the orchard business and my goats were actually pets. Up to now it had been a wonderful blessing to be without a telephone (oh, those housewives in Los Angeles, trying to earn a few dollars, reciting those endless monologues about insurance—how wonderful it was to be free of them), but after the fifth or sixth fruitless journey to find a suitable buck, I began to appreciate that a telephone can save time in addition to taking it. Finally I settled down to going about The search sensibly by writing the Nubian Society, advertised in the *Dairy Goat Journal*, and at last, by mail, located a thoroughbred, registered Nubian billy goat at a distance of ninety miles.

By this time I had talked so much about getting a husband for my does that Luther Biggers, on seeing me receive in the mail a copy of a book called *Goat Husbandry*, said, "You mean there's a whole book just about *that?*"

When a cow is ready to be bred, the whole world within hearing distance knows it, but goats are very different. So far as I could tell, they kept all this knowledge to themselves. Between September and March, roughly, they are supposed to be in heat every twenty-one days, but none of the subtle signs that are supposed to indicate this repeated themselves at any such intervals. In my inexperience, I concluded the only thing to do was bring the buck to the does and leave him for twenty-one days on the theory that if I couldn't figure the signs out, the goats could. So it was arranged. We took the truck and made the 180-mile trip, and on the way back, through each little village, the people really took notice. He was a tremendous black creature, that buck, built like a buffalo. His name was

Beau Chic Amity and he stank for miles and miles. Healthy
does have no objectionable odor, just a sweet woodsy smell, and
though I had read of this buck smell, I had never experienced it
before.

For all his gigantic size, he was quite manageable, though
frisky, and at the barnyard he was delighted to get off the truck
and have his feet on solid ground. He was thrilled at the sight of
my two beautiful does. Alas, the attraction was not mutual.
Both does let out dreadful cries of alarm at the sight of him (if
they had had on aprons, they would have thrown them over
their heads) and they ran to me for protection and tried to hide
behind me. Beau Chic Amity, with his great bulk and his
twenty-ton odor, was in front of me. We all did a fast little
dance there in the cold winter air and somehow nobody got
hurt. I wanted terribly to tell my does that it was *all right*, they
could be old maids if they wanted to. I loved them even if they
never had babies, if they never gave milk. I loved them, and if
they were so afraid of this terrible smelly monster, I would take
him away.

But all that journey for nothing? I steeled my heart and shut
the gate on the three of them and turned my back, feeling just
like one of those ambitious Hollywood mothers who turn their
sixteen-year-old daughters over to horrible old men and look
the other way while they dream of fame and baby's name in
lights.

That night, guiltily, I stole down to the barn. That black
monster stood in possession of the corn trough and the hayrick,
he strutted back and forth, gorging himself between threats,
while my two beauties cowered in a corner, seeking consolation
from each other. ("Oh, sister, dear sister," you could almost hear
them crying.)

Sister, dear sister, my foot. In two days they were butting

each other's brains out, trying to get Beau Chic's undivided attention. All of a sudden he looked wonderful, everything he did was marvelous and cute, and to them he smelled divine, just divine.

They cried when he left, too. I didn't. I was thrilled to be rid not only of Beau Chic but of concern over the whole problem for a year. His memory lingered on and on and on, in the truck and in the barn. Through sweeping, scrubbing, soapsuds, sunshine, disinfectant, it lingered on. But in a few months it appeared that all the trouble had not been in vain. My two does quit leaping so gaily in the woods, they became somewhat sedate, and it seemed to me the black one (who was a little undershot and whose teeth showed at times) smiled mysteriously. I counted ahead to the estimated five-month gestation period and began to study the chapter on how to assist at normal and abnormal deliveries.

Shelled corn was $2.50 per hundred pounds that year.

3

Long before the babies were born I had my basket packed with maternity supplies: old, clean Turkish towels for cleansing and clearing the nostrils and rubbing the bodies dry, paper towels and sacks for disposing of the afterbirths, and the essential iodine for the umbilical cords to prevent entrance of that terrible virus from the soil which sometimes causes painful swelling of the joints and even death. I had the soap and scrub brush for my hands and fingernails and the big diagram of abnormal presentations, in case it should be needed.

But it wasn't needed, thank God. Within a few hours of each other, Kathy, the black goat, gave birth to two billy goats (which I later sold for pets) and Miss Dude, the brown goat, had

twin does. I was trembling with anxiety and excitement, rubbing the squirming babies with towels and seeing their incredible beauty as the mothers licked them all over until their coats
were dry and shining. The babies seemed to be all ears. One of
the baby does was a rich brown in color like her mother, but all
the others were black like Beau Chic Amity. Babies are born
with eight lower teeth already complete, and their tiny hoofs,
about the size of dimes, are a translucent yellow. The little faces
are unbelievably delicate, with long pointed noses. Close to the
mother they lie and she, intent in her maternity, suddenly
develops a new vocabulary: *mm mm.* It is a sound not heard
before, which comes with the babies.

I was tremendously gratified that the mothers did not mind
my presence, did not seem alarmed if I picked up a baby. The
does drank buckets of hot water and hungrily ate bran, just as
the book said they would. They permitted me to get the stall all
cleaned up and filled with fresh shavings.

Worn out with the excitement of it all, I sat down to watch
the babies search for the milk. Contrary to what I had believed,
instinct does not lead them directly to the spot, but I felt that I
was not supposed to interfere. So I sat watching them suck the
mother's neck, the chest, the belly, at last get a mouth on the
swollen teat and slip right off it, only to regain their wobbly legs
and stumble drunkenly up the mother's neck again. After what
seemed like ten thousand tries, the babies still hadn't made the
right connection by the time I left the barn to go to the house
and start supper. As soon as King came home we went directly
to the barn and the moment we entered we could hear the
sucking noise. All four of the babies were nursing and all the
time that the sucking goes on at the front end, the tails are
wagging frantically back and forth at the other.

At first the mothers nursed the babies lying on their sides, but by the next day the babies stood up to nurse and their little stick legs not only held them up, but allowed them to run and even jump without falling.

For the first five or six days the milk contains colostrum and is yellow in color from vitamin A. It is rich in all good protective things for the babies and is said to have an unpalatable taste for people. I let the babies have it. After six days I began milking in the mornings. Starting off right with milking is very important and requires great patience. The goat jumps onto the milking platform to get to the food you have already put into a pan that can be reached only if the goat puts her head through a keyhole-shaped opening. While she is eating, you close the stanchion bar so she can't get her head out again. Then very gently, with petting and soft talk, you sit beside her on the milking stand, put your bucket in position and begin to milk. When she kicks, you stop milking and pet her. No matter what she does, you keep your temper. After a few days, if you have been very patient and gentle, the goat will stop kicking and everything will settle into a routine. Miss Dude settled down much faster than Kathy did.

Goat's milk is homogenized in the goat and pure white in color. The taste is very similar to cow's milk, perhaps a little sweeter. It was a great thrill to have our own goat's milk for the first time, though I had as yet no idea of the yield because the babies were getting most of it. When Kathy's kids were a month old I sold them for pets and started shutting Miss Dude's babies away from her at night. Between the two does we had a gallon a day and Miss Dude's babies continued to nurse during the day, although they were eating corn and hay and all the wild plants Miss Dude browsed on in the woods.

I named Miss Dude's babies Rosie and Viola for friends of mine. In the woods, if they strayed too far from her, Miss Dude had only to utter her *mm* sound and they came to her side instantly.

By the time the baby goats were born we were already in the second year of the daisy problem and still fighting. Every time it rained that first winter King watched the raw plowed soil washing down the hill and hoped no severe damage would be done until he could get orchard grass sown. As soon as it was warm enough that first spring he bought the fescue seed. He tore a green tag off the seed sack.

"Keep this someplace," he said.

"What is it?"

"That's the guarantee," he said. "It's certified seed. The dealer has to make it good if anything's wrong."

Not only was the orchard grass needed to keep the soil from washing down the hill, but by the time the trees were large and bearing it was supposed to produce a solid turf over which one could drive a truck loaded with apples and not get mired down. King sowed the seeds by hand from a sower ($3.86), which is a canvas bag held by a strap over one's shoulder. It has an opening in the bottom which can be adjusted to emit more or less seed, and it holds about twenty pounds. As one walks, one turns a vertical crank which throws the seed in a circle. Around the edge of the orchard King could hear the seed hitting the leaves of the trees in the woods and it would help him believe what he was doing. The rest of the way the seed, too small to be seen on the earth, fell silently, and on the contoured rows it was hard counting paces, trying to remember where he had and had not walked before. The whole process, rhythmic and seemingly endless, produced a kind of hypnosis. From a distance I would watch him against the sky, pacing back and forth, his hand turning steadily, until it seemed he stood still and the earth moved.

Rains came in good time the first year and we saw with
excitement the rough brown earth softening into a soft green.
Suddenly there was—here! over there! another!—a white spot.
Then, like corn popping, there were daisies in bloom all over
the orchard. I didn't realize the import of this at first. Rob
Herman, who had sold us the seed, explained apologetically
that he had bought it from Old Jim Hollander up in Stewart
County, rather than from a regular seed house. Jim's fescue field
must have been full of daisies that year. Since Rob had "certified" the seed, he gladly gave us another bag of "certified" fescue
seed. But there was no replacement for the days of lost labor.
There was no remedy for the mad fecundity of the daisies.

A daisy, in Tennessee, is classed a noxious weed. You not
only cannot build a solid turf out of it, but it will drive out what
will make turf. Desperately, before they went to seed, we tried to
find someone to mow the orchard. Unfortunately, everyone who
did custom mowing was, at just that time, occupied with the
necessity of getting his own hay cut. It was an impossible task to
pull off all the daisy heads by hand. We got the orchard mowed
as soon as possible but, alas, the next year there were even more
daisies. I stood in a sea of daisies where fescue was supposed to
be and thought of the money I had spent at florists' for these
hated things. To think I had once, in cities, loved to see daisies
in a florist's window.

Despite the discouragement of the daisies, in September of
the second year King had more woodland cleared for orchard by
a man with a giant bulldozer ($137.50) and we decided to start
building our own house. It would be on the top of a hill, surrounded by apple trees, with a view that seemed limitless. On
one side there was a good blacktop road, on which, in future,
would come the apple customers.

In October we built the new goat barn within sight of where

the house would be. It was only eight feet by twenty, with a
fenced enclosure, but it was on a hill with good drainage. The
old tobacco barn had been built on a swampy ground, a constant threat of foot rot. There was a small feed room, easily
accessible from the road (those hundred-pound sacks of feed get
heavier as one gets older). There was one stall for the goats and
a room with a milking stand in it. Each room had a window on
the south to let in light and whatever sun warmth was possible
in winter. The barn was built of old scrap oak lumber with a
galvanized roof, and it looked very tiny, but to me it was beautiful. I covered the floor with loads of bright-yellow shavings and
could not wait to move the goats in.

In November the fillings started falling out of my teeth.
There was a regular shower of fillings. And King discovered he
could no longer see what he had to see at his job with his old
glasses. We were reminded of the high price of disintegration,
not only in money, but in the traveling distance and time
necessary for repairs.

Yet we resolved to stick with the plan of the house. We
were too committed to the land to back out now and in December we deposited fifteen dollars with the local electric cooperative to have an electric pole installed so that the carpenters
could operate their power tools. The only way we could manage
to have a house was to pay, over a twelve-year period, ten
thousand dollars for a five-thousand-dollar house, built by a no-
down-payment firm. We found one that would forsake their
standardized design for our design, and went into a bad bargain
knowingly.

That New Year's Eve at midnight we stood high on our hill,
on the spot where the house would soon be. It was to face the
North Star, not for romantic reasons, but because the best view
was north. To enjoy it, we planned for that side of the house to

be mostly glass. I can get glass clean enough to enjoy a north view, but not any other, and I did not intend to spend the rest of my life being reproached by streaks on glass shown up by direct sunlight. The house was to be nestled among the apple trees, with its back to the road, eight feet high on the road side, rising to twelve feet on the view side.

Would this be it, I wondered, the last home? There is always one house where you die. A sobering thought at midnight on New Year's Eve, standing under the stars in the snow. I thought of all the other homes, some fleeting and rented, others more permanent. Some entered with illusions of emotional security, of romanticized sheltering, some simply endured. And this one?

Physically, it was to be essentially one large room, glass on the view side, a huge fireplace with raised hearth at one end, small alcoves for kitchen and bath with closets between—only the essentials, and undemanding to keep. On the view side the glass doors were to give onto a large patio, where we expected to do much of our living.

And spiritually? Well, really, were there any illusions left? Well, it would be . . . it would be what it would be.

"Are you cold?" King said.

"No," I said. "I was just shrugging off some old thoughts."

Some bitter old thoughts I had carried from some restaurant where we had stopped on the journey here. In what town? As you cross the country, all towns fuse into one. But though I did not remember the town, I remembered the waitress very well. A small body, deformed by tuberculosis of the spine, I suppose, such as one rarely sees any more. She had fine blue eyes with fatigue smudges under them, and the long, thin bones of her hands showed the size of the body she had been meant to have.

On long motor trips I stare out the window and become philosophical. I remember I was speaking of how essential it is for women (meaning me) to think they have made or can make some man happy, and how tenaciously they cling to this belief. On long motor trips King sits at the wheel and drives, and *he* becomes tired.

"It seems unrealistically romantic," he said. "Couldn't you compromise in the belief you had made someone a little less *unhappy?*"

Well, no. No, I could not compromise for something not good enough to have spent a life on. No, I could not. If I had a choice.

But I did not really have a choice, I was thinking that New Year's Eve in the snow. For we were irrevocably committed to each other somehow. In sickness and health? That was the least of it. In grandeur or pettiness, wit or stupidity, fascination or screaming boredom, in truth or lies, meeting or worlds apart, drunk or sober, listening and deaf—we were committed.

And now we were also committed to the land.

In January King ordered a pair of lopping shears ($8.75) from Seymour Smith Hardware, confident that those tiny trees would really have growth they didn't need, and in February he ordered thirty more trees ($16.00)—ten Red Delicious, ten Winesap and ten Red Haven peaches to replace the ones cut down accidentally by the man who had mowed the orchard. Now that the secondhand tractor was paid for, King bought a bush hog for mowing the orchard grass. This year he planned to beat the daisies and not be dependent on someone else's haying time. I bought a registered thoroughbred red Nubian billy goat already named Clintwood Beau's Buddy. We had to go eighty miles to get him, but it would be better to have one of our own.

Clintwood Beau's Buddy (registration number N141824) was one month old and altogether beautiful. I held him on my lap all the way home. We arrived after dark and, rather than take him to the barn to be among strangers, I put him in a cardboard box with hay in it in our bedroom. After all, I had never owned a registered thoroughbred anything before. It was his first night away from his mother and he cried without stopping. Finally I wrapped him in a bath towel and took him to bed with me. Instantly he fell asleep. How warm he was. It was hard to believe that within a year he would grow to be a huge, sex-oriented monster with that pungent odor so repulsive to human beings and so alluring to lady goats.

He would be herd sire, husband to Miss Dude, Rosie and Viola. I would sell off Kathy, the black goat, and any future babies not of his reddish-gold color. I could see it now, my future herd, all uniformly red-gold, running through the green woods, their harmonizing bells making sweet music. And when I had made all the mistakes and was full of wisdom and experience, I would buy him a thoroughbred registered doe of the same color. And there would be milk, gallons of milk, and cheese and yogurt and tiny fawnlike golden babies dancing sideways and leaping in the sunlight.

In April we arranged with Mr. Norman to begin digging the well. The house was very nearly finished by this time and we were eager to get in. But of course we had to have water first. The region abounds in water witches, who locate water with peach twigs, willow twigs, practically any kind of twig, and we heard of many famous ones. I would have loved to see one working, but before we had made arrangements, Mr. Norman came with his rig and started to drill. Mr. Norman laughed about the witches. "There isn't hardly anyplace in this region where you *can't* find water," he said. I had noticed there seemed to be an awful lot of witches mentioned in relation to the population, while I had never heard of one when I lived on the desert. "In twenty-five years of drilling in this area," Mr.

Norman said, "I never had but one dry well. I had a few with sulfur water, but only one with *no* water. If you don't get any water, the well's on me." That's what he kept *saying*, but what he had actually written on the back of his card, and King later said he vaguely remembered reading, was that *half* of a dry well was on him.

Even far below the site, in the house where we were staying, the sound of the drill was impossible to ignore, just as if it had been inside my head. After the first hundred feet it sounded louder. I know of no other experience to equal it, hearing the drilling that means $4.25 every foot it continues into the earth, and knowing that at some spot you must decide to say *stop* because that's all the money you have or all you can borrow. But then if you said *stop*, and by going one foot more you would have had water . . . ?

Day after agonizing day it continued. The pump belched up blue colored clay and yellow colored clay and gray colored clay and fine flint-rock dust, and a rainbow of different colors and textures went cascading down the hill. But no water. Finally the decision had to be made. At three hundred feet there was still no water, and Mr. Norman let us in on the news that we were to pay half. There is something about staring at a $1,275 hole in the ground that stops conversation. Mr. Norman said he was so *sure* there was water there that he would go fifty feet more at his own expense before he pulled the rig out and started at another location. By this time the whole county was interested. We heard nauseating stories about people who had struck thousand-gallon-per-minute flows at one hundred feet, eighty feet, seventy-five feet.

We heard no sympathy, though; they had *told* us to get a witch. We were really more comfortable with Mr. Norman, even if, when he pulled his rig out, we owed him $637.50. For it

was not doing his business any good, either. He moved his rig
150 feet to the east and we started the whole thing over again.
There was really nothing else to do but to go on trying. The
house was built, the orchard was in, and we had to have water.
Of course, all around us, below, were creeks, springs, little
rivulets, swamps. But the trees had to be on a ridge. And we
wanted to be with the trees. In the new location Mr. Norman
found water at 150 feet—not any miraculous amount, but
sufficient for two people if they were careful. So now we owed
Mr. Norman another $637.50 and it would take $275 more to
install a Jacuzzi pump to get the water to the surface. Into the
house—well, that was another problem.

Our lives were, of course, tremendously changed by all this.
Mr. Norman probably only changed his opening remarks to new
customers. "In twenty-five years of drilling in this area, I only
had *two* dry wells."

We made the first house payment ($71.36), paid J. L. Sykes
fifty dollars to dig the cesspool and ditches, Luther Biggers
hooked up the water connections to the house, and in May we
moved in.

We had a bed, two card tables, a few borrowed chairs and a
hot plate for making coffee. The rest of the cooking we did in
the fireplace, over charcoal, for the kitchen had all been
predesigned for a wall oven and a countertop unit, which we
could not afford because of the well, and I had decided I would
rather have nothing than something I didn't want. We never
tired of charcoal-flavored meat, as I'd thought we would. I
suppose if there were charcoal-flavored ice cream I would like
that, too. The raised hearth was exactly the right height for
comfort (twelve inches), the draperies from the California
house fitted perfectly, and the view was magnificent.

The floor, though, was unfinished raw boards, constantly

covered with red mud. The topsoil had been removed to make a level place for the house and the exposed red clay clung like glue. And it rained and rained and rained, while the spaces that would someday be the patio and the back porch ran rivers of red mud. Every time King could spare a half hour from the orchard, we drove along the road hunting the places where large gray slate rocks were exposed in the hillside, and these he lifted and carried home. There seemed never enough to keep people's feet out of the mud. Sometimes I thought that in the night the mud ate up the rocks we carried in the daytime.

But the view, as I said, was magnificent, and spring unfolded before us and, alas, so did the goddamned daisies. Maybe not quite so many as the year before, but enough, enough. One thing I knew, and that was that the author who wrote

> At evening when I go to bed
> I see the stars shine overhead.
> They are the little daisies white
> That dot the meadow of the night*

was not a Tennessee apple farmer. From this height we could see redbud and sarvis and dogwood miles away, spotted all through the grays of other trees, and now it was a thrill to wait for events we knew were coming, to celebrate the first whip-poorwill, the first violets, the croaking frogs, the first poke sallet.

The peach trees had been sprayed with Bordeaux mixture against peach leaf curl in February and in March with lime sulfur against rot. In April they had to be sprayed again with lime sulfur, and the routine spraying of the apples with Captan and Ferbam every two weeks against fungi began. There were

---

*Frank Dempster Sherman, "Daisies."

DDT sprayings, too, for Oriental fruit moths and other insects this year, though in later years, when there would be fruit, this would no longer be used. Dalpon was used to inhibit the growth of grass around the trees, where it stole nitrogen and made inviting nests for mice and rabbits. The trees had put on a magnificent growth, though it would be two more years before they would bear any significant amount of fruit. Still, you didn't have to tie red rags on them to see where they were any more. Some of them actually had blossoms, heavenly sweet and promising.

The orchard, of course, was forbidden to the goats, so in our walks we went the other way. Miss Dude, even a year after the birth of her two does, Rosie and Viola, had continued to give nearly half a gallon of milk a day for our use and it appeared that she would never go dry. Now there was an abundance of free food in the woods. Miss Dude and her daughters and Clintwood Beau's Buddy and I would go every day from their pen into the deep woods, where I would sit on a rock or lie on the ground while they browsed on hickory and hackberry, elm and maple, cedar and sassafras, wild grasses and blackberry bushes. The sound of the wind was completely different from that in the lowlands. You got so much more for your money. Beau (Clintwood Beau's Buddy was too much to say) was growing beautifully. He had two white wings on his face and was much more affectionate and playful than the does. He was still delicate and fawnlike that summer and I dreaded the time when he would have to be separated from the others and put off by himself. Life cannot be all pleasure for a herd sire. I must be in charge of the breeding schedule, not he. And I must be sure that the does' milk was not contaminated by his odor.

I decided not to risk taking him to the country fair, since I had never been to one. I would take Miss Dude and since Viola

would never stop bleating if Miss Dude were out of sight, I
would take Rosie and Viola, too.

The day of the fair, King stood in the early-morning darkness checking the last items off my long list by flashlight while I
put the remaining things from the barn into the truck. There
was a currycomb and brush, a milking stand, disinfectant, fly
spray, a rake to keep the stall clean, food, water bucket, copies
of *Dairy Goat Journal* for display, hammer, nails, two clean white
coats for me, an ice chest, a supply of small paper cups. . . . Oh, I
had been a long time preparing the list.

At last everything was ready. The old truck was a pickup
with low sides. I climbed into the truck bed and held out a
peanut for Miss Dude (the goats had all been trained on peanuts, which they ate shell and all) and she jumped right up after
it. Rosie and Viola followed Miss Dude just as they were supposed to. It seemed best to stay in the truck bed with them. So
we all settled down together and King started the motor. At first
the goats jostled about unsteadily, but after a few miles they
relaxed and lay down. We had the world all to ourselves at
sunrise. Early-morning birds were singing and honeysuckle
cascaded over the road banks. We were on our way to the fair. I
had actually raised these beautiful creatures who gave real milk
in abundance and I could handle them in strange surroundings
with confidence. There are some moments so joyous that, even
while one is experiencing them, one knows they will be the
remembered ones. Such was that early-morning ride through
the deserted county roads at sunrise, with the cool wind blowing
at my hair and the warm, shining, golden bodies of the goats
around me. Some hours you'd like to live over again. That's one
of mine.

There wasn't even any class for goats at the fair because the
farmers, being used to ordinary scrub goats, held them useless if

not worse, so there was no competition and no prize, but they let us enter and choose a stall. The cattle judge, imported for the occasion, though he said he wasn't much of an authority on goats, did realize they were Nubians and beautiful, and he thought I ought to have a blue ribbon for making the effort to get there.

Miss Dude jumped up on her milking stand. I washed her udder carefully and dried it, discarded the first six squirts from each teat, which might have harbored bacteria in the teat canal, then milked her into a sterilized container, filtered the milk into another sterilized container, and stored the milk in the ice chest.

People began to come up to see what Miss Dude and Rosie and Viola were. "Goats? I never seen such as that. What kind are they?" After I'd given my short lecture on Nubian milk goats I would offer a small sample of milk in a paper cup. "Oh, no! I don't like goat's milk," each person would say.

"Did you ever taste any?" I'd say.

"No. I never did. But I don't like it."

"Aw, come on," I'd say. "Live dangerously."

Very gingerly the tiny cup would go to the mouth, a cautious taste would be taken (oh, high adventure!), the rest would be gulped. "Tastes just like cow's milk," the drinker would say, with surprise. Then he'd disappear. Ten minutes later he'd be back with a friend. "Give *him* some of that goat's milk," he'd say.

"Not me," the friend would say. "I don't like it."

"Didja ever try any?" the now experienced one would say.

"No, but . . ." and so forth, and so forth. The same words, the same result, a hundred times that day. The county was soon full of people congratulating themselves on their courage and coming back to pet the goats. Miss Dude took all the admiration with her usual grace, but Rosie and Viola had never seen so many people or had so many peanuts or so much attention. Rosie became a ham in a very short time.

About ten, the schoolchildren came. They brushed the goats and drank up all the samples. One little boy was particularly enchanted. "I'll be your advertisement," he said, and he stood outside our booth yelling, in a loud voice, "It's *bettern* cow's milk! It's *bettern* cow's milk!"

The fair was almost the end of the hot weather. The humid summer heat sat on one's chest like an ancient paralyzed relative that one is required to carry on an endless march and can't cast off. Some days I did the very minimum of chores and endured the rest of the day in a tubful of cold water, reading. After sundown, though, the wind would rise and it would seem possible to live again. There were wonderful, wild, life-giving thunderstorms followed by days of hot steam and more red mud. We did manage to get tile on the kitchen and bathroom floors, but the raw board floor of the rest of the house was still a nightmare of reddish glue.

October, in Tennessee, is truly superb. The air sparkles, the sky is high and clean and blue. Every day the autumn colors change and become more exciting. The goats and I rattled through the fallen leaves in the woods. Beau was now mature and eagerly courting everybody in sight. In October it seemed an excellent idea to have left California, it seemed the orchard would certainly prosper, that the circles of nitrogen King was scattering around the trees would sink and rise with the water level, doing good.

It certainly didn't seem possible that I would walk into the house one Sunday to find King helpless on the bathroom floor in excruciating pain, unable to move.

He could tell me the pain was in his back, that it had happened when he bent over to tie his shoe, and that was all. In the cracks between the living room floorboards the cold winds whistled up and sailed into the bathroom, where King's legs held the door open. I could not lift him; I could not even get him all in one room so I could shut the bathroom door and cut down the draft. I put blankets over him and tucked them under him the best I could and then I started walking in the cold rain for Tennessee Ridge, where the nearest telephone was.

The doctor, when he came, hopped from one stepping stone to another over the red mud. "Who carried those?" he said.

"King did," I said.

"Well, let those be his last," he said.

After an injection, the doctor and I managed to move King a few feet onto a pallet on the floor so that he was at least all in one room. He was to stay on the floor until the pain eased enough for him to be taken to the doctor's office for examination.

Word got around very fast because, of course, the doctor's car had been seen on our road. I never ceased to marvel that little children who could not even learn to read could instantly identify every car in the county. Very soon people from all around our region began to come.

The design of the house as one large room, which had seemed so simple and right before, now seemed terrible, for there was no way to protect King from the visitors. When I am sick I find a visit exhausting after five minutes, and it has always seemed to me absolute insanity to allow visitors in hospitals. As soon as I opened the door to a knock, there was King, exposed on the floor, in full view, and it was impossible to tell a well-meaning neighbor that he couldn't come in after King had just greeted him. But to my amazement I saw that it would have been a mistake anyway.

What the doctor's injection and repeated medication by mouth had failed to do, the men who had taken time away from their fields and cattle and chores did accomplish. I saw King's rigid leg muscles relax slightly. I saw him dare to change his rigid position, and I knew that eventually he would be able to get into a shape that could go or be pushed through a car door and be taken to the local clinic for x-rays which would allow an assessment of the situation. All we had now was King's first spontaneous gasp (studiously not repeated): "My God! Every cent we have in the world is sunk in the orchard and I'm absolutely helpless." Also, each day he didn't work at the factory was a day he didn't get paid.

"Why, they're doing you good, these visitors," I said. "I thought it would be agonizing for you with no bedroom to go to, no door to shut. . . ."

"Oh," he said, "yeah. They're—they're such an improvement on daytime television." What goes on on weekdays on TV he had never had a big dose of before, and while *anything* had been worth trying as an escape from his first sweating anxiety and intense pain, he had in horrified disbelief found out that even well people who can walk about and are able to hold up a book expose themselves to such hours.

I suppose we were too self-conscious or too close to tears then to admit the miracle it was to see real concern in the honest eyes of these taciturn and clannish neighbors, where kin and family appear to be *all*. I thought of the civilization we had left and the many bedside scenes I had witnessed of people being witty, being elaborately casual, of how impossible it would have been to hear someone say, as Priestly Irwin had just said, sitting on the floor by King and looking directly at him: "I sure feel bad about this, King."

There were plenty of people to get groceries, too, knowing I did not drive, and to go into the county seat for prescriptions and to see that the wood supply was always there when I needed it. Genuine concern for one's friends and relatives (being careful not to "intrude") we had, of course, experienced before, but not this look in the eyes, so naked and so real. These men knew the gamble it is to put everything into a crop that won't pay off for years, in full view of everybody, and they knew what it would be like to fail at it and lose to the "bresh and briers."

One of the most concerned was Monroe Allsbrooks, who came with a bottle of liniment he had found very helpful for his lumbago. "It's really mule liniment," he said, "but it taken all the hair off my mule so I had to quit usin it on him. But now, for a man, you take that and rub it on him. . . ."

King's skin over the whole affected area was so sensitive he could not have tolerated distilled water if it had to be applied by a human hand, but I thanked Monroe and put the liniment away. He stayed on longer than usual; past chore time, in fact. "I wish you would hurry up and put that on him," he said. "I got to go. Hit's past feedin time and radio says snow tonight. I'd like to leave here thinkin somethin had been *done* for him."

I had to tell him the truth, that King simply couldn't tolerate the pain of being touched, and he left with my promise to try it as soon as possible. For once, it was not kerosene. I don't know what it was and neither did Monroe.

"I'll tell you what," I said to King after Monroe left. "I'll try it on one of my legs so you can describe its effects by the next visit." Whoo-ee! I certainly was alive, alive-o in one leg for a while, though as a depilatory I found it inferior. Mule hair, I guess, is softer than I had realized.

Very slowly King managed to graduate from the floor to a board on the bed. The rains quit and heavy frosts began. Visitors became rare. Three Chinese chestnut trees which King had ordered arrived and lay on the floor in his place, their roots growing dryer and dryer every day. I knew the sight of them dying there was driving him mad and one day I went out with a shovel to the space that was later to be the patio, where we had planned to plant them (so as to beat the squirrels to the nuts), and tried digging holes in the frozen red clay. Though there was a freezing north wind, sweat flowed from my forehead, but after an interminable time only an inch or so of soil had been removed. I simply didn't have the strength. I felt King beside me. In slow motion he sank to his knees and took the shovel from me. "Go in the house," he said. "I can't bear to see you."

On his knees, he dug the giant holes and stretched each root tendril out to its full length. He crumbled the lumps of clay to fine dust and covered the roots. *Me* he allowed to stomp out the air pockets.

That night he slept and it snowed. Next day he was driven by a friend to the clinic for x-rays and was advised to continue medication and get to Nashville for an orthopedic surgeon's consultation as soon as he could stand the trip, unless he got so much worse he would have to be taken in an ambulance.

The Nashville surgeon said if it were his back he'd put up with it this time and have it operated on the next time it happened. Anyhow, he'd wait a few weeks and see if it didn't very slowly improve. The next big physical demands would come in February, when the new trees should be planted and by then . . . well, who knew what might happen?

Moving carefully, as though stitched together with thistles, King began going to the office half days. He would emerge from the car white-faced and sweaty-palmed, force himself through the recommended exercises, and fall asleep, only to dream that he had an examination in a college course he had completely forgotten about, the lectures for which he had never attended.

By Christmas he was working full days and we considered the day of rest to be holiday enough without, for the first time in our lives, any special celebration. We got a present, though. Someone dumped off another dog.

I don't remember whether Bosco was second or third in the long procession of dumped dogs. He stood on the road watching and watching for *the* car, dangerously approaching each vehicle that came by. I heard screaming brakes until I could endure it no longer and finally went out to the road with food. With one last look back to the road, he gave up the search and followed me to the house. I could tell there was something wrong with one ear and I brought him in to examine it. Once the door was shut, the stench arose in a powerful cloud of proof that kerosene and bacon grease (with which he had probably been treated) are not antibiotic. The condition of rot was indescribable. The dog, obviously familiar with houses, offered no resistance to treatment. He lay on his side on the hearth and submitted to the application of a warm antiseptic solution with a deep sigh and immediate sleep. Working my way through the encrusted, suppurating mass, day by day, I finally got down to the skin itself. One day the ear just came off in my hand. What remained was a little black ruffle, clean and healthy. It gave him a very rakish air, the long, floppy black ear on one side and the little ruffle on the other, something like a roly-poly baby playing George Raft with daddy's hat.

Bosco took a great liking to Murray Webb when he stopped by one day and Murray, whose old dog had recently died, took him home with him. Murray still wore his look of bafflement which preceded his resignation to the fact that he could no longer lift anything. He had been a giant of a man, working in the sawmills and raising ten children on his farm. He only wore his teeth to funerals and square dances and the year before he had still been able to square dance all night. Now, of a sudden, he could hardly walk from the house to the barn and if you drove by his place you would see him all awkwardly angular, trying to teach his great height how to lean on a fence. "I need this dog," he said, stroking Bosco. "There's three things a farm ain't a farm without: a crowin rooster, a bawlin cow and a barkin dog."

It wasn't usually that easy to find a home for the dumped animals, though, and when I began to inquire into the situation locally I was horrified to find that most farms around us had suffered for years from this practice. There was no Humane Society in the county or in any adjoining county. Near the lake in the picnic table areas, there were packs of starving dogs roaming about hunting for the picnicker's tidbits that had suddenly stopped after Labor Day. B. N. Stoker, I learned, used to go all winter to take food down there, but there was never enough, he said.

It seemed idiotic to me that the country people had to submit to this dumping of every ailing, pregnant, sick or unwanted animal from the town and I saw no reason why the county court couldn't authorize the sheriff to shoot animals brought to him. I wrote such a resolution and took it to the Community Club, where people were willing to sign it, each signer telling *his* irate story. Some people had as many as thirty cats. But they signed without any hope. They told me nothing would be done and the resolution would fall into the same pit of inaction that previous complaints had. The resolution was duly published in the local paper and, sure enough, nothing happened. Finally I went to the county agent's office, the only sensible place I had so far found to take problems.

"Well, you're in hunting country," the agent said. "You shoot a man's hunting dog by mistake, and you're in real trouble. It's not just a matter of a few cents for shells for the sheriff's gun. The law says a found dog has to be advertised and it has to be confined for two weeks before it can be disposed of. This is a poor county. This county is not able to build an animal shelter for confining dogs the necessary period, hire a man to take care of them, feed them, advertise them, and all that."

I can fight city hall all right. I just decided, for the time being, I didn't know how to fight county court in hunting country. In time I hope, the Department of Public Health will find it has the necessary means to do so, since Tennessee leads the nation in cases of rabies.

The night the warning came on TV that there was a severe cold spell on the way and that it would be wise to let pets into the house, I thought about Bosco and knew Murray would have a warm place for him. In the barn I put out extra hay for the goats, moved their water bucket inside the stall and decided to shut them in for the night. Miss Dude, Rosie and Viola were all pregnant. Old Beau had hugged off the warmest place for himself and the does were lying as close together as their bulging sides would permit. Their winter coats were all fluffed out and they were clearly anticipating a cold night. The tiny barn was already full and if each doe by some chance had *twin* does, we'd need an addition to it very fast.

The sky was riding darkly on my shoulders as I left the barn and snow started falling before I got to the house. I loaded up the woodbox with logs and built a big fire in the fireplace. By the time King got home from work the snow was already very deep. We sat by the fire eating hot soup and worrying if the car would start in the morning and if the snow tires would get him up the hill.

What we should have been doing was checking the foundation of the house, where, it turned out, a small access door had been left propped open and through which the freezing wind whistled in a fast path, bursting all the pipes under the house. Innocently we slept in King's ancient GI underwear while the wind whistled higher and higher, the snow turned to ice and the temperature went to a fifty-year record low. In the morning the electric power was off (we assumed temporarily, from the ice on the wires), so we had no means of getting news of the situation. The electric pump would naturally be off, too, so we assumed this explained why we had no water.

Oh, well, what matter? We were surrounded with deep snow. We would melt some of that. And that is how we learned that a *great big* bucketful of pure white snow, after hours of blocking the fireplace heat and sweating and slobbering and dribbling all over the hearth, will eventually yield a very small cup of very dirty water.

It is amazing how the city dweller's concept of *they* persists. As we melted snow and tended the fire and listened to the whining of the wind, we never doubted but that *they* were out there somewhere, working day and night, to restore electric service, to clear roads, to ensure food and water supplies. Well, they were, within their limitations. But *they* also had some persistent concepts and one of those was that country people know how to take care of themselves. What none of us had counted on was that, in addition to the countless isolated places where the weight of ice or falling trees had broken wires in rural areas, a car in the county seat had slipped on the ice and sheared off a power pole, knocking out the electricity for the entire county. The town, of course, had to come first. We knew nothing of this at the time. We knew nothing at all. The road was deep in snow, unmarked by any tracks. The mailbox was buried.

In the morning, when there was a lull in the wind, we took

our precious bucket of dirty snowmelt and, dressed in many layers of clothing, started for the barn. We plowed waist deep into a strange, dry snow such as I had never seen. King, holding the precious bucket over his head, made a tunnel with his body for me to follow in. The noise of our progress and of our breathing made jagged violations in the solid silence. It seemed indecent to move with such struggle and awkwardness. To be a white bird, slowly gliding, would have been the only fitting solution, I thought, and realized there were not even any birds moving. There were no rabbit tracks.

We stopped to rest before attacking the huge snowdrift which blocked the barn door. The shovel we needed was inside the barn. A cracking sound, without rhythm, was all about us. We stared at each other in question.

"What's *that?*" I whispered.

The sound was coming from the big trees in the woods, but it was not the sound of breaking branches, and corresponded to no visible motion. It was a perfect lesson in the essence of terror. Had there been a giant sitting there cracking giant English walnuts, it would not have been a frightening sound. With no giant, wild thoughts ran through my head: Not fire, then. Not a flood. And Chicken Little was wrong. *This* is the way the world will be destroyed; it will crack apart. I could see the globe with tiny cracks spreading in crisscross networks. My teeth were chattering like mad.

"It must be the sap in the trees," King said, "frozen and expanding or contracting. I never heard anything like it. God, it must be much colder than I thought. We'd better get done and get back to the house." He began to clear the barn door with his hands and feet. It was frozen solid. "I'll climb over the fence," he said, "and push open the door from the inside." That worked.

The door to the goat stall was frozen, too, but here we had

tools to work with. As soon as we had pried the door open, Miss Dude, Rosie and Viola burst out of the stall and began eating snow, but Beau went straight for the bucket (which already had a sheet of ice on top), stuck his mouth in and—there went a whole night's work. I could have cried in exasperation.

Beau pawed at the empty bucket for more. "Eat snow!" I said. But his stubborn posture clearly said that he was accustomed to having his water provided and that snow-eating was for does.

As soon as we put hay and grain in the stall the goats all returned, so we decided to shut them in again and return with more water as soon as possible. We put some dairy feed out for the wild birds and started back to the house. The wood supply was completely covered with snow and the logs were all frozen together. Each one had to be pried loose to be put in the woodbox. Whenever we stopped for breath or rest, we heard the random cracking sound of the big trees.

Our fire was still going inside the house and we tried to find drying space for our gloves and boots and caps. The hearth was a mess from all the snow-melting buckets and I was trying to think how to clear a space for cooking breakfast when the pain of thawing out set in. Being in the cold outside had been surprisingly painless. We had just been congratulating ourselves on having managed all we had outside, when suddenly, excruciatingly, the price of it began to tell.

Thawing out was a new experience. I would have writhed in agony if writhing had not been impossible. I had on so many layers of underwear that I couldn't bend. But apparently I hadn't worked out the right combination for my feet. Tears of pain ran down my face. Worse was the knowledge that it all had to be done again in a few hours. And *how many* times? When would the power come back on? When would the road be broken through? When would the temperature moderate? Eventually I was breathing normally again and realized the terrible pain was gone out of my feet. It was possible to touch them. It was possible to wrap them in a warm blanket. The toes would move. In a short while I could stand on them and face the problem of getting enough mud off the hearth to make room for preparing a meal.

The meals became stranger as our food supplies dwindled. We ate the frozen food first, for safety, glad that we had not bought a large freezer. Then we began on the canned goods. Whatever we could we ate out of the cans they were heated in, in order to save the water for drinking. By the fourth day we were living on cereal and pancakes and tea. We were very dirty but we had learned how to make the outdoor trips efficiently, how to sleep in short turns and keep the fire going. We had been out of coffee for two days, but on the fourth day we ran out of cigarettes.

The sun was out. It did seem warmer, but still the car was frozen, the tractor was frozen, the truck was frozen, the pipes were all frozen—or so we thought, learning only later that they had all burst and would have to be completely replaced. There were some tire tracks on the road. Somebody had made it through the snow.

"Well," King said, "I'll try to make it as far as Self's place. Maybe he's got his truck running and I can get a ride to the Ridge. What do you want besides cigarettes?" What did I want? I wanted a cigarette so badly I couldn't think of anything else.

The hours went by. I tended the fire. I melted snow. I tended the animals. And I waited. And waited. And waited. After about five hours King came back. He carried a bag of groceries and his pockets were bulging with cigarettes. "I guess we can stop worrying about my back temporarily. Anybody who can walk ten miles through the snow lugging these boots step after step must be all right."

"You *walked?*" I said. "All the way?"

"Self was all frozen up, too. I kept thinking somebody would come along. There were tracks up to the big curve and then there's just a mess of cars piled up in a big drift. The damnedest thing—I saw a mule out in the snow. His breath had crystallized on his whiskers and he had a huge doughnut around his mouth like a misplaced halo. I never saw anything like it. *Do you know it's been thirty-five degrees below zero for four days?*"

At the store he had learned of the knocked-out light pole, that the whole region had been without power, including the factory where he worked.

That night, power was restored. We had electric heat and light and a functioning hot plate. We could start the cleaning up of spilled candle grease and food while we waited on the only plumber in the county to get to us on his list. Eventually the road would be cleared, the car would start, King would return to work and water could be hauled. We had survived and we had not lost any animals.

But what had happened to the trees we did not yet know. At the store there were people who told of young trees which had simply burst open. In later times, whenever a tree broke in a windstorm or had to be cut down for any disease, there was a black ring inside to mark that year. I have always felt that if one of us should have an accident in traffic necessitating an amputation, the black ring would prove to be in us, too.

4

The goat Rosie had been a virgin milker. Long before
Clintwood Beau's Buddy had reached maturity, Rosie's udder
had filled out. In my inexperience I let it go for a long time,
knowing she could not be pregnant. Finally, with the aid of
peanuts, I got her to climb on the milking stand and I emptied
the udder of a gray, watery fluid. Rosie seemed perfectly well.
The next day the udder was again full, and this time the con-
tents looked like milk. The current crop of dumped kittens and
dogs lapped it up happily. I came into the house and began to
study my book. Yes, there it was, the "maiden milkers." Not too
unusual. My Rosie had a little excess thyroid.

Whether this explained other aspects of her personality, I
don't know. She never attained the size of Miss Dude, her
mother. Her legs remained delicate and slender all her life. Her
hoofs were small. On our walks in the woods I was accustomed
to stop at my "couch," an ancient tulip tree which grew horizontally for some ten feet before turning abruptly vertical for sixty
or seventy more. Here, on the horizontal part, the goats would
jump up in single file to receive a peanut and Rosie was always
first in line. She held her head at a different angle than the
other goats, the nose pointed high, and she was different from
them in her need for affection. When I sat down she would rub
her head against my hand. When I stood up she rubbed up and
down against my leg. I treated her for lice, although neither she
nor the other goats had the telltale bare spots at the edge of the
ears or anyplace else. There was no diminishing of her need for
affection. When I approached the barn Miss Dude and Viola
would call a greeting to me, but Rosie always yelled in a high,
demanding voice. When I left the barn the others took note of

and accepted the closing of the gate, but Rosie yelled until I was out of sight. When she grew tall enough, she leaned her head over the fence and stretched after me as she yelled.

I had begun taking them to the woods when Rosie and Viola were two weeks old. They would follow behind Miss Dude and chew on whatever she chewed on, whether they were actually eating or not. When Miss Dude came to a poisonous plant, she would snort and make the sneezing sound of alarm. At any strange noise in the woods, the appearance of a dog or cat, the shadow of a buzzard, Miss Dude would give her *mm mm* signal and Rosie and Viola would stand close to her, motionless. Sometimes they stood under her. Once when a helicopter flew over (nowadays the revenuers use helicopters to hunt for moonshine stills) Rosie ran to me instead of to Miss Dude and I was terribly touched. I stood still and said *mm mm*, too.

It turned out that Rosie had been the first to avail herself of Beau's new maturity, too. She did not bulge out at the sides in the fashion of her mother and it was with complete surprise that I found her solitary baby lying alone and neglected on the icy ground. It was a billy, marked exactly like Beau. Rosie had paid him enough attention to get his fur licked dry, but nurse him she would not. *Me* she paid a lot of attention. I checked the baby's eyes and nostrils and put iodine on his umbilicus. I left him very close to Rosie, closed the door of the stall and went to the house to get her hot water, molasses and a bran mash. When I got back, slipping over the thick ice, she had kicked or pushed the baby as far from her as possible, up against the door. I brought him close to her to nurse and she kicked him out of the way. She wanted her hot water and molasses. She wanted a little nibble of bran mash. She wanted to be stroked on the head. But her baby she didn't want.

I might have left everything up to "nature" if it hadn't been the time of the second worst blizzard of that year. I waited until I was so cold I couldn't endure it any more. By this time Rosie had still shown no interest in her baby. He was no longer even trying to nurse, and night was getting close. I made the decision, right or wrong, to take the baby into the house. Rosie didn't object when I picked him up and put him inside my coat.

Bending against a fierce wind full of sleet, I made my way to the house and put the baby on the hearth in a warm basket. As soon as my hands were thawed out, I collected clean utensils and went back in the sleet to milk the precious yellow colostrum out of Rosie. I carried this into the house, found a bottle and began to feed the baby. In the warmth he had begun to move again. He was terribly hungry and, after an hour or so, he began to look alive.

In the morning I took him back to Rosie. With a lightning movement I couldn't forestall, she butted him clear across the stall. I gave up. Later, when the ice was off the road, I learned of other farmers' raising lambs and even calves by the kitchen stove (nothing ever happens for the first time in the country). It is not only in humans that maternal responses do not always appear automatically after birth.

Back on the hearth, the beautiful red-gold baby thrived and danced on his toothpick legs. Since his mother had been a grade goat, I would not be able to sell him for breeding purposes and, for the same reason, I would not be able to keep him with my herd. Butchering the golden baby was unthinkable and therefore I was happy to see that the plumber (who was still working on the burst pipes from the blizzard before) was falling more in love with him each trip he made into the house.

During these first days, the baby had a bright-orange waxy

excrement. Miss Dude constantly licked this off her babies so that they were at all times immaculate. I did the best I could with Kleenex. He loved the fire without caution, and though I got larger and larger cardboard cartons from the crossroads store, I never got one that he didn't eventually leap out of, so that each time I had to go out of the house I would shut him in the bathroom. It was a great relief when I finally got him weaned and the plumber took him home to his little boy. It was also a great relief to have hot running water in the pipes once again.

I scrubbed the whole house with soap and hot water. I had a great bonfire of all the baby goat's successive cardboard boxes and urine-soaked hay. It is amazing how, if you put a pint of milk in a baby goat, you get a gallon of urine out. Then I took a deep hot bath. We were back to normal, and if there had been anyplace to go, we would have gone out that evening to celebrate. One thing we did miss in the country, and that was an occasional good movie.

"Well," King said, "we'll go to the restaurant across from the plant and I'll show you the beautiful girl." Several weeks before, he had come home with the news of this beautiful girl who worked as a waitress in the café where he ate lunch. She had long black hair, a rarity in this region, and deep-violet long-lashed eyes. She also had a beautiful body with an ungirdled, high-riding behind which had all the male customers drooling with excitement.

But she was not in the restaurant. "Where is the beautiful girl I came all this way to see?" I asked Dixie Sugg, the proprietor.

"I suppose you mean Darlene Hackett," Dixie said. "Well, your guess is as good as mine. I give up on her. Ever time I turn around, she's missin. I imagine you'll find her at the Highway Thirteen Bar. That seems to be where she spends her time. Yesterday she said she had to go down to her trailer to take care of her kids. When she didn't come back, I went down there and there was them two kids in that trailer alone, nothin to eat all day. Dirty as could be. They're beautiful chirren and she told one of the girls here she don't want them. They ought to be took away from her."

"These children," I said. "How old are they?"

"The little girl, she's five, and the boy's just not three years old yet."

"And they're *alone* in a trailer?"

"Right this minute, far as I know. Somethin just got to be done. They're just beautiful chirren, and smart, too. And she just don't want them. I don't know how many would take the little girl. She's just lovin as she can be. She just cuddles up to anybody. But nobody don't want the boy. He's wild. Can't nobody do nothin with him. And it seems awful to separate them."

"Wait a minute," King said. "Is this trailer over behind the factory? There's a little boy out in the middle of the road there all the time. I don't know how many people said they nearly ran over him. I nearly did myself the other day."

"That's Robbie," Dixie said. "He stands out there and just screams. Why, somebody told me they seen both those kids in the creek. Wonder they haven't been run over or drowned before now."

"Well, where is their father?" I said.

"He took off," Dixie said. "Just disappeared about a month ago. Don't nobody know where he went. She come in here cryin, sayin she didn't have no money for food. I give her a job. Then she said she didn't have no clothes. I taken her to Clarksville and bought her two dresses. Cost me fifty dollars. She could work here and take care of those chirren, all right. But she won't work. Right in the rush hour I turn around and she's gone again. She says she's goin out for twenty minutes and at closin time she ain't back yet. This happened over and over until I just can't put up with it any more. There's plenty of people'd help her if she'd just do right, but. . . ."

"That little boy," I said. "They mustn't do that to him. To have his father gone, and his mother, too. And then if somebody's going to take his sister away—why, she's all he's got. They mustn't do that. Would you know it if it happened?"

"I reckon I would," Dixie said. "There's one woman wants that little girl so bad she'd just do about anything to get her. And there's others, too."

"Listen, King," I said, "is it all right with you if they come to our house?"

"Well . . . ah . . ." he said, "I guess so. Where would you put them, though, with our one room?"

"Dixie," I said, "don't let them be separated. If you find there's a chance of that, bring them to us. We'll take care of them."

"Somethin's gotta happen," Dixie said, "soon. Because she's already three months behind in the trailer payments and when they come to take that trailer, those chirren goin to have to go *someplace.*"

"Bring them to us," I repeated.

That night was a sleepless one. I was haunted by that wild little boy standing in the middle of the road, screaming and screaming, and possibly about to lose his sister. Yet by daylight it seemed melodramatic to make this our concern. We were strangers. There must be many local people of good conscience in the town who would have better knowledge of the situation and who would act. And if, as Dixie said, the mother actually wanted to give the children away, there would surely be younger and healthier people who would come forward. And somewhere in the picture there must be "authorities." Weren't there "authorities" even in remote corners of this civilized country who were charged with the responsibility of children? And if I sought them out and asked what they were doing about this matter, wouldn't I be a "busybody," and a foreign busybody at that?

For we would always be foreigners, we knew that now. If someone mentioned a Mrs. So-and-so, we could not say, "Oh, yes, she was a Such-and-such, daughter of old Bill Such-and-such. She married George So-and-so," for we did not know these things, and even when we were told, we could not keep the ancestry straight. It was all meaningless to us. But more important, the natives could never know this ancestral information about *us*. Therefore, we were never really *located* in their minds and remained unassigned, in polite limbo.

At the factory, King heard that Roy Hackett, the children's father, had returned, and we assumed that there had been a reconciliation and that the care of the children could not in any way be our concern. To be truthful, we received the news with some relief. The prospect of going suddenly from no children to two children in middle age is not something to be considered lightly, but from no children to two wildly unhappy children is an awesome thought.

By contrast, the goats were happy, docile and easily managed. In February both Viola and Miss Dude had babies. Just before Viola's were born she did a strange thing. She walked over to her mother and leaned against her. They conversed a moment or two in low tones and then Viola got down on her knees and began to nurse at Miss Dude's udder. Miss Dude stood still for this. She turned her head and watched Viola with maternal solicitude. Then Viola got slowly to her feet, went into the barn and began to tread a circle in the ritual that precedes birth. Finally she lay on her side and began to strain. I closed the door so that she would not experience cold drafts or sudden alarms from dogs or cats, and went to the house to get my basket of maternity supplies and hot water. Viola gave birth to a doe, Eunice, and later the same day Miss Dude gave birth to twin does, Mattie Mae and Emma. All three does were of the glorious red-gold color I had hoped for. All were marked with the white wings on the face Beau had.

Three does in one day! All perfect, beautiful and healthy. I had ten bath towels hanging frozen on the fence before I had rubbed all the babies dry. Snow was falling again when I left the barn for the last time. Viola and Miss Dude, each with her own babies tucked under her, lay side by side. Rosie stood watching them as they constantly licked and mothered their infants.

Now I had six does, and four of them had the color and markings I wanted. In a few days I would be milking three goats every morning and in a few weeks, when the babies would most need it, there would be fresh, green, *free* food in the woods for them to eat and warm weather to relieve the dangerously crowded space in the barn. If only we could avoid pneumonia for a month. If only spring would come early this year.

When King came home we took a flashlight and went down to the barn. We sat down on the clean shavings by Miss Dude and Viola and they let us hold their warm, golden babies without alarm. Pushed out of the golden circle, Rosie leaned in, demanding, demanding her share of love.

"I'm going to put those golden babies in the St. Patrick's Day parade," I said to King.

"How would you manage them in all that noise and confusion?" he said.

"Well, I'm not really the manager, in case you hadn't noticed," I said. "Miss Dude is the queen."

There was no doubt about that. Even though Viola was now a mother, too, she still kept her old place in line behind Miss

Dude when we went to the woods. Miss Dude was simple, straightforward authority. She had a curious loping gait so that when she ran, her udder flip-flopped from side to side. Still, somehow, she managed to look impressive. Her shoulder-length ears were marked with white. Her Roman nose was long as a hound's and her amber eyes were gentle and velvet wise.

In the woods she walked daintily, sampling the goodies as though at a ladies' club buffet: a few red buckberries, a mouthful of crunchy hazelnut catkins. She would bend down for a piece of dark-green bamboo bramble or stand on their hind legs to tear off with the strong lower teeth a piece of orange sassafras bark, topping it all off with a little bright-green cedar. Miss Dude was always a dainty eater. Her appetite satisfied, she would lift her head and turn in a different direction. "We have had enough of this," she seemed to say, and she would begin to move ahead. The others would all stop eating and fall into line. She was the queen.

Monroe Allsbrooks, with his giant hands, built a little cart for Miss Dude to pull and he fashioned a harness for her and trained her to pull the cart. We decided to fill the cart with apples, which we had to buy in the store because the orchard wasn't producing yet. When it came time for King to paint the cart, we realized that the moment had arrived at last for deciding what we were going to call the orchard. It was the only orchard in the county, so some people just called it "the orchard," and other people called it "the orchard on the Cooley Ford road," but most people who had seen King planting the first little trees in the snow and had watched them take shape and grow called it "King's orchard." I left King standing with the paintbrush in his hand. "I guess the time has come when I have to make up my mind," he said.

The next time I saw the cart, there it was, in neat letters:
KING'S ORCHARD. "You made up your mind," I said.

Miss Dude walked in the St. Patrick's Day parade as though she
had been trained for parades since infancy, her two latest babies in a
straight line behind the cart full of red apples. Miss Dude looked
neither to right nor left, paid no attention to high school bands,
Shriners on motorcycles with shrieking sirens, or barking dogs. The
little red beard she had grown after the birth of Mattie Mae and
Emma in no way detracted from her impressive manner.

5

The green felt hat worn by a friend in the St. Patrick's Day
parade was still hanging on the fire irons when the children
came. Their grandmother brought them.

"I'm Grace Hickerson," she said. "Dixie Sugg told me you
said you'd take these kids. I'm about out of my mind over them."

"Well . . ." I said. The little boy broke loose from his grandmother and dashed across the room to the hearth, where he
picked up the green hat and put it on his head.

"Put that back, Robbie," the grandmother said. "See how
they are?" she said to me. "Just wild. Poor younguns. Ain't had
no care taken in so long. Robbie's hair was down to his shoulders. I had it all shaved off. Can't nobody get him still enough
to comb it and he don't like it shaved, I guess."

"It's all right, Robbie," I said. "You can wear the hat. It got
wet in the parade and I had it there to dry. It just fits you now."

"Yeah," he said.

"This is Marilyn," the grandmother said. "She's five. She's a
sweet little thing." Marilyn smiled up at me, her green eyes
sparkling under bright-red bangs.

"Won't you sit down?" I said to Mrs. Hickerson. "It's been so long since I heard about the children, I thought surely they were being taken care of." I sat down myself, hoping that somehow the situation would become reasonable. Robbie had discovered the old cat and was pursuing him under the bed. Marilyn was quietly circling the room, taking everything in.

"Well, I got to go to work," Mrs. Hickerson said. "I'm cook at a restaurant down on the lake. You see, I got a boy of my own to take care of. He's thirteen and I have to work to support him. I'm divorced from his father and his father don't send child support. The husband I'm married to now, Tom Hickerson, he won't keep these children. He won't have them in the house. It's just an awful situation. I got to leave them with an old uncle of mine, Jack Ussery. He's sick and crippled and he can't chase after them. He lives right on the highway and I'm scared to death Robbie'll get run over. I go over there at noon and take them dinner, but then I got to go right back to work.

"I had a house in Stewart for them. It wasn't much, but at least it was a roof over their heads when they took back the trailer. I told Darlene—that's their mother—that she could move in there with them and I'd do my best to help her. I took them all over there and then Darlene said she was going in to the electric company to get the lights turned on and she walked out and she never came back. She just left."

"Perhaps we ought to discuss this later," I said to her.

"Oh, the children heard so much already, from everybody, they can't be hurt more than they been already. Roy—that's their father—he's my own son and I'm ashamed to say it, but he just didn't do right by these children. Don't nobody know where he is. I don't know. Don't *nobody* seem to care. And the way I am right now, I can't do nothing, either. If I just knew they had a good place to go while I was trying to figure out something. Just right now seems the worst time she could of took off."

Marilyn came over and sat on my lap, leaning her head against me. I put my arm around her. "I want to stay here," she said.

"Well, darling," I said, "this is all so sudden. I had no idea. . . . I have to talk to my husband and we'll have to make some plans. I. . . ." I remembered the houseguest due to arrive the next day. "How about Easter?" I said to Mrs. Hickerson. "That's just a few days away and it would be a nice day to start. Would that be all right?"

"Robbie's pulling the cat's tail," Marilyn said. The poor old cat, having endured all he could, escaped Robbie and ran to me for protection. Why he had not scratched the child was a mystery.

"Well, I guess then," Mrs. Hickerson said, "If that's the soonest you can take them. I'll try to manage until then. Come on, Robbie, I got to go to work."

"You can keep the hat, Robbie," I said.

He took it off and hung it back carefully where he had found it. "No," he said. "I'll leave it there for when I come back."

"All right," I said. "I'll keep it for you."

"I wish Easter was now," Marilyn said.

"I know, dear," I said. "I'm sorry. It's just a few days. Then we'll have a good time with Easter eggs and everything. And I'll take you down to see the goats."

I really had a lot to do. Even though we could somehow not quite gasp the reality of suddenly having a family, still we had to locate two cots and find someplace to put them. The immediate need was to prepare for the houseguest, a student in an emergency situation, who had been promised a quiet place to study for examinations which were crucial to her career.

Before she arrived, Roy's father, Garner Hackett, came to see me. Visiting from Detroit, where he lived, he tried to press me to take Marilyn and Robbie before Easter. He seemed a direct person, much concerned over the children.

"It's really a shame about these children," he said. "I just can't understand their parents acting this way. I'd take them myself, but I live alone and go to work every day. There wouldn't be anyone there to care for them in the day."

"When we first heard about the children," I said, "it was from Dixie Sugg, and that was weeks ago. We had the idea that they had nobody, but now I keep hearing of relatives. Even Dixie herself, I found out, is related to them."

"Yes," he said. "She's my other son's mother-in-law."

"So I understand now. There's Dixie and there's Mrs. Hickerson and your other son and his wife and I don't know who else. Why didn't any of these relatives take them?"

"They've all got children of their own to take care of," he said, "and I suppose it's because of the parents. Everybody is so disgusted at the way the parents acted, nobody wants to do anything for them. But if you and Mr. Baker will give the children a home, I certainly will help out. Anything they need—shoes or clothes or anything—just send me the bill."

At my request Hackett returned that evening to talk to King. He brought the children and they came into the house with me while Hackett and King talked in the orchard. Jack Ussery, Mrs. Hickerson's old uncle, had stayed in Hackett's car. He appeared badly crippled, and when I realized that he had been watching the children, I was truly horrified and wished we could take them right then.

King liked Garner Hackett, too, and the three of us, later on, had a good understanding. What we agreed was that we intended to make a good and permanent home for the children, but that there would certainly be surprises in it for us, inexperienced as we were, and because of our age, we might find it too difficult.

"I'll be coming back here in July," Hackett said, "and we can talk it all over then."

Well, that much we felt we could guarantee—the children would have a place that would not change for three months. Even if it should turn out to be too much for us to handle, we knew we could do it for three months. Then in July we would be much better able to make long-term guarantees. And so, with my promise to write to Hackett and let him know how the children were doing, we felt it was all settled that they would come Easter, as arranged, and we would have a responsible person to deal with if there were emergencies.

A few days later Hackett came again to see if we couldn't take the children immediately. He found me in the barnyard with the goats. He hated to ask me, he said, but Jack Ussery was just too old and feeble to handle the children, particularly Robbie. Mr. Ussery's house was right on the highway in Stewart and Robbie kept running into the street.

"But I have this student here," I said. "I told you she was coming. And we have promised her quiet to study for her examinations. We gave our word. The girl has no place else to go. Her whole career depends on these examinations. Besides, I wanted so much to start off right with the children, to give them all my attention at the beginning. You know how small the house is."

"I have to go back to Detroit," he said, "and I was just hoping to get the kids all settled before I left. Grace thought maybe a few days wouldn't matter. . . ."

"To tell you the truth, Mr. Hackett, this kind of pressure is really irritating to me. There are all these people who have

expressed concern over the children—there's you and Mrs.
Hickerson and Dixie Sugg and her daughter. We're going to
relieve all these people of responsibility for those children all
the rest of their lives perhaps, and it does not seem too much to
ask that they find a way to look after them for these last few
days. I just simply cannot take the children until Easter."

"That's all right," Mr. Hackett said. "I understand. And I'm
really grateful for what you and Mr. Baker are going to do for
these kids, believe me."

The night before Easter, while he was carefully removing a
wet paper stencil from an egg, King said, "We ought to be
sleeping."

"I know," I said. "It may be the last night's sleep we'll get."

But we might as well have stayed up all night painting even
more intricate designs on eggs, for all the sleep we had. My
wakeful fantasies alternated from joy to apprehension. By the
light of his cigarette I saw King sitting on the edge of the bed. I
put out my hand to touch him. "My God," he said, "what have
we let ourselves in for?"

The first thing we had let ourselves in for, it turned out, was
an agonizing Easter. The children didn't come. Among the
colored eggs and toy rabbits, we waited. We had lunch, and
after many tired hours of greeting each car sound with disappointment, we finally ate the Easter dinner I had so carefully
planned. Worn out with waiting, neither of us had an appetite.

"What could have happened?" I said.

"Ultimately we'll find out," King said.

I fed the goats and stayed watching them a long time. The
evening light seemed filled with sadness. I was surprised at the
quality of the disappointment I felt, for by dwelling on the
responsibility the situation held for us, I had managed to keep

hidden this unknown hunger. Back in the house, it seemed really very silly that I had even believed the children were coming. People don't just give away children like that, after all. The grandmother's visit must have reflected a moment's desperation and later she had thought better of it.

"Surely they wouldn't come this late," I said, beginning to get ready for bed.

"Maybe the parents changed their minds," King said. He wound up one of the Easter toys and set it going on the floor. It was a mamma rabbit wheeling a baby rabbit in a carriage. Over the top of the carriage was a bright-blue parasol from which colored balls hung. As the carriage wheels revolved, so did the parasol, sending out the pink and yellow balls in a bright whirl. For a plastic toy it seemed to have been made unusually well. I thought it would never run down.

King stood beside me, watching the toy, his hand on my shoulder. "Maybe it's better this way," he said.

The mamma rabbit wheeled her baby around and around in a bright circle. I began to think there had never been any visits, that I had made the whole thing up. If I had not been so tired, I would have packed the whole Easter mess away and hunted out all the eggs from their hiding places.

Next morning when I was milking Miss Dude, I sat beside her and leaned my head against her warm side.

"The children didn't come," I said. "I have to go put away all those Easter toys and store the cots and everything."

I released the bar that held her head and waited for her to jump down from the milking stand. After I milked Viola I stood leaning against the door while the whole herd came up for their morning stroking and feeding.

"I don't feel like going to the woods today," I told them. "I'm sorry."

They all followed me to the gate and called after me as I started toward the house. In the driveway stood a man, holding Robbie by one hand and Marilyn by the other. Each child had a paper bag. The children seemed extremely subdued and looked at the ground.

"I'm Grace's husband," the man said. "I'm Tom Hickerson."

"But," I said, "yesterday. We were expecting the children yesterday. What happened?"

"Oh, well," Hickerson said, "they was invited to a Easter egg hunt at the church and Grace thought. . . ."

How absurd to waste time in this talk. It was obvious he could not possibly imagine or care about the day of waiting King and I had spent. I put out my hands toward the children. Immediately they dropped Hickerson's hands and took mine. We started moving toward the house.

"Well, you can have Easter all over again," I said to them.

"The boy, now," Hickerson said, "he's got a terrible habit suckin his thumb. I tell him it'll turn into a nigger thumb and *that* stops him."

I quelled an impulse to run into the house with both children. "Thank you for bringing the children," I said. Could he hear me screaming in my head: *Go! Go! Just go!*

"Well, Grace thought," he said, " better I bring them. If she did maybe they'd cry and that be hard on everbody."

I squeezed the children's hands. How cold they were. "We'll be fine," I said. "We'll just take our time getting to know each other." *Go, for God's sake, go!*

Inside the house I leaned against the closed door and restrained a desire to clutch the children to me and vow they would never have to see that awful man again.

"I'm very happy you came," I said.

Robbie broke away from me and ran to the hearth. "My

hat's still there, Marilyn," he said. "Look!" He put on the green
St. Patrick's Day hat and gave me a wicked smile.

The old cat was stealthily making his way under the bed, but
he was not quick enough. Robbie hit the floor and slid after
him, his cowboy boots sticking out from the bed. Were there
eyes in the boot heels or radar? I wondered, for as soon as
Marilyn, who had seated herself, reached soundlessly into one of
the brown sacks, Robbie emerged. I don't know how he pro-
pelled himself, but he simply flew through the air and landed
like a bird of prey, Marilyn's wrist clamped in his mouth. Then
he bit. Marilyn screamed and kicked him in the ribs. He released her arm, grabbed his ribs and began rolling on the floor,
screaming. Marilyn jumped up and down, crying, "He bit me!
He bit me!"

All this took place in the time it took me to walk about five
steps. With a pure genius I did not know I possessed, I picked up
both paper sacks. Instant silence. "I'll write your names on
these," I said, "and put them away for you. Here we eat candy
after lunch."

As long as I held on to the sacks, I was ahead. I treated them
with great respect, carefully printing the children's names on
them and putting them (in clear view) on a high shelf. Marilyn
had been cheated out of her big scene and now she tried to
summon back her tears. She held out her arm to me. "Look,"
she said. Sure enough, there was complete dental impression of
her brother's mouth, a sign I would come to know well. I would
later find it on the arm of a chair, on my husband's back, on the
base of a silver candlestick. . . . I touched her arm gently and
told her I was sorry. The skin was not broken, but a large area
was fast turning blue.

I wound up the mamma rabbit toy and set her going on the

floor and while the children were discovering the other Easter things, I started preparing lunch. Whether it was because they thought of them as my toys or because they just hadn't had time to plan out a battle, they were not fighting. While the peace lasted I was working fast, setting the table, getting things ready.

Suddenly Robbie threw himself on the floor and began yelling, "Kay yoggs! Kay yoggs!"

"What does that mean?" I asked.

"Aw, he can't say Kellogg's," she said. "That's what he calls cereal. He wants cereal. That's all he eats."

"Go in the bathroom and wash your hands before lunch," I said to her. Robbie got up off the floor and followed her. As I was soon to learn, he could not tolerate having her out of his sight.

Lunch was a great education. Marilyn was most interested in the dishes. "What's this? What's that?" she said, over the pepper mill, the sugar bowl, each object. Her hands were extremely graceful and sure, like those of a connoisseur handling priceless antiques. I had no idea that five-year-olds could possess such coordination. The food, all being unfamiliar, she didn't care for. Clearly, she was a picky eater. She did not know the names of any vegetables, apparently. And she didn't care to know the taste.

"Tell me," I said, "what you *do* like and maybe we can have it for supper."

"I like hot dogs," she said.

Robbie was a different matter. He ate everything in sight, steadily, rapidly, as though it would be snatched away if he stopped. But I hadn't really seen anything yet. For dessert, I brought out a bowl of fruit. Robbie ate a banana, an orange ("What's that?" he said), an apple and an entire bunch of grapes, holding his free hand protectively around it.

"More fruit," he said.

I found a box of raisins, and if I had not objected, he would have eaten the whole thing. I feared he would be sick from overeating, but an hour later he threw himself on the floor again, yelling, "Kay yoggs! Kay yoggs!"

Marilyn waited a respectable interval, then she gave me a direct and studied smile. "You *said*," she said, "that we could have our candy *after* lunch."

I produced the sacks. Carefully she took out all the items— the squashed marshmallow chickens, the jelly beans, the colored eggs—and lined them up in a row. She would eat one slowly and then study the line for the next choice. She also kept a careful watch on Robbie's store. I knew I dared not leave the table until the possessions were returned to their proper sacks and put away.

Both children seemed to be a little more relaxed and their hands, when I touched them, were getting warmer. Marilyn walked to the patio doors. "Look!" she said, and I was pleased that at least one of them had seen the magnificent view, a solid fifteen miles of uninterrupted trees to the sky in all directions. "Oh, look, Robbie," she said. "A radar tower!"

Well, yes, it wasn't solid trees. There was one structure.

"At night it has a red light," I said. "You'll see."

The thought of night, when the radar tower light was visible, suddenly made me think of King's homecoming. What a surprise he was going to have! Having no telephone, I could not warn him. An early supper was indicated, followed by an early bedtime. Surely the children did not fight all night, too. Already I longed for night and sleep. *This* tired after four hours; what had ever made me think I could care for two children? I tried to believe that things would quiet down in time and I went to the kitchen to see what I could prepare for that early supper. Both children followed me.

"What's that?" Marilyn said.

"Celery," I said. I finished washing the celery and reached for the butcher knife to start chopping it. "Would you like some?" I turned to the children and saw Robbie, white-faced, shrieking, his chest heaving up and down.

"Why, what's wrong?" I said, moving toward him. He screamed and stumbled backward in terrible fear of me. I retreated and looked in question to Marilyn.

"It's the knife," she said.

I had not even realized that I was holding a knife in my hand and hastily I put it down. I walked away from it into the living room and sat down on the bed. "What is it about the knife?" I said to Marilyn. I patted the bed beside me and she came over and sat down.

"Uncle Jack is going to cut off Robbie's goober with a big knife," she said. "He's got a big knife to clean fish with and he's going to cut off Robbie's goober."

Although I'd never heard it called that before, the meaning was instantly clear from the way Robbie now held his hands protectively before him.

"Oh, *no*," I said. "Absolutely not. King would never let anybody do that to you, Robbie. You just wait until King gets home and he'll tell you he would not let anybody hurt you. Tell me," I said to Marilyn, "about Uncle Jack."

"He's some kin to Maw," she said, "our grandmother that brought us here the first time. Maw took us to Uncle Jack's place when Tom Hickerson kicked us out. He's a ole man. He's crippled. All he does is fish."

When King walked in the door I wished for one of those fine

cameras that are able to catch instantaneous changes of expression: zip, zap, click, clack, eyebrows up, eyelids accept, smile on,
smile off.

"Ah. . . . well, hello," he said. "We have visitors."

"More like a family," I said.

Twenty-two years of intimacy shot to hell, I thought. Lost in
an instant. All our ease of speaking freely to one another, gone.
I suppose when people have their own children they can keep
on talking to each other right over the baby's head (well, the
first one anyhow) and gradually they develop their times of
privacy when the baby is asleep, when the baby runs out to play,
when the baby is in its own room.

Now there *was* only one room and we were all in it and if,
please God, the children ever fell asleep we would be far too
tired for conversation.

I suppose we all had supper that night. I can't remember it,
though I'm sure Marilyn picked at this and that and announced
she didn't like it and Robbie ate everything in sight. I do remember asking if they'd like a bath, setting off a duet of delighted screeches. A bath, it turned out, was their idea of the
greatest thing going. I filled the tub with bubble bath, to their
extreme delight, and when they had settled down a little, I
began to bathe them. And thus I found out about the rashes
around the anus, the bad sores that Marilyn had behind her
ears. Robbie's fingernails were very long and very dirty, but
Marilyn's were bitten right to the quick.

I improvised some sleepwear out of King's undershirts and in
these the children danced around, giggling and pulling at each
other's gowns. While I made the cots, Marilyn sidled up to
King. He took her on his lap. "You look just like a princess," he
said. "I guess I'll have to call you Princess."

"What's a princess?" she said.

"Miaou," Robbie said, "miaou, miaou." He was on all fours, crawling at great speed back and forth in front of King. He really gave a wonderful imitation of a cat, arching his back, stretching, holding his head on one side. I stopped the bedmaking long enough to scratch him behind the ear. "Hello, Kitty," I said. "You crawl into bed now."

I sat on the floor (would I ever be able to stand up?) by Robbie's cot. He crawled over and got into the bed. I took one of his feet in my hand and began to say this little piggy with his toes. When I finished that one he said, "Nothergen," and held up the first. I did them all again, to rapt silence, and then I pulled the sheet and blanket up over his legs. "Now I'll give you a bellybutton kiss," I said.

"I want one, too," Marilyn said.

"Get in bed," I said, "and King will give you one."

King's bellybutton kisses were louder and better and Robbie wanted one of his. So I left them, with King on his knees moving from cot to cot and back again, blowing great smooches into bellybuttons until he was purple in the face.

He came into the kitchen, to find me stupidly dropping things, trying to make some order. Behind him I saw both children out of bed.

"Why are you out of bed?" I said.

"Me and Robbie generally see the late movie," Marilyn said.

"You get right back into bed, both of you," I said. I put the covers over Marilyn and sat by her bed. "You aren't going to be an imitation grownup here," I said to her. "You're going to be a real child and we're going to take real good care of you. Wouldn't you like that?"

"I don't know," she said. "What do we do?"

"First, we see that you get to sleep early and get a lot of rest, the way children are supposed to." I leaned down and kissed her. "Pleasant dreams," I said.

Then I went over to Robbie's bed. "There's a light on in the closet, Robbie, so you can see to go to the bathroom if you need to in the night. I'm going to leave it on all night. And we'll be right here in that bed. Right here with you all night."

King followed me to the kitchen, where the sinkful of dishes and all the supper disorder waited, but as I started the dishwater running I thought I heard another sound. There they were, both of them, out of bed again. They seemed to be flitting in all directions at once, like butterflies. I turned off the water and went in to the children. "What in the world are you doing out of bed *again?*" I said. Marilyn turned and started weaving a serpentine course with high footsteps. Immediately Robbie fell into follow-the-leader. King and I sat down on the hearth in disbelief, watching this puzzling dance. Finally Robbie turned and pointed at us, never missing a step in the ritualistic dance.

"You wait till we're asleep and then you slip out," he said.

"No!" King and I shouted in unison. "We wouldn't do that."

Robbie just smiled mischievously. He knew all those games, his smile said. Nobody seriously stayed home to do the dishes. He wasn't taken in. Marilyn said nothing, just kept up her prancing steps in a circle, Robbie following. As Robbie came near King in his dance, he pointed to him and said, "He got his coat on." Thus we learned that if a man is home to stay, he takes his coat off.

"I think," I said to King, "it would save time in the long run if we just went to bed and worried about the kitchen later."

"A great idea," he said. "You don't have to sell me."

So we got into our nightclothes and into our bed. By the

closet light we could see the children hopping into theirs. "Good night," we said.

We heard a funny little snore from the direction of Marilyn's bed. I felt the bed shake with King's suppressed laughter. I exhaled. I closed my eyes.

The next thing I knew, King and I were standing in the middle of the room listening to the most hair-raising scream I have ever heard. It was Robbie. I ran to his bed and and knelt down by him. "I'm here, Robbie," I said, "I'm here. What is it?" But I could not wake him. "Mamma!" he screamed. "Mamma! Mamma! Mamma!" I touched him very gently. His body was rigid. I sat saying his name quietly, saying I don't know what that I thought would be reassuring. Suddenly he put his thumb in his mouth and began to breathe deeply and slowly. I crawled back to our bed.

"My God," King said. "How often is that going to happen, do you suppose?"

It turned out to be roughly once an hour. The screams never disturbed Marilyn. She slept straight through everything.

In the morning I found a note from King by the coffeepot. "Didn't have the heart to wake you. I'll bring home some food tonight but I'm too stupid to shop for underwear. K."

Gratefully I saw that both children still slept. If only I could have a cup of coffee in solitude. It helped, and I debated whether to dress first or tackle last night's kitchen disorder. I decided, in the blessed quiet, to have another cup of coffee. How beautiful the children were, asleep. Robbie on his side, his thumb in his mouth, his long black eyelashes against his too-pale skin.

Cup in hand, I moved over to Marilyn's bed. Her gorgeous red hair lay in a halo on the pillow. Her mouth was a little

open. Her bright red cheeks . . . *that* red? Were children supposed to have cheeks *that* red?

An inch away from her body I could feel the heat. Alarm
signals swept through me, banishing my drowsiness. Suddenly
she sat up and vomited in an arc, covering the sheets, the
bedspread and her makeshift nightgown. She began to cry.

"Sh-sh," I said. "It's all right. It's all right." I got a washcloth
and cleaned her up. I found an old shirt of mine and put it on
her. When I started to lift her over to our bed I discovered my
arms were trembling.

"Come over here," I said. She tottered over to our bed
drunkenly and fell on it. I covered her up and while I was
stripping her bed she sat up and vomited again, all over our bed.
Dear God, why hadn't I thought to get her a basin after the first
time? Now she was having a severe chill. Finally I had her in
one clean bed, wrapped in a clean blanket with a hot-water
bottle. There was mountain of reeking soiled bedding in the
bathtub. In my head, like a bunch of crows after a piece of
bread, horrendous thoughts flapped their wings for attention.

Don't panic, I told myself. *Don't panic.* With gratitude I saw
that Robbie still slept. I sat down by Marilyn's bed. Her teeth
had stopped chattering. She looked at me with frightening
question and I tried to smile reassuringly. "You'll feel better
after a while," I said. "Tell me where you hurt."

She put one hot little hand outside the blanket and
clutched my dress. "Don't leave me," she said.

"Why, no," I said, "of course I won't leave you. I'll be right
here beside you. Now I have to take your temperature." I
unclenched the hand, finger by finger, and went to find the
thermometer.

"What's that?" she said.

"Haven't you ever seen a thermometer?"

She said she hadn't. Well, I wasn't going to take the chance of her biting it in two. I put it in her armpit and while I held her arm close to her body I could feel the little heart racing.

It said 104. One hundred and *four!* My God, what would I do? No phone. I could not call a doctor. I could not take her to the doctor, either. If I went out to the road to flag down a car, I might stand there for an hour. But it was idiotic to think she would let me leave her to stand on the road. Oh, if only someone would come by. Where was the Avon lady? The Avon lady had been all the way out to see me once. Why hadn't I bought a great big order then so she would come back often?

Or even the Watkins man. He had been there once with all his bottles of extract and other things I didn't want. True, he hadn't meant to come; he'd been lost trying to find the road to someplace else.

But somebody. Anybody. I went to the door and looked hopefully at the road. *Rain?* When had it started to rain? Now, of course, any thought of dragging that child out on the road to walk or be carried, if I could have done it, was impossible.

Stop! I said to the black birds fluttering in my brain. Give up the road. The Avon lady is not coming. The Watkins man is not coming. Nobody is coming until five o'clock, when King gets home. Get to work on the child.

How much aspirin were you supposed to give a five-year-old? I didn't have children's aspirin, of course. I decided to try half a tablet and another half in an hour. Marilyn swallowed it and it came right back up. But we had the basin this time. So I couldn't have any help from aspirin, as of now anyway.

I stuffed all the reeking bedding into a plastic bag and put it out of doors. Later, later, I would take care of it. *Now* I had to take care of the child. Fortunately, I did have alcohol. I set the clock by the bedside.

"Marilyn," I said, "you have a high fever and I'm going to sponge you off so your fever will come down. Every fifteen minutes we'll try to swallow a little water. I'm going to take care of you. When King comes home from work we'll take you to the doctor. Can't you tell me where you hurt?"

"Don't leave me," she said.

I sponged and sponged. When she was cold I stopped and covered her up. Every fifteen minutes I got a teaspoon of water down her. After an hour I tried half an aspirin again and this time it stayed down. Half an hour later I tried another half tablet. After an hour her temperature was still 104 and I graduated to whole aspirins and continuous sponging.

The mess in the kitchen from the night before was still there and I was constantly adding to it. The goats were unfed and not milked. And Robbie woke up.

"Listen, Robbie," I said, "Marilyn's very sick and I have to be with her all the time to take care of her. You find yourself some fruit to eat and as soon as I can I'll get you something else. I want you to be quiet."

"I wet the bed," he said.

"That's all right, Robbie. Don't worry. You'll get over it when you feel safe here, I expect. We have more sheets. I think we have more sheets."

"What's wrong with Marilyn?" he said.

"I don't know, Robbie. She has a high fever and I'm trying to cool her off. I'm going to take care of her the best I can."

"It's raining," he said.

"I know, I know."

In the afternoon I changed from water to orange juice. It

stayed down. At last Marilyn volunteered some information. "My throat hurts," she said. I took the flashlight and looked. It was a red mess down there. Well, at any rate, I could forget about appendicitis and other emergencies below the neck. Shortly before King got home she fell into a deep sleep. The redness faded from her cheeks. I took her temperature. It was normal. It seemed stupid to waken her and take her out in the rain and into town to try to locate the doctor after hours when what her body so obviously wanted was sleep. We decided to postpone the decision until morning. By morning she was very hungry, her temperature was still normal and yesterday seemed unreal.

I gave both children some paper and pencils, mentally adding crayons to the interminable shopping list. Then at last, I tackled the mess in the kitchen. It was a long time before I saw the countertop glimmering through. I stopped for a cigarette and sat down where the children were drawing. Robbie was scratching on one piece of paper after another, making them as black as possible. Somewhere on each sheet there was a white circle. "Moon," he said. "Moon, moon, moon."

Marilyn handed me one of her drawings. "I drawed Roy with a mustache," she said. "Here I drawed him again when he shaved it off. I can't make his legs good."

Roy, the father, we heard about. Maw, the grandmother, we heard about. Tom Hickerson, who, we learned, had threatened to cut off Robbie's dingdong, we heard about. Uncle Jack, who threatened to cut off Robbie's goober, we heard about.

But Darlene, the mamma, was never mentioned.

I hoped that when it did come, if ever, I would be alert enough to hear it.

However, in the stupor in which we moved about like

zombies (Robbie's nightmares continued on the hour night after night), I was not even alert enough to catch the cause of Marilyn's guilty behavior. Every once in a while, while blushing, she would give me a big, insincere smile. After this had happened a number of times I realized that she was always standing by the table when it happened. King and I were both in the habit of dumping change out of our pockets and I thought the poor child had perhaps found a dime and was suffering unnecessary guilt over having taken it.

By accident I discovered, while making up Robbie's cot, that the table was reflected in a door mirror. The next time I saw Marilyn gravitating to the table, I turned my back on her and pretended to be fixing Robbie's bed. Unaware that I was watching, she looked at my back, then stealthily stuck her finger in the open salt dish and licked it. When I turned around I got the blush and the big smile again. Robbie, too, stuck his finger in the salt dish and licked it. A steady diet of Kay yoggs, I thought, leaves something to be desired.

"Some people like salt on apples," I said. "Would you like to try it?" I sliced up some apples (putting the kitchen counter between Robbie and the paring knife, of course) and sprinkled salt on one slice for myself. Mostly the children licked the salt off the apple slices, but some apple got eaten. I hoped that when salt was no longer such a valuable thing that one had to steal it, their own bodies would tell them they didn't need any more.

How like the baby goats they were, I thought, remembering the deep channels worn through the salt blocks in the barn. If only I could think of the children as I did the baby goats—little warm creatures made happy when their needs were met.

"Let's go and see the goats," I said.

Buffeted like a Ping-Pong ball from one children's crisis to the next, I had neglected the goats terribly. Snatching a moment when King could be with the children, I had dashed to the barn and thrown down a little food each day. Now I had hopes that, in time, the barn could be clean again and the leisurely walks in the woods resumed. To reach the barn, though, there was a short stretch where we must walk on the public road and that part of the road approached a blind curve.

"Now, Robbie," I said, "when we come to the road you must take my hand. That's the rule and that's the road."

I had absolutely no conception of how they would act on the road. If they simply began to run, I had no faith that I could catch them. And if they took off in opposite directions . . . what would I do then?

6

To my great surprise, Robbie stopped at the road and put up his hand. "That's the road and that's the rule," he said. "That's the rule and that's the road." And he chanted it all the way to the barn. It was a very educational experience.

The goats had gone off to graze on the hillside and the barnyard was empty. Dry black pellets of excrement lay in little piles about the unraked stalls. Unfortunately, the pellets resemble raisins and Robbie, who loved raisins madly, thought he had discovered their source. Quicker than I could say *No!* he had a handful in his mouth and was chewing. Then he was spitting. Then he was crying. In his anger he struck at the stall door. It swung back, hitting him on the head. He began screaming.

The goats, having heard my voice, were now returning to

the barnyard, leaping into the air, their bells jangling. I had
taken many visiting children to see the goats, and if they were
city children, they usually hung back timidly until they were
convinced that the goats were gentle and then, at my urging,
they would hold peanuts in their hands for the goats to eat or
they would pat them gingerly on the heads. But not Robbie. He
flew through the air, careening into Miss Dude's side. Utterly
flabbergasted, the hair on her neck rising in alarm, Miss Dude
began to run in a big circle, Mattie Mae and Emma bleating
behind her. Robbie gave chase, and very soon tripped on the
uneven ground and fell. He fell right in the path of Viola and
Eunice and Rosie, all of whom now followed Miss Dude in a
milling circle. The barnyard seemed filled with goats, all wildly
excited and bleating in panic and running, running, running. In
the midst of this was Robbie, screaming on the ground, up again
before I could reach him. In desperation I grabbed him, lifted him in
my arms, stood still and began to sing "Rock-a-bye-baby."

Instant peace from Robbie. In my aching arms his body
relaxed. I stood perfectly still, singing, until the goats calmed
down.

"What's that?" Robbie said, smiling.

"What's what?"

"You singing."

"That's a lullaby," I said.

"A yuhyaby?"

"Yes. Didn't anybody ever sing you a lullaby?"

He shook his head no. "Nothergen," he said.

Earlier I had taken my eyes away from Robbie long enough
to see that Marilyn was leaning against the barn, still and
unfrightened and in no danger. All my muscles now trembling, I
managed to get Robbie into the milk room, closing its door to

the goats. Over the partition separating the milk room from the adjoining stall I now watched, fascinated, through the stall's open door to the yard, as Marilyn moved ever so quietly toward the goats, who had stopped running and were huddled together. She was without fear and they permitted her to stand among them. Miss Dude stood looking at Marilyn and Rosie went over and leaned against the child. Marilyn put out her hand to Rosie's head and began to stroke her.

"You see?" I said to Robbie. "That's the way you must be with the goats, just like Marilyn, You must *never* chase the goats again. You must never wave your arms or move fast or make a loud noise."

I managed to get one stall raked and part of the yard cleaned. I put out dairy feed and wondered how long it would be before I dared try milking with the children present. Fortunately, with the babies there to drink it, no harm was being done the does, except that they might have to be trained all over to jump up on the milking stand.

While the goats' attention was riveted on the dairy feed, I quietly took Robbie out of the milking room. At my command he stood still, watching the goats eat. With horror I saw that I had left the rake leaning against the barn where one of the children could step on it and run a rake tooth through a foot. I quickly moved to put the rake away and the moment I let loose his hand, Robbie was kneeling at the food trough, eating of the dairy feed, goat fashion. It was a big improvement over the "raisins," I guess. Something like, and maybe even better than, Kay yoggs.

Back in the house once again, the dairy feed and mud washed off Robbie, I sank onto the bed. Marilyn came and leaned against me.

"Am I too big?" she said.

"For what?"

"For a lullaby," she said, "like you give Robbie."

"Why, indeed no," I said, "except I don't think I can lift you. You lie down here and put your head on my lap. O.K.?"

"Me, too," Robbie said, crawling on the bed. The two of them pushed skulls for space on my lap and before they got to the skull-cracking stage I began to sing in my cracked cigarette alto. Like angels they lay, eyes closed, receiving, receiving.

The teeth of the rake haunted me, though, and from wondering about tetanus I progressed to polio, diphtheria, what else? What else? Had they had any immunization at all and how would I find out? I decided on a trip to the County Health Department in Erin to find if they had any records on the children. I no longer feared that Robbie would run away from me or throw himself in front of trucks. The children had gained weight so rapidly that the clothes they had come in were already uncomfortably tight and hot. It was so warm now that they just wore underpants around the house. A friend with children near the same ages had managed to find us some shorts and shirts, and these would do for the trip into town. King came out on his noon hour and took us to Erin.

On the street we met an attorney we had consulted before about the deed to our land. "I heard you had these kids," he said, "and I'm glad."

"Yes, we'll be in to talk to you about it as soon as we get everything calmed down," I said. "Right now we're going to the Health Department to see if there's any record of immunization."

"Where you should go is the Welfare Department," he said.

"Well, I wanted to ask you about that, among other things."

"Other things can wait," he said. "You get over there today. You need to be on record as having been there."

"O.K.," I said. "Just as soon as I can."

"Go today," he said.

At the Health Department they, too, had heard we had the children and were glad, they said. There was an earlier record of Marilyn's having had some immunization and that was how I learned that she had been left before, as an infant, with the grandmother. There was no record that Robbie had had any immunization at all, so it was decided to get him started off with a diphtheria-whooping cough-tetanus shot, as well as one for typhoid and an oral polio dose. Marilyn, for this time, was to have only typhoid and oral polio. I began to try to explain to the children how this would help protect them, but Marilyn had caught sight of the needle and she simply went wild.

The nurse, experienced with this kind of behavior, moved very rapidly and efficiently and got it all over with. It was a wild time and I dreaded the return visits scheduled later.

I took the children to the dime store and bought a doctor kit and a nurse kit for them to play with at home. Then we headed for the Welfare Department. Here, too, the people expressed their great relief that the children were with us. Everybody seemed to have been very worried, but nobody seemed to have acted. With the children there listening, I could not ask what I would have liked to ask. Annabelle Norfleet, the welfare worker, said she would be out to visit the children at home.

At the shoe store we discovered that the boots Robbie was wearing were two sizes too short. They must have been painful; yet he had never complained. How in the world had he been able to move with such speed?

Though they had lived in this town for some time, Marilyn

didn't recognize any of the buildings or any of the people in the stores on the square. Except one—a local beer place. "That's Billy Joe Rumfelt's bar," she said. "They sell some bad kind of beer in there. It makes you mean. Me and Robbie had to stay out in the car. There was snow all over and me and Robbie got so cold and so scared of the dark."

I found I was too exhausted to tackle the supermarket without King, so we went early to our meeting place. While we were waiting, Marilyn rather hesitated about saying "Mrs. Baker," as she had before, and I asked her if she wouldn't rather call me something else. "I know Rachel is hard for children to pronounce sometimes. What would you like to call me?"

She leaned against me and gave me her fetching company smile. "Well, if you don't *mind*," she said, "I'd like to call you Mamma."

"I'd like that fine," I said. "I just didn't want to push you into it if you didn't feel like it."

"Mamma, Mamma, Mamma, Mamma," Robbie said. Marilyn had given me the stamp of approval; that was all he had been waiting for.

When King came, we went to the market for groceries. It took one person's full time and attention to replace what Robbie could pull from the shelves while the other one shopped. And Marilyn, unless restrained, tried to take away from Robbie whatever he had grabbed. That led to a bite, followed by screams, tears, a retaliatory kick, howls and, of course, the dropping of the merchandise (mercifully, it was not always glass).

War-torn and weary, we started home in the car. Because of the children's noise it was impossible to have a conversation with King. The only remedy was to sing. They loved to sing in the car and this magically stopped the mayhem. Robbie especially liked "Yankee Doodle" ("and cawed it macawoni"), but

Marilyn's favorite (from an old song book I had found in the house) was "Union Maid" ("Oh, you can't scare me, I'm sticking to the union!").

At home, we had our own song (made up by the children) for supper:

> The radar tower is working
> And supper's on the table.
> Light the candles, blow the match,
> And wait!
> Till Daddy sits down.
> And then, *eat!*

Before supper they fought over whose turn it was to sit on the kitchen stool and after supper they fought over who got to put out the candles with the candle snuffer. But in between, Robbie ate and even Marilyn, this night, courageously tried a small sample of something that wasn't a hot dog. And milk, milk, milk. They couldn't get enough milk.

Gone was the leisurely cocktail, gone was listening to the evening news, gone was conversation. There was only one way when the children were awake that we achieved any quiet at all and that was, after supper, to put them in the bathtub. There was a short interval when the bubble bath soothed them and they played together without fighting over their bath toys. If you waited thirty seconds too long, though, the fight started again. We got to be masters at timing this.

Bathed, dry and in clean underpants, they were ready to play cat and mouse. They had discovered a rack of King's city-life neckties hanging in the closet and these they tucked into their pants for tails. Then they were mice. King was the big bad cat who chased them.

"Save me, Mamma," they yelled, hurling themselves at me. I

let the big cat threaten until the screams reached a point beyond which I couldn't live. Then I got a Q-tip, dipped it in
magic (witch hazel) and touched the cat on the forehead. He
crumpled slowly into a heap. And it was time for bed.

Not sleep. Just bed. Bed with this little piggy and
bellybutton kisses and bedtime stories and nothergen and
nothergen and then for each one a little Chinese bowl full of
raisins and almonds and the bedtime song:

> To my little one's cradle in the night
> Comes a new little goat snowy white.
> The goat will trot to the market
> While mother her watch will keep.
> To bring you back raisins and almonds.
> Sleep my little one, sleep.*

At the Health Department I had picked up a free booklet
called "Your Children's Quarrels" and while I was leafing
through it one afternoon Marilyn asked to see it because it
contained pictures. "What is it?" she said. "Oh, it's a book for
mammas to read about children quarreling," I said. "Do you
think if I keep studying I'll learn how to be a good mamma?"

"Oh, yes," she said. "Besides, you have something that no
one else has."

"What's that?" I said.

"Why, you can laugh and cough at the same time," she said.
"I never knew anybody who could do that."

Ah, to be appreciated. Sweet balm.

---

*"Raisins and Almonds," Jewish folk song from *A Treasury of Folk Songs,*
edited by John and Sylvia Kolb (New York: Bantam Books, 1948).

Robbie's cot was a narrow one which we kept against one wall out of the way, but Marilyn's was a larger, folding cot which we put up each morning in order to have room enough to walk around. Our bed served as a couch during the day and was back against the wall opposite the fireplace. So Marilyn was accustomed to taking her naps on the couch. She did not always nap, but was usually content to sit or lie quietly on the couch, looking at her books or drawing or playing with a toy. It was Sunday, so King was at home, and it was he who first noticed that Marilyn was crying. She made no noise, just sat perfectly still with tears rolling down her face. This was very unusual. King went over to her.

"Why, Marilyn," he said, "what is it? What's the matter?"

"It's my dog," she said. "I miss my dog."

King sat beside her and held her in his arms. "What's this about a dog?" he said. "We never heard anything about a dog before."

She made big swallowing efforts to get her tears under control. I took her some Kleenex and she wiped her nose and rolled the Kleenex into a ball. "*Our* dog," she said. "Robbie's and mine. We had him when we lived in that trailer."

"What happened to him?" King said.

"I don't *know*," she said.

"Well, darling," King said, "it's been an awfully long time since you were in the trailer. I don't even know where to start looking for him. Do you?"

"I think he went up Stavely Holler," she said. "We stayed up there with Virgie Stavely after they took the trailer away. And I think he went up Stavely Holler someplace."

"I don't have the faintest idea where Stavely Holler is," King said. "Do you?"

"I think I could find it," Marilyn said. "I think I could show you."

"Well, we could go out in the car and look around," King said, "if you think you know where it is."

"*Can* we, Mamma?" she said, already putting her shoes on, the tears now vanished.

"It won't hurt to look around," King said, "and have a drive and maybe stop at the Dairy Dip."

"You and Daddy can go try," I said, "but, Marilyn, please don't get your hopes up too high. I don't think the chances are very good, really. It isn't likely that the dog would be there in the same place after all this time, you know. It's been weeks and weeks since you were there."

"Come on, Daddy," she said. "Let's go."

When Robbie woke up we took the goats to the woods. The trees were beginning to leaf out now and all the lovely soft greens of spring were out. Robbie was mad for flowers and he picked a bouquet of wild phlox.

At home we put Robbie's flowers in a vase and I started to prepare supper. Still there was no sign of King and Marilyn. I hoped King had not had car trouble on some deserted back-country road. I was sorry this had happened on his Sunday afternoon, for the back roads were dreadful and I feared Marilyn would be pressing him to try another and another and just one more. I knew it would be hard for him to decide on the moment when they must give up the search and accept the fact that the dog was truly lost.

Suddenly the car was there and Robbie was outside, jumping up and down and screaming. I could see Marilyn, red-faced, sweaty and laughing, trying to get out of the car, and King, leaning over the steering wheel, looking very, very tired. Marilyn ran to me and began pulling at my dress, yelling, "We found him! We found him! And he's got the same name as your husband."

And there he was, slowly emerging from the car, wagging his tail, licking Robbie in the face, an old, flea-bitten, black-and-

tan hound dog with perhaps a police dog grandfather in his
ancestry. He was big and evil-smelling, with sad amber eyes.

"Oh, King," Robbie yelled, "King, King, King, you hum."

King (my husband, that is) gave me a sheepish look. "Well,"
he said, "much to my surprise we found him."

"Just what I needed," I said, sitting down on the back steps.
"An old, flea-bitten hound with the same name as my husband."
King (the dog, that is) came over, leaned on me and slobbered
all over my face with his tongue.

It was to be a source of endless confusion. I would go out to
call the dog to be fed and my husband would dash up, out of
breath, from work in the orchard. "What's the matter?" he'd say,
thinking there was some emergency with the children. Man and
dog were both too old to have their names changed.

Not that there was really any sense in calling the dog for *his*
meal. He much preferred rotten carcasses to dog food. Rotting
'possum, dead birds, castaway fishermen's catches, ancient cow
skulls, dead cats—it was unbelievable the amount of rotten
booty that dog found and brought home. Apparently he rolled
around on them a bit before he began chewing. He always
offered them to me with beautiful devotion shining out of his
great amber eyes. Where did they all come from? I came to
believe that dog could find a rotten carcass at a formal wedding.

For our social life, we went to the launderette in the evening
after supper. What was for us a tedious necessity was, for the
children, a place of wild excitement because of the penny slot
machines. The prizes were miniature plastic toys, and the trick
was for King to dole out the pennies so that the children's
attention was held while I had my eyes on the washers and
driers. While the clothes dried we would examine all the loot
and sometimes make songs about it. I remember one that began:

A beetle, a crutch, three flies and a pistol,
A spider, a horseshoe, a fish and a snail.
A bucket, a hot dog, a roulette wheel.

The clothes to be folded and carried to the car, a look around, checking for left articles and, alas, there must have been a split second we had our eyes off Robbie. Suddenly there was a column of water shooting horizontally at great pressure, Robbie was screaming hysterically, King was running next door for the owner, who came running very fast with a wrench in his hand. No children or clothes, fortunately, had been in the direct path of the stream of water (at this hour we often had the launderette all to ourselves), but the entire floor was running water.

To our surprise, the owner didn't seem angry. As soon as he had followed the stream to its source underneath some machinery and turned off the water, he came crawling out through the wetness and got to his feet. "I been hunting for that outlet faucet ever since I bought this place," he said. "I knew there should be one someplace, but I never could find it."

When Robbie realized he was not going to be punished he recovered very quickly, and he and Marilyn started rounding up their prizes, which they had dumped in the excitement. It took King and me longer to recover from the shock. Back home, lying in bed, waiting for that first sleep before Robbie's first nightmare, I was still shaking.

It so often seems to me now, when ever-new madnesses lurk waiting behind the TV switch, that the key to the lock that holds the universe together has been misplaced and forgotten somewhere at the eye level of a three-year-old. And any day now, the right-level eye is going to see it, the right-sized hand is going to reach out . . . and turn the key.

7

After about a month Grace Hickerson came to visit her grandchildren. Robbie was asleep, but Marilyn, excited to see her, ran
to her to be kissed and hugged and to be allowed to look in her
purse and inside the sack that had presents of candy and gum.

"Oh, Maw," Marilyn said, "I just got so much to tell you.
You know, we have three meals here every day and they're
called breakfast and lunch and supper."

"And I see you been eating them all," the grandmother said.
"My," she said to me, "I couldn't believe children could look
that different in a few weeks. How they have filled out. How
you been getting along?"

"It's been pretty hectic," I said. "Now we're all settling down
some and getting a little calmer."

"I know they're not easy," she said. "I been wanting to come
every day, but I thought if I came and they cried it would make it
harder on you. I didn't know how you'd feel about my coming."

"Maw," Marilyn said, "look. I can tie my shoes. See?"

"That's fine, baby," she said, and then, turning to Robbie,
who had just started to awaken, "Come here, Robbie. Come
give Maw some sugar." She held out her arms to him and
Robbie became a cat who slipped off his bed and crawled into a
corner of the room.

"Why, ain't you gonna come give Maw a kiss?" Mrs.
Hickerson said.

"Nope," Robbie said.

"It always seems to take him a while to wake up," I said. But
Mrs. Hickerson could not wait. She pursued him to his corner,
where he tried to burrow into the wall. She tickled him and
pulled at him until she finally got him to laugh, but he would

not leave the corner. Finally she gave up and went back to her chair. "Aren't you going to come look in the sack and see what Maw brought you?" she said.

He left his corner and walked over to the sack. He looked in at the candy and gum and then he said defiantly, "You give it to Mamma. Mamma put it away. We eat *after* supper. We don't eat candy between meals."

"Oh, I'm sorry," Mrs. Hickerson said. "I didn't mean to go against . . ." and she handed me the sack.

"Well, I'll put it away for after supper, then," I said. "I didn't know my ideas were getting across that well, to tell you the truth. And that—that calling me Mamma, you know . . . I didn't press that. It was their idea."

"I think it's fine," she said. "You don't know what it means to me to see these children taken care of and happy and filling out the way they are. I've just been sick with worry about them for so long, and I've not heard one word from Darlene or Roy, either one. Not one word. And right now—"

"Maw," Marilyn said, "look at the pictures I drew and I can write on the typewriter, too. I can write my name. And look here. I can sew. See that? And I'm gonna learn to milk the goat, too."

Marilyn continued to bombard her with each detail of our lives, but Robbie said very little and when Mrs. Hickerson rose to leave, saying she had yet to take food to Uncle Jack, he came and stood behind me, holding on to my leg.

As soon as Mrs. Hickerson's car was out of the driveway, Robbie pointed to the sack of candy, on the kitchen counter. "Me want! Me want!" he yelled.

I didn't argue. I gave it to him, only checking to see that it was shared equally between the children. Robbie gave me a huge, conspiratorial smile. He had made his grandmother an outsider and he had defended the ways of the house before the outsider. It was a gesture and we both knew it. How he had been able to sustain it for the length of her visit, I didn't know.

After he had tasted the candy he gave me the remainder to put away again. Then he stood looking out the door. I went and stood by him and he leaned against my leg. Then he pointed out to the road and said, "You hold my hand on the road. That's the road and that's the rule. That's the rule and that's the road."

That night he stopped wetting the bed.

I had said to Mrs. Hickerson that things were getting calmer, but it was only a matter of degree, something like moving from a hurricane to a windstorm. Outside in the woods I knew the brilliant red stars of the fire pinks were stabbing the soft spring air, the blue phlox would be everywhere. The hidden lemon-scented white flowers of the May apples were dangling down to the earth, where the violets would be thick: purple and yellow and white. And trillium and spring beauty and hepatica and the clean bluets in the mossy places—I was missing them all in this wild confusion of cooking and washing dishes and cleaning up spills and bathing and cooking again, to the accompaniment of the children's interminable fighting, fighting, fighting, like a constant barrage of random firecrackers.

The goats had only the minimum of care necessary to sustain life. By one o'clock each day I was exhausted, so that naptime barely saved my sanity and coming out of the nap took heroic effort.

"I can't understand why they don't go out to play," I said to one of our visitors. "At first I was afraid they would be dashing out and I would be chasing them all over the place, but I can't *get* them to go out. They're holding on to my legs while I scrub the floors, even. There's that gorgeous fresh air and sunshine and they're in here every minute."

"Oh, I understand it," she said. "I know a woman who lived in that trailer court. Every time a boyfriend drove up in a car the mother pushed them out the door and locked it. Rain or snow, it made no difference. They used to go to this woman's trailer and say they were locked out."

Not only could I not get them out of the house unless I went, too, but we could not get them into the car unless, each time, we reassured them that yes, we were coming back home after we finished the errand. They seemed never quite relaxed until we did get in the car to return home and then, as we approached the house, they would begin to say, "Hum, hum, hum, we're going back hum." Each piece of terrible knowledge we learned like this ate further into our hearts. Each sign of happiness or security made it more unthinkable that they would have ever again to be uprooted.

From the comments visitors made, it wasn't apparent that Robbie's frenetic activity was changing any, but to me it was perceptible that some kind of pendulum inside him was very gradually slowing down. He did not *always* scream that whatever Marilyn picked up was his. He could play contentedly with a toy car for as long as five minutes. One day it was his turn to sit at the typewriter with instructions to hit only one key at a time and to have paper in the machine. He made no complaints, asked no help, had no questions. After a long interval I heard one key struck. Then another. After half an hour I looked over his shoulder and saw ROYAL typed on the paper. He had copied it from the nameplate on the typewriter. Since he did not know his ABC's, I found this remarkable.

My own pendulum was slowing a little, too. I no longer felt always, every minute, in *crisis*. Some days there seemed to be a little time for something other than cooking, washing dishes, preparing food and forestalling accidents. Now and then we would read some stories, learn some songs, cut paper dolls. There was even a day when we didn't have to go to the clinic or buy clothes or wash clothes or go to the grocery or the barbershop, and we went to the woods. We took the goats, now that Robbie was able to refrain from chasing them. Miss Dude went first, as always, being the queen of the herd. Behind her were her babies, Mattie Mae and Emma. Next came Viola and her kid doe, Eunice. Next came Rosie.

We found a good place to make a playhouse in a little clearing. There was a fallen log for me to sit on and a tree with two low branches for Robbie to climb. The goats went off to browse nearby, always keeping in range so that as soon as I stood up or moved, Miss Dude would alert them all and they would return to me. Marilyn and I were making dishes out of acorn cups and we were "arranging" the small logs or branches which were to be the furniture.

"Knock knock," Marilyn said.

"Who's there?" I said.

"Madame."

"Madame who?"

"Madame foot's caught in the door," she said, and laughed and laughed.

Robbie came out of his tree and sat on the log by me. He picked up an acorn cup and I poured him a pretend cup of tea, which he drank.

"Is there a devil?" he said.

"A devil? No, I don't think so. Why?"

"There is," he said. "A devil that jumps out from behind and *gets you.*"

"Where did you hear about devils?" I said.

"Mrs. Johnson said there was a devil," Marilyn said. "And if you don't be good the devil will throw you in hellfire."

"Oh, I think that's terrible," I said. "People just say that to frighten children. I think it's wicked to frighten children. Why would she want to frighten you, Robbie? Who is Mrs. Johnson anyway?

"She was our baby-sitter sometimes," Marilyn said. "She wanted to watch television and Robbie wouldn't be quiet."

I put my arms around them both. "There is no devil," I said. "Bad people say things like that just to scare you. It's not true. Besides, you are *not* bad. You know Daddy wouldn't take bad children into his tent to play Indian. Every night he asks if you've been good children and every night I—"

"Heap good papoose," Marilyn said.

"Heap good brave," Robbie said, and they began to yell their Indian chants and dance around.

"Don't scare the *goats*," I said. Miss Dude had given the alarm sound and moved the whole herd out of sight. "Let's be very still, so they'll come back."

"Can we have marshmallows in the tent tonight?" Marilyn said. (The Indian ritual with King in the tent included holding miniature marshmallows on toothpicks over a candle flame.) I hoped no Indians ever witnessed these inaccurate games of Indian life being perpetuated every night. They would surely be more irate than I was over devils and hellfire. However it had grown up, out of expedience, it allowed me fifteen precious, childless minutes every night while the children, we hoped, learned to be less afraid of the dark and had a good time with King.

Slowly the goats ate their way back into my circle of vision and Marilyn walked over to them to play with her favorite, Eunice.

"Could Eunice be my goat?" she said.

"That would be nice," I said, "you and Eunice growing up together." Her red hair was very close to Eunice's color and the two of them together were very beautiful.

"I want to stay here with you and Eunice," she said.

"There are ghosts," Robbie said.

"No, Robbie. Ghosts are not real, either. I suppose there is another baby-sitter who wanted to watch TV and she told you about ghosts to scare you."

"Earline," Marilyn said. "She said if you don't shut up and go to sleep, they come out in the dark."

"They all white," Robbie said, "with holes for eyes."

"Oh, poo!" I said. "They're just for fun on Halloween. They aren't *real*."

"They go *wooooo wooooo*," Marilyn said.

"There *are* monsters," Robbie said. "I saw them on TV."

"I'll tell you one very important thing about devils and ghosts and monsters, Robbie. It's a big secret."

"What?" he said.

"They're afraid of laughter. It *scares* them to *death*. Did you know that? Ho ho ho, Devil," I yelled. "Hah hah hah, Ghost!"

Both children began to laugh very loud. We laughed and we laughed and we laughed. We scared the goats so that they all ran off again and we had a long wait until we got them started for the barn. But we scared off all the devils and ghosts and monsters. I hoped we had. I hoped we had.

That evening when the children were in their pajamas, a friend dropped by the house for a few moments. I said good night to her at the door, but King escorted her to her car. Instantly Marilyn grabbed me. "You've got to get him back," she said. "He's going to get in her car and go away with her and he'll never come back."

She was crying and jumping up and down, absolutely terrified. There was no possible way to reason with her. "Put on your shoes and go see for yourself," I said. "He's only putting her in her car."

She heard that about the shoes. Tears still streaming down her face, she ran out of the house, In a few minutes she was back, holding to King's hand, a little embarrassed about the scene she had caused. "He was just putting her in her car," she said.

"Of course," I said. "Daddy would not go off somewhere without telling us first."

Marilyn's wild scene had riveted Robbie in silence, his eyes wide violet pools of fear. Now he went over to King and held him about the knees. "You no go," he said.

"Go?" King said. "I'm going to bed. You're going to bed. We're all going to bed."

But sleep was another matter tonight. The bellybutton kisses, the stories read, the yuhyaby . . . and still the need to be reassured. So, without thinking, we were back in the always-never business again.

I don't believe I'd ever had any philosophical discussions on relative degrees of reassurance. I just learned all at once, in an instant, that there isn't, for a frightened child, any such thing as a conditioned reassurance, a promise with the fingers crossed or a modicum of security. There's no such thing as being half safe. Before you have time to consider, you're saying, I'll never leave you, I'll always stay with you. The reason you guarantee what can't be guaranteed, the reason you speak in absolutes, is because children absolutely have to have it.

Maybe with children of your own, that you learn on a day at a time, who develop by steps from saying one word at a time to a few words at a time—maybe such children give you an E for effort and can afford to go by your actions. But with instant families, frightened instant families anyhow, who really don't believe that you will act tomorrow as you acted today—they've got to have the *words*.

And they don't ask if you will always love them, which would be easy to answer. They ask if you'll *take care* of them, if you'll stay with them, if you'll return to them. They have to hear it in so many words that you won't dump them, leave them, walk out on them or trick them. And because they have to hear it instantly, you give it instantly.

You see, behind the frightened eyes, a tiny soul drowning in a sea of fear and you throw that rope. Not half a rope, not part of a rope, but *whatever rope is necessary* to reach the distance.

And before you know it has happened, a family exists, and certainly it seems that it will always be because it feels as though it has always been. While you're not looking, it is created; while your back is turned, when you bend over to pick up a sock from the floor, perhaps. While you're reading a thermometer, while you're shaking the soap bubble mixture, while you reach out with a towel to the little body stepping out of the bathtub.

Or, as King said, when you take them into town and everybody says how pretty they are.

I thought I watched the children every minute and yet I found MARILYN written inside the cupboard door, on the closet wall behind the clothes, inside the woodbox and, one day at the barn, under the sliding latch on the milk room door. When had she come to the barn with a pencil in her hand? Apparently I was not as all-knowing as I thought. I knew Robbie always yelled "Stop, stop!" at the stop sign when we were in the car, but I thought he recognized it by its shape and its position. Yet on our third visit to the clinic he pointed to a sign on the wall:

STOP BIRTH DEFECTS, and said, "Stop, stop!" And he was not yet
three. Marilyn could print KISS, LOVE, MAMMA, DADDY, MARILYN,
ROBBIE AND CAR, and she could recognize those words in print.
She could count to thirteen and then to twenty and very shortly
to one hundred. Robbie counted, "One, two three, and a whole
bunch."

And so the piggy banks (necessary to get their pennies and
nickels out of sight to avoid the endless arguments over possession) became money-for-college banks ("cawch" Robbie called
it). The local pressure for high school marriage, followed by the
Detroit factory job to support the car payments and the unwel-
come babies, was so great one couldn't begin to fight it too
early.

There we were, talking about college just as though we had
a right to a future. It's like eating peanuts, this commitment
business; once you start, there's no stopping. Commitments bred
like rabbits. They slipped off our tongues. It gets to be like
breathing, this feeling for the future.

Marilyn developed a great interest in rocks all of a sudden.
The whole road to the barn was paved with chert from the
creek bed and rarely did she step on it these days that she didn't
find a rock more beautiful and "innaresting" than the last. She
had a whole collection lined up on the window sill. "Marilyn is
going to learn all about rocks," I said to Robbie one day. "She
says that's what she's going to study in college. Then she can
come home and tell us all about them. What do you think you
might like to study?"

He was quiet for a long time, his eyebrows working in their
intense pattern. Finally he jutted out his little chin and made
his pronouncement.

"I will study the dark," he said.

8

So, in what seemed then natural steps in progression, we found
ourselves, in June, talking to our attorney about how best to
protect the children. Hugh Crane, the attorney, had an office
on the town square of the county seat and King and I took turns
sitting in the outer room with the children or sitting in the
inner room with Crane. He was a tall, very thin man in his
forties, with a face that appeared to have been hurriedly hewn
out of slate. It was all hard planes and angles except for the
deep-blue eyes, which had two absolutely horizontal shelves
over them. On these shelves the eyebrows had been lavishly
whipped and swirled out of excelsior. I always expected a miniature bird's nest to show up in one of them.

"That boy," Crane said, "he's a live one, all right. I'm really
glad you got those kids; they've been worrying me crazy. I was
an orphan myself," he said. "Brought up in foster homes."

"Was it pretty bad?" I said.

"No, not really," he said. "It was just me, I guess. I just kept
running away. The people were probably good people. I don't
know why I was so crazy about running away. You want to adopt
them, is that right?"

"We want to do what's best for them," I said. "We've never
even had *time* to discuss adopting them in any rational way. We
just survive through one crisis after another and then, suddenly,
we're planning to make a room out of the carport and the
children keep wanting to be reassured that they can stay forever
and that nothing will change. And then, the other day—well,
Marilyn is crazy about cars, especially big cars. We were at the
laundromat and she dashed out the door and into the street
after a car, yelling at somebody. She said it was one of their

mother's boyfriends. And I realized if the man had stopped the car she might have got in. I guess anybody has as much right to pick her up in a car as we do. It gave me an awful scare and then I got to thinking what if she needed an emergency operation or something. We don't have any legal position at all."

The essence of the matter, Crane said, was that adoption depended on proving abandonment by the parents and, in Tennessee, abandonment was defined as four months time without visitation or support on the part of the parents. When had the mother left? We had had the children two months by this time and would have to find out from the grandmother when the mother had left. In the meantime, since it was so difficult for me to get into town, Hugh Crane would prepare the necessary notices for filing. These would have to be published for four successive weeks in the local paper since we did not know the location of the parents.

The fine details didn't concern me. When the notice appeared in the local paper I thought the four weeks publication time gave us an added month.

IN THE MATTER OF THE ADOPTION OF MARILYN HACKETT AND ROBBIE HACKETT, MINORS IN THE CIRCUIT COURT OF HOUSTON COUNTY STATE OF TENNESSEE, HOUSTON COUNTY

Personally appeared before me, Avis C. Walker, Clerk of the Circuit Court for Houston County, the undersigned, Hugh Crane, who made oath in due form of law that he is agent and attorney for the petitioners, King Baker and Rachel Baker; that Roy Hackett and Darlene Hackett are non-residents of the State of Tennessee, and requests the clerk to have made proper publication for the defendants; that the facts and statements made in the foregoing petition, as of his knowledge are true, and

as to those statements made on information and belief, he
believes to be true.

Hugh Crane
ATTORNEY FOR PETITIONERS

Sworn to and subscribed before me this 13th day of June, 1963.
Avis Walker
CLERK OF THE CIRCUIT COURT

STATE OF TENNESSEE HOUSTON COUNTY CIRCUIT COURT

IN THE MATTER OF THE ADOPTION OF MARILYN BAKER
AND ROBBIE BAKER (MINORS)

In this cause it appearing from the Petitioners' bill, which is
sworn to, that the Defendants, Roy Hackett and Darlene Hackett
are non-residents of the State of Tennessee: It is ordered by me
that publication be made for four successive weeks, as required
by law, in the Stewart-Houston County Times, a newspaper
published in Erin, Tennessee, in said county, notifying said non-
resident defendants to appear before our said Circuit Court, at a
court to be holden at the courthouse in Erin, Tennessee, on the
third Monday in September, 1963, and make defense to said bill,
or the allegations thereof will be taken for confessed and this
cause set for hearing ex parte as to them.

This 21st day of June, 1963
Avis Walker, Clerk

At a court to be holden at the courthouse. In any case, it
was Hugh Crane's worry. My job was with the children. I had,
though, intended to give Mrs. Hickerson warning. However,
when next she came to see the children, she said it was all right,

that Hugh Crane had got in touch with her and she thought Darlene had left in February. She remembered it was very cold the day she left.

"I don't know if you know or not, but I've left Tom Hickerson," she said.

"Yes, I had heard," I said, "but I haven't mentioned it to Marilyn. I thought you'd prefer to tell her yourself."

"Well, I've known I had to for some time," she said, "but I just had to wait until I could choose a time when he wasn't, well, violent. He's really all right to get along with when he's not drinking. I don't know what it is. His mother said he never had these crazy spells until he came home from the war."

Later she said to Marilyn, "Baby, I'm not livin with Tom no more. I've moved into that old house near the restaurant."

"So?" Marilyn said. "Who are you with now?"

Mrs. Hickerson looked at me and blushed. "Well, I guess I had that coming to me," she said. "Poor younguns. Don't nothing stay the same six months at a time. I'll sure be glad you get this adoption through and they can settle down and stay someplace without being took off here and there."

I remembered the day Marilyn had asked me in exasperation, "Don't you have no boyfriends *at all?*" And I had tried to explain to her what I thought a family should be, while she listened with an expression of utter boredom on her face.

"This place I'm in," Mrs. Hickerson said, "it's all run down, in awful shape, but I can stand it for a few months, I guess, until I can get straightened out. I've got a perfectly good house in Stewart," she said, "standing vacant. It's tied up in a property settlement with my first husband and my lawyer says I dare not go in it until the property settlement is final. It's a shame. If only Darlene and Roy had waited just a few more months, then I would have had a place to keep the children myself."

"I didn't know this," I said. "There's such a lot I don't know. Mrs. Hickerson, I should be honest with you, I know. You see, I had such a bad impression of Mr. Hickerson. I didn't know you were afraid of him and I didn't know you were trying to leave him."

"I know," she said, "it must have looked awful to you, but. . . ."

"Then when Roy's father, Mr. Hackett, came he seemed so different, talked so responsibly, offering to help with the children, I told him I'd rather deal with him about the children."

"I know," she said. "Garner could always make a very good impression. I know just what you mean. But he's not taken care of his own child. I can't get one cent of child support out of him for his own without taking him to court over it and if he don't take care of his own, you can be sure he won't take care of Roy's."

"Well, he did offer, and after I saw how bright the children were I wrote suggesting he take out insurance policies or start savings accounts for college for them, not only for the financial help, but to give them the feeling their own relatives cared."

"Did you hear from him?" she said.

"He sent us a box of chocolates."

She laughed. "That's like him," she said.

"But, Mrs. Hickerson, what I wanted to say, now that you've left Mr. Hickerson, is that I've had time to be with the children and to know something about how they feel. And the person *they* trust, the one *they* talk about, is you. When I talk about Garner Hackett, they just look embarrassed. I've had time enough now to tell who it is the children feel close to and trust. . . . Mr. Hackett told me you could go into that house in Stewart and—"

"My lawyer told me he'd try to get me to do that and if I did I'd lose the house. If he wanted me to have it, all he'd have to do is sign the property settlement. If he wanted his own son taken care of, all he'd need to do is pay child support. As it is. . . ."

"An outsider never really knows anything about somebody's

divorce. I just wanted you to know that I'd been in touch with
Garner Hackett about the children and that I can see now that
you're the one who really cares what happens to them."

"Maybe it's better for the children I didn't have the house
yet, because then they could have done just what they did
before. When Marilyn was only six weeks old, Roy and Darlene
dumped her on me. I was living with Garner then, in that
house, and we didn't hear nothing from Roy and Darlene. I
thought we had Marilyn to raise. And then one day, when she
was about one, why, here they come. 'We come for our baby,'
they said, and they just picked her up and took her. It like to killed
me, having her all that time and then they just taken her off. Not
even a thank you. Just 'We come for our baby.' Like she was some
kind of a doll to play with for a while and then put away when they
got tired playing with her. Wasn't nothing I could do.

"Next time they had a big fight, here Darlene comes again,
only she's got Robbie, too, this time. Roy, he took off, didn't no
one know where, and one day Darlene, she was supposed to be
with the children, I thought, and when I got home she was
gone. Walked up to a neighbor's house, I heard, and he took her
off to Detroit. Left that baby and told nobody. Left the door
open, even. That baby crawled out of the house, down a path to
the woods. I found him crawling on the ground. He could have
put his hand right on a snake or anything.

"A few months later Roy and Darlene got together in
Detroit, I guess. Somehow nobody can't ever find them, but
they can always find each other. And here they come back and
picked up their babies again and took off. Now, you and Mr.
Baker, you get it all legal and they can't do that no more—just
walk in and pick up those babies anytime they feel like it. I
don't understand them."

It bothered me that the children were hearing all this and

every other conversation we had, but there was nothing I could do. They stayed very close to me, kept coming up to show me a toy, using any excuse to be touched and to touch. Grace Hickerson worked long hours in the restaurant. She and her son were absolutely dependent on the job. She still had to make daily trips to care for her uncle Jack, and she had to make trips out of town to see her lawyer. I simply had to use whatever time she had when she made the trip to see the children.

"Mrs. Hickerson," I said, "since the legal notices have been in the paper, all *kinds* of people have been talking to me. Strangers stop me on the street and start talking. I thought these children had nobody, and here I keep hearing about cousins and uncles and aunts and. . . . Why, they have all kinds of relatives around here. Even Dixie Sugg is related to them. Why didn't any of these people take these children? Why didn't your son and Dixie Sugg's daughter take them?"

"Everybody's so mad at Darlene and Roy and the way they did," she said, "don't nobody want to help *them.* My other son, he says he takes care of his own children; he don't see why he should take care of Roy's. Roy's just as able to work as he is."

"But nobody's thinking of the *children,*" I said.

"I know," she said. "That's the way people are. Don't nobody want to do anything for Roy and Darlene or get mixed up with them at all."

"But the *children* . . ." I said.

"That's the way people are," she repeated. "Even Darlene's mother, Mrs. Swoboda. I wrote to her. I thought she'd help me out, the fix I was in at the time. I thought she could at least send some money or help feed them. She's married again and got a little girl of her own, two years old. She and her husband both work, got good jobs and a big house. She said she would take Marilyn to be company for her little girl, but that Roy would have to send her eighty dollars a month before she'd do it, and she won't take Robbie *at all*. Said she couldn't handle him. Well, I didn't think Marilyn and Robbie ought to be separated—"

"No," I said, "absolutely."

"So I wrote her I'd keep them together, then, if she'd just help me out a little, but not one cent have I had. From anybody."

Marilyn went over to Mrs. Hickerson and gave her one of her "company" smiles. "Maw," she said, "isn't it about time for you to be going now?"

"Well, baby, I guess it is," she said. "I still got to take Uncle Jack his supper. But I just can't tell you, Mrs. Baker, what it means to me to see these children the way they look now, happy and fed and in a home with people who love them."

"We hope to keep it that way," I said. "Annabelle Norfleet, from the Welfare Department, comes to see the children once a week and she said that in most cases the judge goes along pretty much with the Welfare report and it's going to be favorable to us."

Grace Hickerson and I walked out the back door together, past a huge pile of cement blocks.

"What's that for?" she said.

"They're for the cistern," I said. "It's going to be ten feet deep and the top of it will make a back porch. The well does just fine for the two of us, but now it's showing signs that four is too heavy a burden, and so we thought we ought to be getting all this wasted rain water. We'll hook it up to the hot water."

Though I longed to have the extra water, I dreaded the building of the cistern, It seemed to me a certainty that if there was a hole eight feet wide, twenty feet long and ten feet deep just outside the back door, Robbie would certainly fall into it. After they got concrete in the bottom, it loomed that much more dangerous. I kept the back door locked all the time it was being built and Robbie was not even allowed to look without holding my hand. He was surprisingly cooperative. When they finally got the inside coated and sealed, and the top in place, I breathed a great sigh of relief. When the cistern top was covered with cement, the job would be finished.

"Could the children put their footprints in the cement?" I asked Ed Stone.

"All right," he said. I'll let you know when it's right."

"And you," I said. "Would you put your handprint in it somewhere?"

He was a very shy, quiet man. "Why would you want my hand?" he said.

"Because you built it," I said.

"Oh, well," he said, "if I don't forget."

It took several tries to do the children's footprints. Ed Stone had to smooth everything out with his trowel, hold the children up in the air and then set the feet down just so, without their wiggling their toes. He was quite a perfectionist, but a patient one. When he was satisfied with the footprints I said to him, "Now don't forget your handprint. Where are you going to put it?"

"Oh, you don't really. . . ."

"Yes, I do really mean it," I said. I turned aside to clean the cement off the children's feet. Out of the corner of my eye I saw Ed Stone carefully washing his hand. Not to make him more self-conscious, I took the children in the house. Later I found the handprint, with difficulty, in the farthest, most inconspicuous corner. But it was there: surprisingly long-fingered and slender for a workingman's hand.

It was amazing how I could keep an eight-by-ten-by-twenty-foot awareness of that hole in my head day and night, along

with a technique for never touching a knife unless it was
shielded from Robbie's eyes by my body, and all the other
esoteric and idiosyncratic anxieties I juggled—and then, when
there was a real and present danger to the children, I walked up
to it smiling, unaware. As Marilyn and I came back from the
goat barn one evening (Robbie was in the house with King), a
woman came toward me from the house. No bells went off in
my head. No strange aura lifted the hair on the back of my
neck. No goose pimples appeared on my arms.

I took her for one of the many people who came to see
about buying goats or goat's milk, or just to look at the goats.
Sometimes people stopped to ask about the orchard, too. And
some came to have books autographed or simply to meet a live
author for the first time in their lives. If I felt anything about her, it
was just a slight annoyance that she had come at suppertime.

"Yes?" I said.

"Hello, Marilyn," she said. "Don't you know me? Aren't you
going to say hello?"

Marilyn stepped back. "Who are you?" she said.

The woman ignored Marilyn's question and began speaking
to me as we walked toward the house. "I'm Darlene's mother,"
she said, "Bess Swoboda. I'm these children's grandmother. My
husband and our little girl are in the house with with your
husband. We drove down from Detroit to see the children."

Inside the house, I looked at King, my eyes saying: *What?
what? what?* His eyes said to me: *I know nothing.* Mrs. Swoboda
introduced me to her husband, a shy man, apparently younger
than she, dressed in a conservative business suit of such a
shining neatness that, had I met him at the crossroads grocery, I
would have known he was on his way to a funeral. Mrs.
Swoboda in her well-tailored, expensive suit and her stylish
coiffure did not look like a country woman going to a funeral.

She appeared very comfortable and confident. Robbie and her little girl sat on the floor playing with a ball. Robbie got up and came over to me. Marilyn stood by King.

The little girl, with her soft blond curls and blue eyes, dressed as though ready for Easter Sunday church services, should have been painted on a china plate inside a circle of gold Old English lettering: "I am Daddy's darling." She sat between her father's legs and the doting way he looked down at her gave me warning, for now and then Robbie, who seemed fascinated by her, pushed his ball toward her. *Don't bite,* I thought. *For God's sake, Robbie, if you bite that little girl her father will kill you.*

The small talk of the Swobodas continued about the weather, the drive down from Detroit, and the state of business in the bakery where they both worked. Who took care of the child? I wondered.

Work on our new room had not begun yet. It was too dark to send the children outdoors. Whatever it was that was going to be said was going to be heard by the children and no help for it. "The children have had no supper," I said. "I expect they are getting hungry. Have you had supper?"

"Oh, yes," Mrs. Swoboda said. "We stopped in Erin and ate after we talked to the lawyer."

There were two lawyers in Erin. "You saw a lawyer," I said.

"Yes," Mrs. Swoboda said, "that Mr. Crane." (*Ours,* thank God. Hugh Crane knew they were here, then, and had we had a telephone, he could have alerted us.) "You see," she went on, "we want to adopt the children."

"*Adopt them?*" I said, though I could feel King thinking: *Take it easy, take it easy.* "Why . . ." I said, "why, Marilyn didn't even *know* you."

"Oh, that," Ms. Swoboda said. "That's because my hair was a different color when she saw me. She knows me, all right. Darlene used to bring them over to see me often."

"Ah . . . well . . ." King said. "Of course if you haven't seen the children for some time, you probably don't realize what an emotional condition they were in."

"Yes," I said, "they were so frightened and upset and insecure. Now we have just begun to get them calmed down and eating well and sleeping. I can't imagine that anyone who cared for them would want to see them picked up and moved again, to go through it all again after they've—"

"Oh, I wouldn't let Darlene have them," Mrs. Swoboda said. "I know she's not done right. I blame Roy, but I blame her, too, just as much. I'd make her sign a paper that she was to have nothing to do with them. I just can't explain it. Of course I didn't want them to marry. Not that I had anything against Roy, but Darlene was just too young. Nobody could talk them out of it. So finally I gave her a wedding. I bought them furniture. Beautiful furniture. I don't know what they did with it. Darlene was *so* carefully brought up. I even paid to send her to a private school so she wouldn't have to be with the colored. She had everything. She had beautiful clothes and she was so beautiful. She could have had just about anything in this world, and how she turned out like she did I just don't understand."

"Well, look," I said, "she's your daughter. I'm sure there is something the matter and she needs help. But right now I think it's best to consider the children, don't you? They're here, right now, and we are doing something for them. What they need is to stay put and feel safe."

I looked over at Mr. Swoboda and there was no way that I could imagine his putting up with any major disturbance of his neat and tidy existence. "And you?" I said to him. "Do *you* want to adopt these children?"

He glanced quickly to his wife and then looked down. "Oh, yes," he said. Was he lying? I couldn't tell.

Mrs. Swoboda didn't give him a very good grade, either, I saw, and she quickly changed the subject. "We have a lovely house," she said. "I don't know if you know Ellington Court or not, but it's a very nice suburb. I wish you could see the house."

Oh, I can, I thought. I can just see it, with mortgage payments you can't afford, full of shining household appliances, and not a scratch on any of it. Maybe I had never met anyone before who really believed it—what they are always trying to sell you: that if you have the things that go with the solid, prosperous people, you will *be* a solid, prosperous person. Mrs. Swoboda did believe it. So long had she had possessions speaking for her that now she was acutely uncomfortable because she could not carry her house and her suburb with her. Suddenly she did not think the expensive dye job on her hair, the carefully tailored suit, the shiny new car, or the hard-working, tidy husband were enough for me. "If you could just *see* our house," she said. "If you could just come to Ellington Court."

"But why *now?*" I said. "These children have been in great need for months. I don't understand, after all this time, why you would want to upset these children and put them through another change *now*."

"They're my grandchildren," she said. "They're the only grandchildren I have, and I can't just let them be taken away *legally*." She managed a few tears at this point.

But they were your grandchildren when they were starving, I wanted to say, when you refused to send help to Grace Hickerson. In all this time, not one letter to the children, one card, one present; not one cent.

"It would be good for the children to have more family," I said, "for them to know you cared about them, to have you visit them and be interested in them. Perhaps they could come to visit you later. But I just can't see uprooting them now. I know it's the wrong thing, just when they're beginning to feel safe and to belong somewhere."

"Oh, the lawyer said we couldn't take them," she said. "I understand that. He said only Darlene and Roy could do that, that you've got custody of them."

"And nobody knows where Darlene and Roy are," I said.

"Why, I know where they are," she said.

"You *do!*" I said. "Nobody has heard a word from them here. Where are they?"

"They're in Chicago," she said. "They're together again. They have an apartment."

"Would you give us the address?" I said.

"I don't have it," she said. "Darlene just told me they were in Chicago. I don't know the address."

Neither Marilyn nor Robbie showed any reaction at all to this news. I was stunned. I simply could not take it in, that the lost were not lost at all, but living together in an apartment in Chicago. What did it mean?

"Seems like," Mrs. Swoboda said, "Darlene's *afraid* to come back here. Do you know why that would be?"

"People do seem to be pretty outraged," I said. "There are other women here without husbands who take care of their children and, you know, she did have a job. All she had to do was stick with it. And then, too, there's the man who took her away from here. She's supposed to have taken some money from him and he's reported to be angry about that. Also, there are quite a lot of people who have seen the children outside the bar in a car in bad weather."

That got them out of the house, all right. Mrs. Swoboda left her address and telephone number willingly, but she insisted she did not know how to get in touch with Darlene.

We had our delayed supper and slowly the children began to

be noisy and active, like themselves again. Bedtime was very late. King had long ago said, "Good night, Chet," and Robbie, as always, had answered, "Good night, David," followed by their saying in unison, "and good night for NBC." When I kissed Robbie good night he said, "This our hum? We stay here?"

"This is your home," I said. "You stay here." What else could I have said, dear God? What else could I have said?

We were anxious to confer with Grace Hickerson to see what light she could throw on the puzzling visit of the Swobodas. She herself had received a phone call from Darlene a few days before, she told us, but Darlene had said nothing about Roy or the reconciliation or the apartment. In fact, Grace had thought Darlene was calling from Detroit.

"She asked how the kids were," Mrs. Hickerson said,"and I told her they were being taken care of by a couple, better care than they'd ever had in their lives. She said she had a job, but she didn't say anything about sending money for the kids or coming to see them. 'Well, tell them I love them'; that's all she said."

"What does it mean, her mother and Mr. Swoboda coming down here, saying they want to adopt the children?"

"Well, *that's* purely a lie," Mrs. Hickerson said. "I know that. He's not about to take on Darlene's kids to support. Not on your life."

"Yes, I felt sure he was lying when I asked him," I said. "But what *were* they trying to do? What did they come for?"

"It must be to get them over the state line," Grace said, "to stop this legal business. Darlene must have asked her to get them or else she thinks she can make Darlene take them. If there wasn't something tricky about it, she would have come to see me."

"But do you think Darlene wants them?" I said. "So many people have heard her say she didn't and her actions certainly. . . ."

"Well, she don't," Grace said, "but if Roy and she are living

together again, if they *are* reconciled, then Roy would want
them, maybe. Anyhow, he'd think she shouldn't have left them,
even if *he* did."

"But if he does want them, why doesn't he call you, or come
to see them, or. . . ."

"Don't worry about it," Grace said. "If they are together
again, it won't last. They'll fight again. They always do. They
won't be together by the time it comes to court. That's the
thing: they don't want it to come to court. Darlene's mother
thought she could just walk in here and pick up these kids and
there never would be any hearing in court.

"You know who might be behind this?" Grace continued. "It
might be Roy's father, Garner Hackett, my first husband. He
lives in Detroit and I know Darlene worked in a bar in Detroit
after she left here, because I've talked to people who saw her
there. People from Houston County stay close together in
Detroit, closer than they do here. What's in the paper here is all
over Detroit by the next day. And if you and your husband would be
free baby-sitters, that would be fine. But putting it in the paper and
making it legal—well, all his friends would know about that."

"Yes," I said. "That's what Mrs. Swoboda said: 'I can't have
them adopted *legally*.'"

Within a few days it all seemed unreal to me, that visit from
the Swobodas. What was real was the children and the minute-
to-minute living that never ceased.

Rains came and filled the new cistern and we got the hot-
water tank and the toilet hooked up to it with a separate pump.
In July J. J. Bird, the state horticulturist, went over the whole
orchard with King. They found three immense peaches; big as a
baby's head they were. Mr. Bird said we'd have a crop the
following year. The apples appeared to be a year ahead of what
he had expected.

And the work on the new room had begun. Monroe Allsbrooks and his helper were building it and Monroe said he remembered where he had seen, long ago, a good supply of cedar boards. Of these we planned a cedar closet and one wall of cedar drawers with a toy chest underneath.

Things were coming along very well. The children could go for hours now without fighting. Mattie Mae and Eunice were beautiful and healthy and Miss Dude and Viola were still giving a gallon of milk each day.

One evening Monroe's helper, Aaron Marable, returned to the house after having left, I thought, for the day. I supposed he had forgotten tools he needed at home, but he asked for King, who was late that night. He didn't come in the house, but walked about outside, smoking cigarettes and looking toward the road. Finally he came to the door.

"I thought he'd be home by now," he said.

"He usually is," I said. "Maybe he had car trouble or something."

"Well, I got to go," he said. "There's someplace I got to be. But you tell him to look on top of the rafters in the shed. A friend of his sent him something. You be *sure* now. You be sure to tell him."

When King came home (it had been a flat tire) I told him. "I think Aaron must have left you some moonshine," I said, "on the rafter in the shed. He was very insistent that you be *sure* to get it. It's supposed to be from a friend of yours."

King came back in the house empty-handed, looking rather strange. "Later," he said. Both children were hanging on his legs. I would have to wait, I saw, until supper, bedtime stories, "Good night, David—Good night, Chet," and finally sleep.

At last the day was at an end. King walked back and forth in the kitchen while I washed the dishes.

"Well," I said, "what was it?"

"It wasn't moonshine," he said. "It was a handgun."

"Loaded?"

"It was," he said. "It's not now. I left it out there."

"My God," I said. "The thought of Robbie and a loaded gun on the same premises. It's enough to curdle your blood."

"Don't worry," he said. "I'll give it back to him in the morning before I go to work."

"But why?" I said. "Why would he do such a thing? Why be so mysterious about it?"

"I'll find out in the morning," King said.

9

That gun turned out to be only the first of many. Guns kept mysteriously appearing. They were never owned by anybody. They always belonged to "a friend." The friend had "sent" them over. We began to feel like a way station in a guerrilla war, only we never found out who was fighting whom. We kept trying to pass them back as fast as they kept coming in. Maybe there weren't really so very many, or, as little as I knew about guns, it could have been the same one over and over again, but it seemed like a lot. *One* gun in the same house with Robbie seemed like a lot to me.

Rifles were carried in cars and trucks by very many people, especially young boys. They were supposed to be for hunting. Some trucks had gun racks mounted just behind the seat. I suppose it was safer than stumbling over them on the floorboard, but I had never lived where this was a common sight or where ammunition was sold in the grocery stores. As the county agent had explained to me earlier, we were in hunting country now. But who was it we were supposed to be hunting with handguns?

Clearly there must have been some threats made. There were some vaguely worded hints of things heard said in a Detroit bar. Everything seemed too nebulous to take seriously and we never had any time from the very intense, one-room *living* that was going on every moment to sit down and try to put pieces of puzzles together in a long, quiet talk. All we had a chance to do was mutter halves of sentences as we flew by each other on urgent, always urgent, errands.

Years later, we began to have a feeling—I wouldn't say a real understanding, but a *feeling*—for this kin-based, clan society. Certainly we didn't then. When I first read Thomas Wolfe's account of his train ride to New York, I thrilled at the solitary excitement of it. I understood *that*. My sister, as a young girl, saved her money and left Wichita for Paris, and I gloried in the excitement of that. My first time in a strange place on my own was a wonderful time. I walked about strange streets in a fine, misty rain, all alone, in a new blue raincoat, and it was wonderful to me that not one person knew me there. I was a stranger, and that was exciting. In a high school vacation King had made it clear across the country to California in an old Model-T Ford, working in the harvests and picking apricots.

We had a hard lesson to learn even to begin to understand people who never want to be the stranger and who never in their lives *choose* to be solitary. When the people of Tennessee Ridge have to leave to go to work, they go to Granite City, Illinois. The ones from Stewart go to Detroit. And when they go, they go to kin and they live with kin until they get jobs. Somewhere between the job and the temporary home (home is always in Houston County and when they retire, they return) there is a bar patronized by other displaced Tennesseans, with whom they feel at home. These nuclei of Tennesseans are as tightly knit or more so than the relatives they left behind. Contact is never lost. They say that gossip about the home county gets to Detroit before it gets from one end of Houston to the other. Hugh Crane told us there was once an attorney from Houston County who found it profitable to open an office on Fort Street in Detroit for two months every year just to make out tax returns for people from Houston County, because they didn't trust anybody else to do it.

The guns, the vague rumors, the visit of Darlene's mother—none of these had we had the privacy to sit down and discuss and try to make sense of. So when, one Sunday afternoon, both children miraculously fell asleep, we slipped outside and sat in the terrible heat of late July on the back steps, where we could hear the children the minute they stirred and quickly reassure them that we were there. Almost immediately Aaron Marable drove up and joined us. We told him the children were asleep and he sat down with us to discuss the new room. The concrete for the floor was to be poured the next day. Soon another car drove by slowly, as though looking for the place, and drove in. A young man and a little boy got out of the car and came over to us.

"Are you the Bakers?" the young man said.

"Yes," King said.

"Well, I'm just down here for a few days visiting my grandfather," he said. "I used to know the Hackett kids. My little boy here used to play with Marilyn in Detroit. He'd like to see her again, and I thought we'd just drop by."

"I'm sorry," I said. "Both the children are taking naps. They played very hard this morning and they just got worn out. They really need this rest."

"Listen," Aaron said, "don't I know you?"

"Why, I reckon you do," the young man said. "You're Aaron Marable, aren't you?"

Aaron went to his car and brought back cold beers. I looked at King and he shrugged his shoulders. It appeared our precious time to talk was going to be eaten up by old reminiscences. But the stranger cut these rather short, it seemed to us. *He* wanted to talk about the children.

"I've got to go back to Detroit tonight," he said, "and, ma'am, I sure would like to see Marilyn before I go."

"Well, I suppose I can wake them up," I said. "I hate to, though."

"I really would like to see Marilyn," he said. "She and my boy used to play together all the time. Did Marilyn's hair ever grow back?"

"Grow back? I don't know what you mean. She has lovely red hair."

"Didn't you know she was bald?" he said. "Why, all her hair fell out."

"No, I didn't know that," I said. "What caused it?"

"Doctor said from not being fed right. Darlene just give her milk and eggs, that's all. Nothin else. Until all her hair fell out."

He began to tell Aaron a long, tedious account of how he had once helped Darlene and Roy move in Detroit. The street names were unfamiliar to me. I despaired of his ever leaving. I was really sorry for his little boy, who had, all this time, said not one word and simply stood, staring at the ground. It was as though he had been commanded not to say or do anything unless told.

"I'll bet you'd like a cold drink," I said to him. "It's terribly hot. Shall I get you some fruit juice, or milk?"

The little boy stared at the ground, but his father took his hand and started toward the house. "We'll just go in the kitchen and get him a drink of water," he said.

"We might as well all go in," I said. "It's just too hot to stay out here and the children have had a pretty good nap by now."

I made cold drinks for all of us and we sat around as the children slowly woke, hot and sweaty from their naps. The man went over to Marilyn and asked her if she didn't remember his boy. "You and Kenny used to play together all the time," he said. "Don't you remember me?"

Marilyn shook her head no.

I asked the man if he would mind telling our attorney the things he had mentioned. "Oh, no, ma'am," he said. "No point in that. I couldn't come back here no ways. This is the last day of my vacation. I wouldn't be able to leave Detroit again for a year."

When they had gone I said to Aaron, "What was the point of all that—do you have any idea? Marilyn didn't know him. If he knew Darlene and Roy, it was a long time ago."

"Something don't seem right about it," Aaron said. "He is old man Pirtle's grandson, though. I know him. And I'm pretty sure he does live in Detroit."

A few days later it made more sense. Aaron got a call from Mr. Pirtle, asking him to come over. Once he was there, the old man questioned him about us and our life and finally asked Aaron if he would go to court and say we had liquor in the house, we drank before the children, he had seen us drunk, and so forth.

"What did you say?" I asked him.

"I said if he was thirty years younger I'd knock his teeth down his throat. Hell, he's a old man; I can't fight him. He hasn't even got any teeth."

"But why?" I said. "I don't even know this man. I never heard of him before."

"I don't know," Aaron said. "I've been studying on it. I told him what good care you take of the children. He didn't seem to care. He offered me money, too, and then I did have to leave or I would have hit him."

What did it all mean? Mysterious rumors of threats, unowned guns, visits from spies, attempted bribes. We could not get a straight, simple story from anyone. Since there was constantly in the air the portent of something violent, it seemed best to have a plan of some kind. One fortuitous naptime I took my problems to Monroe Allsbrooks.

"Mr. Allsbrooks," I said, "do you know some safe place where I could take these children if I needed to? We just don't know what's going on. We keep hearing rumors. I'm afraid there's going to be some kind of scene that would be hard on the children. They've been through so much already. I'd like to have a plan ready in case I need it in a hurry. I know there are resorts around here. Maybe there's a place we could camp out." I had even considered caves, which I had heard of but didn't know how to locate. There was no motel, and even if there had been, we could not afford to stay long in one.

"Well," Monroe Allsbrooks said, in his calm way, "you could come to my place. I'll tell you how to get there."

"That's very good of you," I said, "but I really didn't mean that. You might not want to involve yourself in this. People are sending guns over here. There must have been some kind of threats. I couldn't ask you to get mixed up in anything like that."

"Now," he said, "I don't think anybody is going to take anything off of *my* place unless I want him to. That's all right. You don't worry about me. If you need a place to take these children, you just come ahead."

It seemed pretty wonderful to me at the time, but I was miles away from appreciating the rare courage of that simple statement. "You see," I said to him, "I wouldn't try to keep these children from seeing their mother if they wanted to. I thought maybe Marilyn wanted to see her mother and I asked her. She said she'd run away and hide in our playhouse in the woods. Mr. Allsbrooks, there *isn't* any playhouse; it's just a place we go in the woods and pretend. If she tried to run there at night, she might get lost or step on a snake. Anyhow, she'd be frightened to death of the dark. I can't have them running out alone in the woods to get away. I have to have someplace planned ahead of time to go to in a hurry."

"You come to my place anytime," he said.

"Thanks," I said. "It's just hard for me really to believe in all this. It sounds like a bad movie. Sometimes it seems ridiculous, but most of the time it just doesn't seem real."

A week or so later, about bedtime, Grace Hickerson came over. "I hate to come in on you so late," she said, "but I thought I'd better let you know. I just heard that Roy and Darlene are leaving Chicago in the morning and they're coming here—they say to get the children."

This time, I thought, I'll get some details. I would ask what she meant by *she heard*. How had she heard? Who told her? Who called? How did they—

"I don't know if it's true or not," she said, "but—"

Marilyn had been leaning against me, listening to her grandmother. Suddenly she bent over and began to vomit.

"Whassa matter? Whassa matter?" Robbie yelled, jumping up and down.

I grabbed some paper towels and threw them on the floor and then turned to Marilyn, who was now sobbing. "I'm sorry," she said, pointing to the vomit.

"Never mind, darling. It's all right," I said. "It's all right."

I asked King to bring me a wet washcloth. "Come sit on my lap a minute, Marilyn. There now. There now." I washed off her face and tried to hold her in my arms, but her little body was rigid and the tears would not stop. Robbie was now pressing close, trying to get Marilyn to tell him what was wrong. Mrs. Hickerson had gone to work cleaning up the mess on the floor.

"Listen to me, Marilyn," I said. "We won't be here when they come."

"Where will we go?" she said.

"We're going to Monroe Allsbrooks' house," I said. "First thing in the morning. After you get all calmed down tomorrow, we'll talk about it. Just stop crying now. We're going away tomorrow."

"Me, too?" Robbie said.

"Of course," I said.

"I'm so sorry getting everybody upset," Mrs. Hickerson said. "But I didn't know what else to do."

"You did the right thing, I'm sure," I said. "Thank you for coming all this way over here. I'm so sorry we can't get a phone."

King saw Mrs. Hickerson to her car and I kept on holding Marilyn. "Mr. Allsbrooks has some animals, I think, Marilyn," I said. "He might even have a pony. I'm sure I heard him say he had chickens and I think maybe he has rabbits, too. We'll just go over there and spend the day and maybe even the night. I'll be with you all the time. But we want to leave very early in the morning, so you need to go to sleep now. You, too, Robbie. Get in bed. Tomorrow we'll have a good time and no one will find us unless you want them to."

Marilyn slid down off my lap and went into the kitchen. She came back with a little cleaning rag in her hand and she squatted down before me. "I got vomit on your shoes," she said, and

she began trying to clean them. Up to that time I would have
sworn that there was nothing that could make orthopedic shoes
less attractive than they already were.

King took us all to the Allsbrooks house early in the morning and then he returned alone to face whatever was going to
happen. Fortunately, I did not know at the time, as he *did* , that
Roy Hackett was reported to have said in a bar in Chicago that
he was coming after his children, and that if he didn't leave
with them, nobody else would be going no place.

Ignorant of this threat, I was nevertheless apprehensive for
King; otherwise I would have been in total ecstasy. Oh, the bliss
of having another person in charge for a change. The joy of
having a house with *other* rooms! There was even an attic,
where the children played without quarreling, where there was
nothing they could hurt, Mrs. Allsbrooks said, where there was
nothing they were not allowed to touch and explore. Outdoors
there were rabbits and chickens and even a pony and there were
experienced grandchildren about to supervise all this. The thing
that said it all for me was to see, for the first time, Robbie get
clear through a meal without knocking over his milk. I told
Mrs. Allsbrooks what a compliment that was to the air of ease
in her house; she said the trick was a very heavy glass. But the
fact was Robbie didn't spill anything all the time we were there
and I had a little glimpse of the happy, easier life we would all
have when the extra room in our house was finished, and life
might be allowed to settle down for us all.

Certainly it was good to have the children out of doors and
supervised when, on the second day, King arrived.

"Thank God you're here at last," I said.

"I waited to be sure they're on their way out of town," he
said, "so I wouldn't lead them right to you."

"And they *are* gone?"

"Yes," he said, "they are gone for now, at least."

"What happened? How was it? I've been so worried about your having to face them all alone there."

"I wasn't alone," he said. "When I left here I picked up Aaron Marable and he was there with me."

Aaron Marable was well over six feet tall and weighed about two hundred pounds. "Wonderful!" I said. "What did *he* do?"

"Oh, he was just sort of *there*. He'd be in and out. Once he stood around and ate an apple and kind of smiled and another time he walked in with a measuring tape and took some measurements of the wall and another time he walked in with a hammer in his hand."

Roy and Darlene had come in rather belligerently, King said, declaring they had come to pick up their children. King told them I had taken the children away. Darlene had not believed this. She insisted that I had hidden the children in the woods, that I could not have taken the children away because the car was there. It took King some time to convince her. Finally they insisted that having come all that distance, they should at least be allowed to see the children.

"So I told them," King said, "to go to the sheriff and find out what their rights were and then if the sheriff said they did have the right, I'd take them to where you were, but that it was quite a distance."

"And did they go to the sheriff?"

"They went to the sheriff and I went to Hugh Crane's office," he said, "and pretty soon the sheriff called Hugh Crane. I only heard Hugh Crane's end of the conversation, but I gathered the sheriff thought we had an injunction against anyone taking the children away from the house until the court hearing."

"Did we?"

"I still don't know. Hugh Crane just kept saying he never questioned the sheriff's authority to do anything he thought he should. And then, after he hung up, he said, 'That's the best sheriff we ever had here and he sure does care about those kids.' And then after a while Crane got another call and told me Roy and Darlene were across the bridge and on their way back to Chicago."

It was over now and all we had to do was pack our few clothes in the suitcase and round up the children and go home, but I seemed unable to stop trembling.

The adoption hearing was set for September 10, but Marilyn would begin school in August. We would go on with building the new room, we would get school clothes for Marilyn. She would enroll in the first grade. We would get this thing settled September 10 and then we could all relax and begin to live.

That night at home, after the animals were fed and the children were asleep, King said," You know, I think you'd better consider the possibility that we might lose."

"Oh, no," I said. "How can you believe that? The Welfare Department thinks we'll win. Hugh Crane thinks we will. Everyone I talk to thinks—"

"I'm just asking you to consider it," he said. "There have been some changes. When we took the children nobody knew where the parents were. Now they do. The parents were separated. Now they're together. The picture has changed."

"But the children," I said. "The children are the same."

"But the law is something else," he said. "So you do have to consider the possibility that we might lose."

"I can't," I said. "I simply cannot conceive of anyone's returning those children to people who have already dumped them twice."

10

The day of the hearing got off to a bad start. Having left the children with friends for the day, we went first to Hugh Crane's office, where we learned that all our key witnesses were missing. The man who had taken Darlene out of town and complained bitterly that she had taken all his money and disappeared from the hotel room—he had left the state in order that his subpoena could not be served. Virgie Stavely, with whom Darlene had lived for a while and to whom she had confided her intention to leave the children, had fled to Memphis. Most important of all, Dixie Sugg, who had intimate knowledge of how the children lived, when they were left alone and when they were unfed, had been hospitalized in a neighboring town and had sent a doctor's certificate to court.

"Don't get yourself upset," Hugh Crane said. "That's pretty standard for a country town. These people hate to go to court. What's more important is this time thing. Abandonment is defined as four months and I took Grace Hickerson's word that Darlene left in February. Now the Hacketts' attorney has some kind of proof that she didn't leave until March."

I clung to what Annabelle Norfleet of the Welfare Department had told me—that the judge would go by the Welfare Department report, which was overwhelmingly favorable to us.

We were a few minutes early and I stood outside the courtroom so I could be seen through the glass panel in the door. I still thought that Darlene might come out to me, might say something real and human that would make sense of this. Wouldn't she want to know how the children were, as I, even now, was wondering if Marilyn had started vomiting again? But though I could see Darlene clearly, she would not look in my direction.

The courtroom was full. I saw Monroe Allsbrooks and his wife. I saw Marilyn's first-grade teacher, who had paid a substitute out of her own money in order to be there. I saw others who I knew cared deeply for the children and I was grateful for their presence. Darlene and Roy and Garner Hackett sat together. Garner Hackett spoke to us, but Roy did not. Darlene continued to look down.

"Where is Hugh Crane?" I said to King.

"He's gone to see about the filing of that demurrer, I guess."

"I don't understand that," I said. "Do you? It's way over four months *now*."

"But not before the filing date," King said. "I think he's trying to get a supplementary petition accepted with a later date."

Judge Ogalsbee came in then. Everyone stood up. He had a ruddy, good-natured face. His body had the stance and movements of a person reasonably content with his life and his world. Occasionally his blue eyes flashed as though a curtain had been pulled aside revealing, for a second, the knowledge that this man was in possession of a colossal secret joke which might, someday, split loose from his control, causing him to laugh himself to death. Hugh Crane sat with us at a table near the front of the courtroom and there was no time to talk.

King was called first for direct examination by Hugh Crane. He established his age, his job, his length of residence in Tennessee, his former residence and the fact that he had been married to me for twenty years. Then, under Crane's questioning, King reviewed the whole history of the children from the time we first heard about them in Dixie Sugg's café until the time in August when Roy and Darlene had come to pick them up and King had referred the Hacketts to the sheriff. Twice Judge Ogalsbee overruled objections from Roy and Darlene's attorney, Othel Travis.

"Do you feel," Crane asked King, "that you qualify physically and emotionally to be an adoptive parent to these children?"

"At the present time I do," King said. "I wasn't certain in the beginning, but I am now."

Othel Travis was a short, heavy-set man who somehow gave the impression that he was a reflection seen in a slightly concave mirror which exaggerated the horizontal dimension. He was very light on his feet.

He glided up to King. "Now, Mr. Baker," he said, "you stated you and your wife have no children of your own, is that correct?"

I had a sickening feeling of what I would be in for from Othel Travis—a kind of patronage that childless couples grow very tired of. I have seen women and men knock children halfway across a room because they got on their nerves, and yet feel they were blessed with some esoteric wisdom by virtue of biology. It is a shame children really aren't found under cabbage leaves, though possibly if it were so, much study and exalting of cabbage leaves would take place and many cabbage-leaf laws would be passed while the children crawled blindly into deep pits, unnoticed.

"That is correct," King said.

"Of course," Travis continued, "both you and your wife have alleged that you love these children as if they were your very own."

"Yes, sir," King said.

"Now, you really don't know how it feels to have children of your very own, do you?" Travis said.

"Well, I have a vivid imagination," King said.

"You have never babied little kids from the time of their birth up until they were two or three or five years old, have you?"

And then abandoned them. We haven't done that either, I wanted to yell, but King answered, "No, sir."

Travis then established the understanding we had with Garner Hackett about keeping the children for a three-month trial period before starting adoption proceedings. "If it didn't work out," King said, "I guess Garner would make some other arrangements."

"Now, you developed a strong, loving feeling toward these children, didn't you?" Travis went on. "And you love them, there is no question about your loving them, I'm sure of that, Mr. Baker. But at the time you went to see an attorney, you loved these children so much you were willing to do anything to get them."

"Is that a question?" King asked.

"Yes, sir. Your feelings were so strong toward these children that at the time you went to see Mr. Crane to see how you could keep custody of them, it didn't make any difference to you as far as the concern of the natural parents. You love these children and the only thing you could think of was that you wanted them."

King explained that the natural parents were scattered in unknown parts of the country at the time, and we couldn't very well be concerned about them. Our concern, he said, was the children, and we could not give them a sense of security in the house if we didn't have the authority to keep them there.

Travis then turned abruptly to the question of "inconsistencies" in the dates we claimed the children had been abandoned in our two sworn petitions, dates that were important in establishing the legal period of four months between abandonment and the filing of adoption proceedings. King explained that there was no way we could check the abandonment date beyond what we had been told, and so Travis made sure that the court realized abandonment had not occurred prior to March 19, 1963, and that King no

longer made such a claim. There was a good deal more and it was a
help to me to have King questioned first so that when it was my
turn on the stand, I had some idea of what was coming.

After Hugh Crane had established that I was King's wife, a
petitioner in this case, that I was fifty years old, that I had been
born in Wichita, Kansas, and had lived in Missouri and California before coming to Tennessee, he continued: "Do you know
when you first became acquainted with the children?"

"I remember," I said, "that there was a little green Irish hat
that had been worn in the St. Patrick's Day parade, where it was
rained on. It was hanging by the fireplace drying out. Grace
Hickerson brought the children to the house and Robbie put on
the hat. I said I would keep it for him and he put it on the next
time he came back. So it was shortly after St. Patrick's Day."

"And when did you get the children on a permanent basis?"
Hugh asked me.

"The Monday after Easter."

"How many times had you seen them before the Monday
after Easter?"

"Twice, I believe. They were brought there by Grace
Hickerson. They were brought again by Garner Hackett. He
had Jack Ussery with him."

Hugh then went into the matter of what arrangements we
had made with Garner Hackett about the children, and I explained that we had hated to guarantee something that we
might fall down on concerning children and we knew that,
even if it was very hard on us, we could do anything for three
months. Garner had wanted us to take the children immediately,
but we had a guest in the house and couldn't take them until Easter,
so there was an interval of a week the children had to wait.

"Did you come to any agreement or understanding with Mr.
Hackett?" Hugh asked.

"Yes," I said. "I told him I would make regular reports to him, and give him news about the children, and I said that what we would absolutely guarantee was that they should have shelter and good care for three months, and then we would reconsider how permanent; but it was fairer to say that we absolutely guaranteed something we could do—three months." I went on to tell the court how it became clear to King and me that the atmosphere was going to be good because we found ourselves in agreement about how to handle the children. "We came up against the problem," I said, "that you can't give children a little bit of security. They needed a whole lot; they kept asking for reassurance that they wouldn't have to move, that they wouldn't be changed. Of course we gave it to them."

"Your understanding has been that you were to care for the children for three months, and then reconsider the situation or reach some agreement in the meantime?" Hugh asked.

"Well, I really expected that we would have them all our lives and I'm sure Mr. Hackett knew that, but what I could guarantee was three months."

"Has Mr. Hackett offered to pay any of their bills or contribute in any way to the support of these children?"

"Yes," I replied. "He always offered to help out if we needed anything and I wrote and told him that we were able to handle the expense, and that the children seemed so bright that I knew they should have a college education. I suggested to him that he either take out an insurance policy with them as beneficiaries or an educational policy."

"Was that done?"

"He never mentioned it."

"Has he contributed anything to the support of these children?"

"He sent us a box of chocolates."

"Have you ever received anything from the parents of these children toward their support?"

"No."

"Has there ever been any effort on the part of the parents to visit the children that you know of?"

"On the third or fourth of August; that was the first time."

"Up to this very minute have there been any inquiries as to the health and well-being of these children, or any concern shown about them?"

"Not even this morning," I replied. "I spoke to the mother. I assumed she would want to know how her children are and then I stood there so she could ask and I could tell her they were well, but she didn't say anything."

Hugh then asked if there had been any other agreement as to what would happen to the children if we had not agreed with Garner Hackett to keep them, and I explained that Grace Hickerson had come to see her grandchildren fairly often and we had talked in a general way about what we hoped for them to have—good educations and lots of things in the future—but that I didn't know if that would be called an agreement or not.

"It was your understanding that the grandmother, Roy Hackett's mother, is agreeable to your care and custody?" Hugh asked.

"I am sure she is," I replied, and affirmed Grace's genuine concern about the children.

Hugh next asked me about the appearance of the children at the time they first came into our care. I described as them as very nice-looking children, but that both were pallid and a good deal thinner than at present, and that Marilyn had running sores behind each ear, which I cleaned and oiled and cleared up.

"What was their emotional state?" Hugh asked.

"That seemed so much more important than their physical symptoms, and we concentrated on that," I said. "The most dramatic was the boy, who had terrible nightmares almost every hour or so in which he cried, 'Mamma, mamma, mamma, mamma,' but he was not awake. I would go and sit with him and talk to him and sometimes try to sing to him. He had these nightmares almost every hour all night long for the first three nights and then they got a little further apart and finally they disappeared after a few weeks. His bed-wetting also stopped. He still sucks his thumb and he has had violent spells of crying and rages which have very slowly calmed down."

Suddenly Othel Travis jumped up from his seat. "What was that statement?" he said.

"Violent spells of crying," I said, "and rages at toys that won't work, or any frustration. They have become much less constant. He has stopped biting both animate and inanimate objects. He has long spells of crying sometimes. I couldn't see much sense to them until I realized that he was afraid to go to sleep and to take his nap. He would keep himself awake. He cried at every naptime for a week, and I stayed with him, and once I sang a lullaby to him. He had never had a lullaby, and he didn't know what that was."

"I object to that," Travis said.

"Objection overruled," Judge Ogalsbee said. Travis returned to his seat and Hugh Crane nodded his head at me to continue.

"Well," I said, "then Robbie began to sing a lullaby to a turtle or a toy or himself and he now takes a nap every day. Marilyn, the little girl, on the surface gets along much more easily than the baby. She was sick almost immediately after they came and she had a high fever. Our pump house is only about twenty-five feet from our house. We had trouble with the pump and it was necessary for me to go read the gauge. I couldn't get that far out of her sight. She thought if I stepped outside I wouldn't come back. Sometimes Marilyn would play happily and greet people who came in and seem to get along fine with them, but then . . . sometimes she would cry for a long period of time, and she would say she didn't know why she was crying."

Hugh Crane asked me if I considered them happy, normal children at the present time.

"They are often very happy," I said. "Marilyn's memory is confused somehow. Both children are mixed up on the rhythm of the day and they are gradually getting this straightened out. Right after breakfast they would say, 'Is it time for Daddy to come home from work?' and they didn't seem to notice whether it was night or day."

Hugh Crane wanted to introduce three letters written to me by Garner Hackett, and after demanding to look at them first, Othel Travis made no objection to my reading them aloud. The first one had been written about ten days after Easter, asking if the children were with us. Garner said he had not seen either the children's mother or their father since he had returned to Detroit. He offered to help with expenses and thanked us again for helping the children.

The second letter was written a few weeks later, in May, after he had heard from me. "It is a shame that their mother and dad will not take any responsibility for these sweet little kids," he wrote. "I had written to their dad but his letter was returned unclaimed. He had moved and left no forwarding address, so I don't know where he is at now, nor their mother."

In the third letter, written in July after I had informed him of the filing of the petition for adoption, he said: "I was surprised that you had taken legal action about adopting the children. Roy, their dad, came over here to Detroit from Chicago to get his wife. I talked to him about the kids. She and he are going to try again to make a home. I told Roy to be sure and not bother the kids until he was sure they could make a go of their marriage. He promised not to go after them until he was sure that they could get along, but he did not write and then I have no way of getting in touch with them. I would much rather see him raise his children, and if he feels he cannot I would be willing to see you adopt them."

Hugh Crane then questioned me about Marilyn's school and teacher. Then he said, "You have cared for the children during this sickness and other periods of distress and anxiety."

"In five months I have been away from them about twenty-five minutes," I said.

"Then you feel you are capable of taking care of these children?"

"Well, I think anybody has moments of doubt if you are seriously interested in the child, if you like doing everything right. But yes, I really do feel that I have an understanding of the children now and that I can tell by their actions that they are making progress."

"You feel your age is not a detriment to you?" Hugh asked.

"I feel it would be better if we were younger, yes," I said.

Othel Travis now stood and walked toward me, his head tilted to one side. He left considerable space between us and his manner was so deferential that suddenly I had a feeling of unreality in the situation, as though we were all pretending to be characters in a courtroom scene in a movie. I was pretending to be a proper petitioner and Othel Travis was pretending to be a proper attorney. Any moment some truly sane person was going to enter the courtroom, saying: "Here, here. If this is about children, you can't use a format that children can't understand. Stop all this ridiculous formality."

"Mrs. Baker," Othel Travis said, "you have left the impression before the court here that when these kids came to your house they were afraid or. . . . What was your impression of the kids?"

"Well, the little girl seemed to adjust easily, but the boy did not."

"What reason do you give for that?"

"My impression was insecurity."

"How long did that last?"

"The little girl's seemed to disappear in three or four days and she was playing most of the time, happy and cooperative. The boy was still having nightmares and bedwetting and showing signs of fear for a long time."

"Isn't it true," Travis continued, "that the natural acts of a child with new people and getting acquainted would create some of the same reaction?"

"Yes, some," I replied. "What was noticeable was that they would never mention their mother. Children would ordinarily talk about their mother. I did not want to force it and I waited. Weeks went by and they never did mention her. Marilyn drew a picture of Roy with a mustache and Roy without a mustache, but neither of the children ever mentioned the mother."

Travis changed the line of questioning. "When they came to your house was there any agreement that you would later on institute adoption proceedings?" I replied that there was an understanding that what we hoped for was that we would do the best thing for the children, make a home for them as long as possible. We were reluctant to guarantee something when it might have turned out that we did not have the right feeling for the children. I couldn't guarantee to love a child. However, it turned out that we did love the children right away. Travis then wanted to know if there were any discussions with Garner

Hackett or Grace Hickerson about adoption, and I told him that we had talked about it and that we hoped the children wouldn't have to be changed again.

"So," he went on, "you took them in without any understanding that later on you would institute an adoption proceeding."

"No."

"Well, then you say that there was an understanding."

"Yes. I remember saying, when Mr. Hackett was pressing me to take the children a week ahead of time, I remember saying that I was going to relieve everybody of the responsibility for the rest of their lives and I didn't think it was unreasonable for me to ask just one week. I made that statement; I remember that."

"Did you ever write to Mr. Hackett and tell him that you had changed your agreement and you were proceeding contrary to what the agreement was?"

"Yes. The agreement was we wouldn't do anything without discussing it with him. Yes, I wrote him and said that I knew that was not in our agreement, but for the protection of the children, on an attorney's advice, we had."

"But you did write and tell him," Travis said.

"That I had not discussed this with him first and that there would be publication in the paper. I didn't want him to learn it from anybody else but me."

"Mrs. Baker, is it true that the first time you thought of adopting those children was when you saw attorney Hugh Crane, and he advised you that for the protection of the children you had better start adoption proceedings?"

"Oh, no," I replied. "Months before I had ever seen the children, my husband and I had already talked about it in the restaurant when we heard about them. My husband almost ran over the little boy one time. He was out alone in the middle of the street, crying and alone. King had to stop the car in order to avoid running over him."

"Does your husband drink?"

"No."

"Your husband does not drink?"

"No, my husband doesn't drink."

"You have never known him to take a drink?"

"Oh, yes, I've known him to take a drink. I thought you meant did he drink to where his word is not good on what he saw in the street. Yes, he would take a cocktail."

"Does he indulge excessively at any time?"

"No."

"Do you?"

"No."

"Do you keep intoxicating beverages in the house?"

"Not regularly, no. We sometimes have it in the house."

"You have a rather unique house there, don't you. Somewhat different?"

"It was designed by a woman in Los Angeles to fit our problems before we had any children, and now we have to add on to it."

"How many bedrooms?"

"It is just one large room now. We are making a bedroom for the children out of the carport."

Travis returned to the injunction. "Isn't it true that you didn't want these parents around?" he said.

"I told Marilyn she could see her mother if she wanted to," I said. "I would never keep her from her. If the child wanted to see her, it didn't matter what I wanted."

"You mean," Travis said, "that a decision of this nature should be left to a child that is only five years old, not to mature, grown-up human beings like you are, a person of fifty years?"

"I think a person of five years knows whether she wants to see her mother or not. I told her I would not keep her from seeing her mother, that her mother was in town and did she want to see her. She said she would run and hide in the woods. It was already dark and I told her she could not go hide in the woods, but that if she didn't want to see her mother, it was all right. She began vomiting and I told her I would take her away until she calmed down. By the time she had calmed down her parents were no longer here."

"Where did you take the children when the parents were here?" Travis said.

I saw Monroe Allsbrooks' gentle face in the courtroom and I remembered the guns and the rumors of threats. I turned to Judge Ogalsbee. "Do I have to tell?" I said. "I consider this necessary for the children's protection."

Hugh Crane intervened. "Answer the question."

"I took them to Monroe Allsbrooks' house," I said. "I asked for refuge until Marilyn could calm down and they gave it to us."

Travis now returned to my inability to understand parenthood since I had not given birth to a child.

"I'm an expert on being a child," I said. "I *was* a child and I know what a child is entitled to."

"You love these children enough that you could take them away from their parents, don't you?" he said.

"I love them enough that I can try to do what they ask, which is not to be moved again, not to be left again," I said.

Travis then tried a discussion of my literary works. Since I had suggested in one that people could improve, he wanted me to agree that Roy and Darlene could improve and be better parents. Hugh Crane questioned his right to discuss my books, since he had not read them. The two of them got into a lively

argument over this, which appeared to be straining Judge
Ogalsbee s good humor.

Have you ever had any psychiatric treatment from a doctor? Travis asked me suddenly.

No, I said.

Hugh Crane couldn t leave this hanging on the air, of
course, so we had to go into what treatment I *had* had from a
doctor. Between the literary discussion and my medical history,
the children and what was important to *them* seemed to me to
be hopelessly lost. Finally Judge Ogalsbee said, Do you have
any further questions, Mr. Travis? and when Travis said no,
Judge Ogalsbee said I could step down.

Before the hearing, when we had been standing outside the
courtroom talking with Hugh Crane, Grace Hickerson had
come up to us. She had been very nervous, looking anxiously
over her shoulder. I don t want them to see me talking to you,
she said. But don t worry. Roy and Darlene won t stay together
long enough to get the children. They re ghting like cats and
dogs.

How do you know? I said.

They re staying at my house, she said, and then she walked
hurriedly away.

It is a custom of rural living very dif cult for me to understand: no matter how much you hate somebody s guts, or he
yours, if he is kin to you, you stay with him if you have to be in
the area. Hated kin visit one another and at mealtimes sit down
expecting food to appear and food appears. There were no
hotels in town, but if there had been, nothing would have been
different. True, Tom Hickerson had refused to let Darlene stay at his
house and he had refused to let Grace keep her grandchildren there,
but they were not kin of *his,* or as they say, kin to him.

When Hugh Crane called Grace Hickerson to the stand, it was obvious that she was still extremely nervous, and after his questions had established her residence, that she had been married to Roy's father, Garner, and had divorced him, that Roy was her son, Crane asked if Roy and Darlene were staying with her.

"Yes," she said.

"How do they get along now, when they are living with you in your presence?" Crane asked.

"All right as far as I know," she said.

"Any quarreling or fighting?" he asked.

"Not that I heard," she said.

"Do they fuss or argue or raise their voices to each other?"

"I don't remember," she said.

Hugh Crane took a deep breath and tried again. "Now, Mrs. Hickerson," he said, "have you heard either of them raise their voice in anger in the past week?"

Othel Travis interrupted. "The court please," he said. "I don't know if that is material—what was done the past week." Crane said he thought it was material, showing the present attitude of the parents toward each other and their children, and indicating their ability to care for them.

"Well, go ahead," Judge Ogalsbee said.

But no matter how Hugh Crane worded the questions to elucidate discord between the parents or brought pressure to bear on Grace's testimony, she "couldn't remember," "couldn't tell," or "didn't know." I looked at King. He shook his head. This woman who had been, in our house, so outraged at the treatment of her grandchildren, so disgusted at the conduct of her own son and so voluble at the immoral and disorderly conduct of her daughter-in-law, was here a timid mouse, frightened and confused. Crane finally gave up this line and asked her to tell about how the children happened to be in her care.

"Well, I heard that Roy and Darlene had lost their trailer," she said, "and Darlene was moving into an old house on Virgie Stavely's place. I went over there and they didn't have no cook stove. It was cold at the time and they had no fire or anything. I asked her if I could take the kids home with me and keep them until she got something for them. She asked me if I would keep them until she could locate Roy. I first told her I would, but when I discussed it with Tom Hickerson—that's my second husband—he said I couldn't keep them, so I went back and told her. I was going to help her to move to Stewart; I had an old house there. Not good condition, but it had heat and there wouldn't be any rent for her to pay."

"You helped her move to Stewart?" Crane asked.

"Yes," she said, "with the children. Darlene had to go to Erin for something, she said, and I told her while she was over there to have the lights turned on, and that was the last that I saw of her."

"Was it your understanding that she would be back?" Crane asked.

"That's what I thought," Grace said.

"Did she give you any information whatsoever as to where she was going?"

"Well, later Virgie Stavely told me that Darlene called and told somebody that she had to go, that's the way it had to be."

Crane asked her what she did with the children when Darlene failed to come back. "I kept them until I went to work," she said, "and then I had them with my uncle in Stewart. I'd get up early in the morning and go to cook them breakfast and tend to them and go on to work and then in between times, from two o'clock until six at night, I'd go back and cook them dinner, and at night when I got off from work I'd come back by and cook their supper and put them to bed."

"Your uncle is Jack Ussery, is that right?" Crane asked. "And how long did Mr. Ussery have the children?"

"I'd say a couple of weeks," she said.

And so it went. On her visits to the children at our house she thought there was a difference, that they seemed well fed and happy, but when asked by Crane if she believed it to be to the children's advantage to stay with us, she said she was not capable of saying what's best for children because she didn't know.

Crane asked her about Roy and Darlene's drinking, but Othel Travis objected: "The court please, I'd like to impose an objection that the character of these people is not an issue now, nor is the intent of the law so far as the abandonment." To which Crane replied, "Your Honor, if those questions are proper for one person, they are certainly proper for the other in the same lawsuit."

"I don't know, gentlemen," Judge Ogalsbee said, "How you would separate this question of the conduct of the parties from the question of abandonment, because, Mr. Travis, the conduct might indicate abandonment. The way that they conduct themselves might indicate that they have a disregard for the children and weren't concerned about them, and therefore it gradually grew to the extent that they just walked off and left them. I think it would be admissible to show the state of mind of the natural parents, whether or not abandonment is indicated. I'll allow the question."

But Grace Hickerson said she couldn't tell if anybody is drunk or not.

"Has it been called to your attention," Crane asked, "or do you have any knowledge of Darlene being in any of the beer joints with the children with her, or out in cars?"

"I never saw her in them, but I have heard local gossip that she was," Grace said.

Asked by Crane about baby-sitters hired by Darlene (one had told many people in the town of being stuck with the children until very late), Grace said, "All I know is that her television was up for sale for baby-sitting. I think she borrowed money for baby-sitting. I paid the television off. I have the television."

"Mrs. Hickerson," Crane asked, "have these children been left with you before on other occasions?"

"When Marilyn was six weeks old; I kept her until she was about a year old."

Othel Travis objected again. He said it did not have any relation to the time, the place, or the circumstances. "Your Honor," Crane said, "I think it is pertinent to show that this is not the first time that this thing has happened, in the interest of the children." Judge Ogalsbee told Crane to go ahead.

When Crane's questioning of Grace Hickerson was finished I sought out Roy in the courtroom. He was relaxing his body in obvious relief. He sat back against his seat, put his head down and smiled.

Othel Travis's approach to Grace Hickerson in cross-examination was very different from the distant and deferential manner he had shown me. He stood very close to her. "Grace," he said, "I hope I don't make you mad. I hope that wouldn't keep you from serving me those good meals that you served the other night down at the restaurant."

"I don't think so," she said.

"Now, so far as you know, there weren't any different arrangements made other than the children would just be there with the Bakers. You didn't say, 'Here are the children, take them. I don't want them,' did you?"

"No," Grace said.

Travis then established that it had been winter when Grace took the children from Darlene, and that Darlene could not have come too, because Grace's husband wouldn't have her.

"Now, on or about March nineteenth, were you with Darlene when she came to the courthouse?" Travis asked.

"Yes."

"What was your purpose in coming to the courthouse?"

"To try to get welfare for her and the children," Grace said.

"Do you know that she received any welfare?"

"No, they told her it would be a month before she could get any help."

"Was she in bad circumstances?"

"Yes."

"She had lost her television set, she couldn't find a place to rent and she had lost her trailer," Travis said. "Do you know if she worked any or not?"

"Yes, she worked at the garment factory some. I don't know how long."

"Were you over to the Bakers' recently?"

"Yes."

"What condition were they in?"

"The children?"

"No, Mr. Baker."

"He was all right, I suppose," Grace said.

"Had he been drinking?" Travis asked.

"I didn't see anything."

"Did he act like he had been drinking?"

"I don't know when anybody is drunk and when they're not," Grace replied. "I can't distinguish between that."

In all this weak and ineffective testimony from this very frightened woman, there was one crumb of comfort. Despite Travis's objections, Hugh Crane had got in the fact that this was not the first time Darlene had left her children. If anyone was listening—was anyone really listening?—they knew now that Marilyn had been left by her mother not once, but twice, in five years. Who, in his right mind, would risk the third time or the fourth?

The next witness called was Annabelle Norfleet of the Public Welfare Department. Under Hugh Crane's questioning, she first established, reading from her record book, that a visit had been made March 6 at a house trailer where the children were living, and that Darlene and Grace Hickerson had subsequently come to her office for assistance on March 19, at which time it had been explained to Darlene that the children must be living with her in order for her to receive aid.

Of the visit to the trailer, the only unusual thing she could remember was that Robbie had no shoes on and had gone barefooted outdoors in the cold. Hugh Crane asked her about her visits to our house.

"The first visit I made," she said, "on August thirtieth, when I knocked on the door, the children were taking their naps. Mrs. Baker and I sat on the porch and talked because we didn't want to wake the children and she was afraid to go out to my car because they had been waking and scared when she wasn't close by. They waked while I was there."

"Have you observed any noticeable difference in the children," Crane asked, "from the time of the March sixth visit to the trailer and your August thirtieth visit to the Bakers?"

"Yes," she said, "they have a better color. I checked on the children to see if they were eating well and Mrs. Baker tells me they are, and it is evident that they are because they are certainly blossoming. Robbie has calmed down. At first, I was a little strange to him, of course; when I would go into the room he was just demanding every bit of his mother's—of Mrs. Baker's—attention, and later as I visited he could go on with his play."

"Did you notice any difference in the emotional stability of the children?" Crane asked.

"That's what I was referring to there," Annabelle said. "There was a difference. Especially in the boy."

Othel Travis began his cross-examination. "Annabelle, the only outstanding thing that you saw about the two children at the time of your two visits was that they were in better financial circumstances, weren't they? Isn't that true—the environment was better, they were equipped better?"

"Well, no," she said. "The little boy's attitude—the financial situation wouldn't affect that."

"Did you state a minute ago that when you visited those kids on March sixth, about the only thing you saw wrong was that the little boy didn't have any shoes on?"

"Well, no," Annabelle said. "I did say he was running in and out the door in his bare feet and he was excited."

"Is that too unusual, for a kid of three years to do something like that?" Travis asked.

"Well, mine don't go barefooted in the winter," Annabelle said.

"You said their coloring was somewhat better, but the time that you were there on March sixth, we had just had a rough winter. Would you say that your coloring was perhaps a little better in August than it was in March? You really didn't say that to mean that because of the environment down there their color was different, did you?"

"What I had in mind, Othel," she said, "was this. You can look at children and tell when they are getting better food and when they are getting better care, and when you are around them very long and they are excited and nervous and then when that child has calmed down."

"Didn't you say, Annabelle, that on the first visit to the trailer there wasn't anything unusual?"

"I was referring to the first visit I made to the Bakers."

"I'm talking about March sixth," Travis said. "You didn't make any visit to the Bakers on March sixth."

"No."

"But when you went there on March sixth, didn't you sit right there and tell this court that about the only unusual thing was the boy didn't have any shoes on?"

"That's right."

"That's right," Travis said. "In other words, they are just normal children, in what you saw, weren't they?"

"Normal children, yes. . . ."

"All right, that's all," Travis said.

I began to wonder now about the confidential Welfare Department report to the judge that I had put so much faith in. Was it also a monument to the inconsequential?

Billy Joe Rumfelt owned a beer place in Erin. It was the only building Marilyn had recognized when I had taken her to town, the place where she said she and Robbie had waited in the car when they had been so cold and so scared. Under Crane's questioning Billy Joe said that another bartender was on at night and that he himself didn't know who came in then; he remembered that Roy and Darlene had been in when they lived in the trailer.

"Did you see the children around your place of business, out in the car? Did you ever go outside?" Crane asked him.

"Yes, I carried her beer out to her car."

"Did you see her children on any of these occasions?"

"She'd just drive up there and get it and said she was getting it for another lady," Billy Joe said.

"Did she have her children with her?"

"She had her kids with her," Billy Joe said. "I say her kids—I don't know her kids, but she had two kids with her."

"Was that on more than one occasion?" Crane asked.

"Yes, sir. They were always in the car and the dog was in there with them." Old King-the-dog. I could smell the scene vividly: the children in the car, the windows rolled up against the cold, the old dog helping them wait and keeping them warm. I'd certainly give him a bone when we got home.

On cross-examination, Othel Travis asked Billy Joe if he ever saw King in his place.

"He comes in occasionally," Billy Joe said.

"And has a few beers?" Travis asked.

"He has one," Billy Joe said. "He never drinks but one."

One man who hadn't been quick enough or smart enough to avoid Hugh Crane's subpoena was T. T. Claxton. Crane called him next. T. T. had the small, pale-blue eyes and sandy hair characteristic of the region. His voice cracked answering the preliminary questions and he had difficulty getting it under control. He was very frightened.

"Have you ever on any occasion been in various beer joints and places with Darlene Hackett?" Crane asked.

"Well, I have seen her in beer joints; yes, sir," T. T. said.

"Have you been with her on occasion when her husband was not with her?"

"Yes, sir."

"Have you ever left any of the beer joints with her, in your car or hers?"

"Yes, I have."

"Have these two children, that you know to be hers, been with you and Darlene in the car at any time you have either gone or come from these beer taverns?"

"Yes, sir, they have been."

T. T.'s face began to sweat. He said he had been in Darlene's trailer because he did a lot of work for her. He worked on her plumbing and her oil heater, her air conditioner, her floors, her light fixtures. He said he never stayed overnight, but he worked as late as one o'clock sometimes. And yes, the children were present on these occasions, he said. He seemed very mixed up on when these occasions had happened.

While Othel Travis was questioning him, T. T. remembered that Roy had been present on the occasions when he was in the trailer, but he had already said he was there after Roy had left town. He contradicted himself in one stumbling statement after another. The only thing that wasn't clear was whether it was Hugh Crane or Roy's presence that made him so nervous.

Hugh called Miss Lillian. She had taught school since the days of one-room schoolhouses, and everyone in the community called her Miss Lillian, although she had been married for many years. She was a very beautiful woman, with a plump, unlined face. Her movements had an unhurried quality, a kind of deliberateness. On her way home from school in the afternoons she would stop and chat with children, call on the sick, get out of her car to pick a few wildflowers or wild grapes or blackberries. Her husband said once when someone asked what time she would be home, "Oh, you never can tell with Lillian. Lillian comes home like a good-natured cow, grazing all the way to the barn." Her presence there was a great consolation to me.

She told of having observed the children in our home over a

period of time, in which they had gradually become calmer, and of how Robbie and I would come out to the road to be with Marilyn as she waited to ride with Miss Lillian to school in the mornings.

Othel Travis tried to get her to say that the increased calmness was no more than getting used to us.

"The children are very fond of the Bakers," Miss Lillian said. "You can tell that by visiting in the home."

"Yes, ma'am, I'm sure the Bakers are very fine people," Travis said, "and they have a very nice home there, do they not?"

"A new house," she said.

"Isn't it somewhat unique in a way? In fact, there's no other house like it around these parts."

"I haven't seen one," Miss Lillian said.

"In fact," Travis said, "it's just one large room, other than the bathroom, is that right?"

"Well, they have a snack bar that separates the kitchen from the living room," she said.

"Do they have all the beds in one room there?"

"I've seen some beds there," she said. "They may have beds in different places."

"Do you know any other places they would have beds?" he asked.

"There is a large closet," she said.

"Oh, in the closet," he said.

"Well, it's not exactly a closet. It's large enough they could use one in there, maybe."

"You didn't look in it?"

"I don't investigate that closely," she said.

It was clear now, the picture Othel Travis was trying to produce: a drunk who lived with his wife and two children and

God knows who else in the same room. Was it going to be necessary for us to make a public statement that, spending twenty-four hours a day in the care of the children, we had no sex life, were far too exhausted for any sex life, and that if we ever did get the children's room finished we would look forward to a long sleep in an absolute stupor of fatigue before we could even begin to hope that old intimacies might seem natural again?

And I felt sure these ideas had been fed to Travis by Darlene. Suddenly I remembered how Robbie, when first he came, would, as if by reflex, as soon as I undressed him for bath or for bed, grab his penis and begin a kind of obscene dance such as I had never seen a child do. Then he would stop and look around in a puzzled way. "Why you no laugh and clap?" he'd say. How many people had this poor, frightened, nervous child been called upon to entertain?

All this had faded away, drowned, I hoped, in a lovely confusion of bedtime stories, this little piggy, bellybutton kisses, and "Good night, David—Good night, Chet." The thought that this beloved routine could, in turn, be destroyed and the old "Why you no laugh and clap?" be reestablished was—oh, it was unthinkable.

The case for the petitioners was now concluded and Judge Ogalsbee called a recess.

11

Othel Travis started the presentation of the case for the parents with his direct examination of Roy Hackett. Roy was a large man, very muscular. There was a slumping of posture already evident at twenty-six, indicating that in a few years he might be a very fat man. Marilyn's coloring and features were exactly like his. Robbie did not resemble him at all. He said that he had been married when he was twenty and Darlene sixteen, that his occupation was window-washing and that a year ago he had moved back to Tennessee.

"Where is your wife from?" Travis asked.

"Born and raised in Detroit," Roy answered.

"She hadn't been used to this old Tennessee country, then, when you brought her here. What did you do when you came back here?"

"Well, first I worked at a sawmill and then I started building houses and when wintertime got here I didn't have a job."

"When did you leave here?"

"About the middle of January. I went back to Detroit to find work."

"Did you have any money when you left?"

"I had about fifteen dollars."

Roy said he got a job working for his uncle at a tool shop in Michigan. He didn't send for his wife and after about six weeks he went to Houston, Texas, where he washed windows. At present, he was washing windows in Chicago. "It's a professional trade," he said, "You gotta be a journeyman. You gotta union." He said the buildings were thirty stories high and that he had made from $160 to $250 a week since April. "I've made plenty of good money," he said.

"The fifteenth of June, when you and your wife got back together," Travis said, "did you know anything about the adoption proceeding? Where were the kids at that time?"

"Well," Roy replied, "I had been in touch with my dad and from what I understood the Bakers was gonna take care of them for three months and he said when me and Darlene got back together to see if we could make a go of it and that the children was all right."

Roy and Darlene, living in Chicago since June, had made no effort to see the children until August. At that time Roy had not seen them for seven months; Darlene had not seen them for five.

"We was down here in August," Roy said. "We went out to the Bakers'. He was there and I told him, I says, 'Well, we are down here after our children,' and he says, 'I'm afraid I can't let you have them.' And I says, 'Why?' And he says, 'Well, you'd best go talk to the sheriff about it.' Then he told me that there was proceedings for an adoption, said it was in the hands of the court, and he said that him and his wife wouldn't stand in our way of getting our children back, that's what he told me. So we come over and seen the sheriff and that's when he read this injunction against me and everything and told me I couldn't see my children."

Roy said he had never intended to abandon his children, that he had left Erin for Detroit in order to get work to support his family. He admitted to having made mistakes in the past, but he thought the children would be better off with him.

"You didn't come into this court," Travis said, "to get the children to give them away for adoption or anything like that?"

"No," Roy said. "I've made mistakes like anyone else and I want the children."

Under Hugh Crane's cross-examination, Roy admitted that in the first six weeks after he had left Darlene and the children in the trailer he had sent only thirty dollars home, although he was working all but the first week. He had come back to Houston County before he had gone to Texas.

"What was your relationship with your wife then?" Hugh asked. "Did you get along all right?"

"We didn't get along."

"Where was she living?"

"She was staying with Virgie Stavely, I suppose. I didn't ask her. I didn't see her in a house. She was in a car with Virgie."

"Did you see your children at that time?" Hugh continued.

"No. She wouldn't tell me where they was at. I asked her."

"Did you ask your mother where they were?"

"I didn't know where my mother lived," Roy said.

"Did you and your wife have any trouble while you were here that day?"

"I didn't want her driving my car around. I had an old car down here, and I fixed the car so it wouldn't drive. I tore the wiring out of it."

"Did you give your wife any money or anything for your children while you were down here?"

"She wouldn't talk to me while I was here."

Roy said, in answer to questions, that he had not sent any money from Texas, where he had made two dollars an hour, and that from Texas he had gone to Chicago, where he made $180 a week, but that he had not sent any money from there, either. From January until August he had made no effort to see the children, though he said he had missed them.

Hugh then established through questions that Roy had abandoned Marilyn before, when she was six weeks old, that he could not remember supplying any support money then, and that on his last trip from Houston back to Chicago he had been afraid to face his family and afraid to face his mother and had traveled through Arkansas instead of Tennessee.

Othel Travis next called Darlene. Although she had always worn extremely tight-fitting and provocative clothing before, she wore this day a demure blouse and skirt and no make-up. She answered the preliminary questions about having been married to Roy Hackett for six years, being twenty-two at the present time, having two children, aged five and three. When asked when she had come to Tennessee the first time, she answered a year ago, omitting the time they had left Marilyn as an infant with Grace Hickerson.

Early on in the questioning, Darlene's eyes filled with tears and she began to sniffle. She had no handkerchief or Kleenex and Othel Travis didn't offer her one. She wiped her nose with an upsweeping hand, the first finger extended, as children do. She said that they were buying the trailer on credit and that she had worked for Dixie Sugg for three months, that Roy had left right after New Year's. "He couldn't get any money," she said. "He tried to work and every place he tried to get a job he couldn't and he didn't get paid enough to make our payments on the trailer, so he had to go to Detroit. He didn't leave me any money because he didn't have any and it cost eighty cents a day to heat the trailer so I tried to get a job. I worked at Dixie Sugg's café, but I worked there less than a week. It seemed it was useless to work there because what Dixie paid me was two dollars a night and that's what I had to pay the babysitter, so there wasn't really any point in working there. I had my application in at the garment factory and I kept after the boss. Every time I'd see him I'd ask him when he was going to put me to work and finally he saw me and I went in. I wrote a letter to the trailer sales—the finance company—and asked them if they could wait on payments until I could make enough money where I could make the payments and they said no, and they give me a week to get out of the trailer, so I had to miss work looking for a place to live. Then I lost my job for missing so much work. And when Roy tore up the car I didn't have any way to get back and forth to work."

"When did you move to the Stavely house you were talking about?" Travis asked.

"Well, first I decided to move in with the baby-sitter's family," Darlene answered. "I didn't have anyplace to live and since the girl stayed with the kids while I worked I thought, well, maybe I can move in there and she can help me take care of the kids while I work, and me paying rent, I didn't figure I'd have to pay her so much money, either, so I moved my television in here and some of my other things and then I left the kids there for a couple of days while I was working, and the kids—I don't know, it was just too rough and dirty and everything for them. So I decided to move down to the old Stavely house and Virgie Stavely and me, we went around every place and tried to find pieces of furniture and a stove, and we tried to get the electricity turned on down there and everything, and we just couldn't do anything because I didn't have any money. Then when I was down there one night wondering what I was going to do, Grace drove up and asked me if she could take the kids and I knew it would be better for them, so I let her take them. I said, 'Grace, you won't let nobody take them, will you?' She said, 'No, Darlene, I won't let nobody take them away from you.'"

Travis then asked her about her visit to the welfare office with Grace on March 19. "What did they tell you?"

"They told me that if I had come in a few days sooner I

would have got relief for that month, but since I had waited, I would have to wait another month. They didn't mention anything about coming back or that Grace had the kids. I said, 'What can I do between now and when the month is up?' And they said, 'We don't know. I'm sorry, you should have come in sooner and we could have helped you.' I didn't know what to do or where to go."

There was no mention of Annabelle Norfleet's having said Darlene had to be living in the same house with the children in order to qualify. Grace Hickerson had certainly understood this; that's why she had been trying to fix up the old house in Stewart.

Darlene said that she had left Erin for Detroit on March 22 and that she had gone to her mother's first. "I couldn't live with my mother up there," she said, "because there was no buses. You have to have your own car if you want to get anyplace because she lives out in a new suburb, so I went to West Fort Street and I'd been born and raised around there so I knew my way around. The waitress jobs there don't pay anything, so I went to a bar and asked if they needed a barmaid, and they said yes. They paid at least forty cents more an hour than in a restaurant and I needed money right then so I got a job as a barmaid."

"Did you have any illness during that time?" Travis asked.

"Yes. Whenever I got to Detroit I didn't have any clothes and no place to live so I had to borrow on that first check and rent a place to live and buy new clothes and a toothbrush and things like that. After I paid it all off I got sick and had to miss work and I finally ended up in a hospital, but every trip I'd go to the doctor it would cost at least twenty dollars. Then they put me in the hospital and I didn't have no insurance so I had to pay all of it and I still owe some of it."

"Did your mother and stepfather take care of some of the bills?"

"Yes, they put fifty dollars down and my dad come from Georgia and he put fifty dollars down and give the hospital a hundred dollars."

"The purpose of your working there—was it for your own personal gain or to get your kids back?"

"To get my kids back. I didn't write Grace myself, because I couldn't send any money. I asked my mother to write Grace and Grace wrote back and said the kids were fine and she understood why I had left, that I really didn't have any choice and not to worry about the kids. She had a couple keeping them and they were fine and eating good and whenever I got my trouble straightened out and I got the money I could come down and get them. So I didn't worry about them. I figured that Grace, being their family, that she'd at least take care of them. She promised me faithfully when I was there she wouldn't let nobody take them. My mother could always get in touch with me."

"Had it ever been your intention to abandon the children? Have you ever ceased wanting those kids?"

"No, never, I have always wanted them. It ought to seem apparent that I wanted them. It was just as hard on me as it was on the kids. I mean, if I hadn't wanted them or hadn't loved them I could have walked out anytime, but I stuck with them and I did without a lot of things myself to stay with them. They seem to want to give the impression that I didn't worry about my kids or love them and they want to say that Marilyn is scared of me and she's not."

"Since you and Roy have been living together in Chicago, have you been getting along well?"

"Yes. We don't drink, neither one of us drink or go out. We go out to a show, that's all."

"Now the testimony that you heard from T. T. Claxton a few minutes ago—those things were true, is that correct?"

"Yes."

"And you admit they were mistakes?"

"Yes, I do. I realize that I did wrong down here and a lot of things I did, it didn't seem like I had much choice. Nobody who seemed to be anybody wanted anything to do with me and I had to have company—somebody to talk to—once in a while. I didn't have any girlfriends other than Virgie Stavely. I never meant my kids any harm. I've never beat either one of them. I've spanked them when they needed it, and if I had anything to eat, they had something to eat."

"Did you call Grace after you got out of the hospital?"

"Yes, it was May or the early part of June. I called her one morning at work and asked her if the kids were all right. I told her I wanted to come down and get them and she said, 'Under no circumstances. Don't come down now.' And I said, 'Why?' and she said, 'Well, you'd just upset the kids by coming down now and maybe not being able to take them back with you.' She said, 'Let them stay down here until you get straightened out and then come down and get them.' She said, 'Don't worry about them because they are your kids, Darlene, and nobody is going to take them away from you.'"

Grace Hickerson's account of that phone conversation had been quite different, but of course I had not heard the conversation. I *had* heard repeatedly in Darlene's testimony the refrain "It seemed like I didn't have no choice." This crippling self-pity—was it the excuse for or the cause of her behavior? I tried to put myself in her place, to think of myself as deserted, put upon, mistreated, rejected by "anybody who was anybody." I got as far as leaving the children *without explaining to them* and I stopped. It was impossible for me to imagine not writing the children, not sending them a birthday card.

In his cross-examination, Hugh Crane asked Darlene where she had been living at the time she left Erin. "I was living with Virgie Stavely in her trailer," she said.

"Where were your children?" Hugh asked.

"They were with Grace."

"You say Mrs. Hickerson told you not to go, that she couldn't care for the children, and yet you went anyway."

"I knew she and Tom Hickerson weren't getting along and I figured they would separate and she would take the children."

"And you have been living in Chicago with your husband since the seventeenth of June, is that correct?"

"Yes."

"Is 309 Davidson Place your present address?" he asked.

Darlene said no. I didn't know where Hugh Crane had found this address. Possibly from a driver's license or car registration office in Chicago.

"This is *not* your present address?" he asked.

"No," she said. "That's just a mailing address. That's a girlfriend's house."

First law of the chronic bill-dodger: Never give your right address. Darlene was no longer sniffling. She had changed from the pathetic little misused person under Othel Travis's questioning to someone whose attention was concentrated.

"What is your present address?" Hugh continued.

"I don't know," Darlene replied. "I can't remember. It doesn't matter. I can't afford a taxi to go anywhere, so I don't need to know the address."

"What kind of car did you come down in?"

"A Cadillac."

"A Cadillac is a pretty expensive car. How is it you can't afford a taxi but can afford to drive a Cadillac?"

"Well, Cadillacs are cheap up there but everything else is real high. Roy bought it from a friend. He took up the payments."

"You say your husband is now making good money?"

"Yes, he makes one sixty to two hundred a week."

"But you've never asked him to send any money to the children?"

"No, we were trying to get furniture, trying to get settled."

"Has T. T. Claxton been to your trailer many times?"

"Yes, he came to fix my stove and help me. He was always nice to me, talked to me, helped me with things."

"Did you go to beer joints with him?"

"Yes, one time."

"Have you taken the children with you to beer joints?"

"I left them outside in the car with their dog and I would take them potato chips to eat and check on them and see they were all right."

"How often would you check on them?"

"About every five minutes."

"You saw Mrs. Baker here this morning. Why was it you didn't go to her and ask about how the children were?"

"I have no desire to talk to them. Mrs. Baker is trying to take my children away from me and turn them against me. Everyone is trying to make Marilyn afraid of me. Marilyn is not afraid of me."

I did not know if Marilyn was afraid of her or not. All I knew was that the child vomited at the thought of seeing her and in five months, under all kinds of conditions, she had never once mentioned her mother.

Garner Hackett, quite in contrast to the way I had remembered him, appeared ill at ease and nervous when Othel Travis called him to the stand. He stated that he had brought the children to visit us before Easter and that we had made an agreement "to keep them for three months, like in a foster home, and then in July I was supposed to return and make other arrangements about them if the Bakers couldn't keep them after that." He also testified he did not know we planned to adopt the children until he had a letter from me about eight weeks after Easter.

"Had you discussed adoption of the children with the Bakers?" Travis asked.

"No. They had no right to do that. I always told them to let me know if the children needed anything."

"Do you believe Roy and Darlene can give these children a good home?"

"I do now," Garner replied. "In the past they did not get along, but now they do and I believe they will give them a good home."

In his cross-examination, Hugh Crane asked Garner Hackett if he had known where Roy and Darlene were when he had brought the children to us. "No, I didn't," he said. Then Hugh asked him if he remembered King telling him about how if things worked out well, the children would probably inherit the orchard.

"He might have," Garner replied.

"In fact," Hugh went on, "didn't both Mr. and Mrs. Baker talk about the possibility of a permanent arrangement, including adoption?"

"I'm not sure," Garner said. "They might have. We were going to talk everything over again in July. I hoped in three months Roy and Darlene might get together again."

"But you didn't come back in July?"

"No. I found out I didn't have to come back until September, but I offered to come if I was needed."

"Did you also offer to help with the expenses?"

"Yes, I did."

"Did you ever send any money to the Bakers?"

"No."

"Do you remember Mrs. Baker suggesting that you start an educational fund for the children?"

"Yes, I remember she suggested something like that."

"Did you start such a fund for their education?"

"No."

"Did you in fact send anything at all?"

"I sent a box of candy."

"Now, Mr. Hackett, when Roy left here in January and he came to Detroit, did you see him?"

"Yes. He stayed about a month and then he went to Texas."

"Did you know where he was in Texas?"

"Yes."

"Did you write to him in Texas?"

"Yes, I wrote him one letter."

"Did you tell him where the children were?"

"Yes, I did."

"Did you see Darlene Hackett in Detroit?"

"Yes, she and her mother came to my place."

"Did you tell her where the children were?"

"Yes, I did."

"Was this before the adoption petition was filed?"

"Yes. Darlene thought the kids was with Grace."

It was incredible. If Garner was telling the truth, both Roy and Darlene had known where the children were *before* the petition had been filed. And it had not occurred to them to tell the children that they were reconciled, to send a letter, a card, a message.

Mrs. Swoboda, Darlene's mother, was next. She was dressed much as she had been when she had come to see us, that is to say, expensively and meticulously. I was able to see Darlene's face watching her mother. I watched both their faces and questions I had never had time for kept coming to me. I knew that I would probably never know the answers. Why had Darlene left the children with Grace Hickerson instead of taking them to her own mother, which is what women in her situation usually do? Was it because she wanted to be free of them herself or because she knew Mrs. Swoboda would refuse to care for them? Had she not stayed with her mother because no buses ran from the suburbs, as she said, or because her mother wouldn't have her? Mrs. Swoboda had located Darlene's father to help pay for medical expenses. She had written to Grace Hickerson that she had worried and prayed and cried about the children. But she had not sent any money.

Othel Travis, after the routine preliminary questions, asked her if she had gone to the bar where Darlene worked. "I'm a Christian and I don't drink," she said, "but I knew the people who owned the bar. I always knew where Darlene was."

Mrs. Swoboda said that Darlene was very nervous when she first came to Detroit, that she cried about everything. She said she had got in touch with Darlene's father and they put her in the hospital, where she had a D and C and stayed for two days; she had to be off her feet for ten days afterward.

"Mrs. Swoboda," Travis said, "you and your husband visited the children last July at the Bakers', did you not?"

"Yes," she said. "We went to the welfare office and they sent us to Mr. Crane. Mr. Crane told us we could visit the children, but that we couldn't take them away. He said nothing could keep Roy and Darlene from having the children. But someone told me that the Bakers hid the children in the woods to keep their parents from seeing them."

In his cross-examination, Hugh Crane asked her about this

visit. "Is it true," he said, "that you told the Bakers that you wanted to adopt those children yourselves?"

Mrs. Swoboda hesitated. She was apparently wanting to deny it outright and couldn't quite bring herself to do so. "She must have misunderstood me," she said. "It must be a misunderstanding."

Hugh then quoted from a letter Darlene's mother had written Grace Hickerson: "'I've talked and prayed and cried, so Grace, what are we going to do? Roy has called me about a month ago and he promised to take his children but he and Darlene are two of the biggest liars I've ever saw.' Did you not write that letter and make this statement?"

"Yes, I did. I wrote it."

"Would you say that they are two of the biggest liars you ever saw?"

"They have lied to me. I'll have to tell the truth. They were both our children. I thought I could say that to Grace and she wouldn't go tell the public. I know if I had the children I wouldn't have put them out like she did. They'd still be with me.'

"If you had the children would you have put them out like your daughter?"

"No, I wouldn't, but I'm older than my daughter. I'd know better how to take care of them. She has never had no responsibility of her own or nothing else. She was my baby for several years, so I catered to her a lot."

"Did you ever discuss with Mrs. Baker at any time the possibility of your adopting the children?"

"Maybe I talked to her about it. I'd take the children. I still would take them if Roy and Darlene wanted to give them to me. There's no understanding between us, but if they'd let us adopt them we could care for them."

"Did you say that you would adopt them if you could prevent Darlene from coming around them?"

"No, I would not prevent her coming around, but if I adopted them I'd expect her not to bother or boss them or anything."

Mr. Swoboda was the last witness. It had been a long day, yet he appeared scrubbed, shining and neat, just as he had at out house. It was easy to imagine him in a clean, shiny bakery, wearing a white cap, a little flour on his face, all the loaves of bread lined up in rows. But where had he been, where had his wife been, where had Roy's father been, where had they *all* been when the children were without food? When Grace Hickerson had begged for help from them?

Under Travis's questioning Mr. Swoboda reviewed Darlene's illness and employment and then spoke of the July visit to our house. "When we came to town," he said, "we didn't know if we would be allowed to see the children or not, so we came up here to the welfare and asked them if we could go out and see the children and they said they didn't know, they didn't have anything to do with it. So we went to see Mr. Crane and asked him. He said he didn't think there would be any objection. We also asked if we could take the children back to Michigan with us and he said no, that the only people who could get them would be their legal parents, that grandparents didn't have any more rights to them than a stranger."

"By that," Travis asked, "did he mean, to you, that the parents could come and get the children?"

"That's the way he put it to me," Mr. Swoboda said, "that Darlene and Roy were the only ones that could. We asked him if there would be any legal action taken and he said no, there was nothing to keep them from coming and getting the children."

In his cross-examination, Hugh Crane asked Mr. Swoboda if he would be agreeable to adopting the children, and he indicated they at first had preferred to take Marilyn as a companion to their own three-year-old daughter, but if both children were going to be put up for adoption they would take them both. Hugh then asked if Mr. Swoboda had talked with Roy anytime in Detroit.

"Yes, he came to my house," Mr. Swoboda said. "We asked him about adopting the children ourselves if they was gonna allow them to be adopted and he said that he was not going to let them be adopted. He was going to take them himself."

"Did you come to my office because you went to the welfare and they referred you to me?" Hugh asked.

"Yes."

"You didn't come to see what the law was and to see what could be done?"

"No, we came to the welfare first and they told us that you could possibly tell us the situation."

"And it is your understanding that I said the injunction was in effect? Did we discuss the injunction?" Hugh said.

"No."

"We said nothing about it?"

"No."

"Did I tell you whether or not there was one in existence?"

"No."

"Does it follow that you couldn't see the children and the parents of the children could? On what basis were we carrying on a discussion?"

"We was asking if we could take the children back to Michigan with us."

"Did I tell you that you could not?"

"No. You did come over it sometime that we didn't have any more right to them than a total stranger, that Roy and Darlene was the only ones who could come and get them."

"Did we discuss the use of an injunction or such a legal weapon?"

"No."

"Have you ever visited in Roy and Darlene's home in Chicago?"

"No."

"You don't know where they are living now?"

"No, I don't."

"Have you been married before?"

"Yes, I have."

"How many times has your wife been married before?"

"Three times."

This was news to me. Had Darlene's father been number one or two or three? I wondered.

The testimony was all over. I suppose I had been thinking only up to this day. I cannot really remember now whether I was expecting Judge Ogalsbee to render an immediate decision. I assumed he had already studied the Welfare Department report and was testing what he heard against the findings in that. It had seemed to me that he very well might wish to see the children, even to speak privately with them, and for this reason we had them nearby with friends so that we could produce them on a few minutes' notice. But he did not ask to see the children.

There was a short recess and after he came back into the courtroom Judge Ogalsbee referred to some papers and checked a calendar. Then he said, "The petition review and abandonment actually is based on March twenty-second. One thing I'm interested in—that is, of course, the abandonment itself. The leading case of Tennessee in reference to this section is the Wolfenden case, 348 Southwestern, Section 751. Then the court went into some detail, the Court of Appeals, in setting out what amounted to abandonment under this statute and stated that if the abandonment takes place it must show clearly

that the abandonment did take place. In that case the court
held that abandonment hadn't occurred, but these children
have remained away from their parents for quite some length of
time, and I don't think it will hurt them to stay a little longer,
in the event that there should be an abandonment shown. If
you will now—we ought to do that hurriedly—if you will file me
a little brief on this matter . . . I think the petitioners should file
that by—let's see—by the thirtieth anyway, and then . . . how
much time would you need to answer that, Mr. Travis?

Travis didn't answer immediately.

"Ten days?" Judge Ogalsbee said.

"Your Honor," Crane said, "we have court all next week. . . ."

"Well, now," Judge Ogalsbee said, "it shouldn't take very
long to hand in a brief on that. This is a serious matter and I am
going to treat it as such, and give it every consideration that I
know how to give it. As I mentioned, I don't see as how a little
further delay will hurt, to let the court have time to look into
this matter first. Of course there is a legal aspect that is involved
in this thing. I have this demurrer that is filed in the matter,
several questions that have to be ironed out before I can get to
the question of abandonment. Let me have that as soon as you
can, and then, Mr. Travis, if you will get your reply in the same
length of time, well, then I'll—

Othel Travis had been conferring with his clients. "Your
Honor," he said, "this issue didn't come up in the course of this
case, but if there is going to be some time before the case is
decided, could we get permission from the court for these
parents to visit the kids? Will they be permitted to visit their
kids?"

"Mr. Baker," Judge Ogalsbee said, "would there be any
objection, under the circumstances, to the parents coming to
see the children?"

"No," King said, "that would be all right. I would like to
have some responsible person nearby."

Did Judge Ogalsbee know about the guns and the threats, I
wondered, and why I had been so reluctant to identify Monroe
Allsbrooks' refuge? "Of course if there is any trouble caused," he
said, "that will have bearing on the decision of the case. Actually, I think the parents should be allowed to see the children.
Tomorrow is Saturday. They could all go there tomorrow and if
counsel wanted to go along it would be all right. Anybody could
go along. Mr. Travis and Mr. Crane, could you do that?"

"Yes, sir," Crane said. "I would be glad to."

"Then tomorrow," Judge Ogalsbee said. "Would ten o'clock
be all right."

"Tomorrow afternoon would be more convenient," I said. "I
need to get the children prepared."

"Two o'clock, then," Judge Ogalsbee said.

So it was decided. Hugh Crane's brief was to be in by October 10. It was now the twentieth of September.

We went to pick up the children. They had never before
been separated from me that many hours and they flung themselves into our arms. For the first time it occurred to me that we
might really lose them and I started falling apart. At home, I
fled to the bathroom, where I tried to get under control. I was
shaking and crying uncontrollably and I had one hell of a
headache. I would have given anything to crawl into a bed in a
dark, *quiet* room, alone, and mercifully slip into oblivion.

Tomorrow Roy and Darlene would be here for the court-
ordered visit and the children had to be prepared for it. This
time if Marilyn started vomiting, we could not run to Monroe
Allsbrooks' house.

12

We decided against telling the children that night about the court-ordered visit. All of us would do better if we had a good night's sleep for preparation. Next morning I said to the children as matter-of-factly as possible, "You know, we told you about being in court yesterday. Hugh Crane is our lawyer and he told Judge Ogalsbee about how we all want to go on living together. Well, Judge Ogalsbee is still thinking about it and, in the meantime, he said that Roy and Darlene can come to visit you today."

"*Here?*" Marilyn said. "They're coming *here?*"

"Now, Marilyn," I said, "just calm down. Daddy and I'll be here. We have to do what the judge says, that's all there is to it. Roy and Darlene will come, they'll stay awhile and then they'll go away and it will be over."

"But," Marilyn said, "let's go to Mr. Allsbrooks' again, like we did before."

The child was moving about restlessly. I feared she was going to break and run for the woods and the temptation to restrain her physically was very strong. Yet I was sure that that would increase her desperation. I wished I had chosen a time when King was in the house. Holding my breath, I gambled that she would not run before I could reach her. I sat down on the bed and hoped that I appeared calm and unconcerned.

"It isn't like last time, Marilyn," I said. "This is an order. If Daddy and I don't obey, they could put us in jail. Now, we couldn't take care of you if we were in jail. We have to do this and that's all there is to it."

Robbie had been taking all this in silently. Now he went over to Marilyn. "It's a rule, Marilyn," he said. "It's a rule."

"Besides," I said, "it won't be so bad. What is it that bothers you so much, Marilyn?"

She started moving toward me. I felt sure that if I could just get my arms around her without her feeling she was being restrained, we could get over the worst of it. Robbie moved with her and came to lean against me.

"But," Marilyn said, "I don't know what I'm supposed to do. What am I supposed to *do?*"

"Oh, I see. Well, darling, you don't have to do anything special. Just do what you feel like doing. Maybe you'll be glad to see them. Daddy and I don't want you to do anything in par-ticular. We're going to be right here."

"But what if Darlene wants me to kiss her?" she said.

"Maybe you'll feel like kissing her," I said. "Why don't you just wait and see how you feel? I'll tell you what. If you feel too much, if it's more than you can handle, you run to Hugh Crane. You like Hugh Crane, don't you?"

"Yes," she said.

"Good. That's what you do, then. If you have more feelings than you can handle, you just go to Hugh Crane and rest awhile. Roy and Darlene are going to bring their attorney, too, and I know he's not going to want to stay around here all afternoon. I expect it will be over in a short while. You do the best you can; that's all anybody is asking."

Though I did not expect the children to sleep after lunch, I suggested naps because it was the usual thing and I hoped that they might at least rest a little. To my surprise, they both went to sleep and were still asleep when the Hacketts arrived with Othel Travis. Hugh Crane, the sheriff and King followed imme-diately, in separate cars. Roy and Darlene carried packages. King and the sheriff and the two attorneys stood around awkwardly in the small kitchen. Darlene came into the living room and sat down in a chair. I went over to the bed and woke Marilyn as gently as I could. She sat beside me on the bed and looked at her parents.

"Hi, Marilyn," Roy said.

"Hi," she said.

Darlene unwrapped her present. It was an elaborate plastic miniature beauty parlor. She put the big box down on the floor. "Come over and see your present," she said.

Marilyn looked at me.

"I'll be out there in the kitchen," I said to her.

She got up and went over to where the present was. She sat down on the floor and began to take the furniture and hair driers out of the box. She had her back to Darlene.

Roy walked over to where Robbie was sleeping with his thumb in his mouth. "Still sucking his thumb," he said. "I remember when we brought him home from the hospital he was just like that, sucking his thumb already."

I touched Robbie gently. "Robbie," I said, "better wake up now. Roy and Darlene are here." Robbie sat up and yawned. He put his arms around my leg. Roy had the sense to retreat. He went over and sat down on the floor and took his present out of its sack. It was a large, expensive plastic truck. Roy pushed the truck back and forth on the floor.

I managed to get my leg loose from Robbie's grip. "I'll be in the kitchen, Robbie," I said, and walked away.

By unspoken agreement, everyone left the living room to the four Hacketts. There was nothing to sit down on in the kitchen. The sheriff stood at the back door. Othel Travis tried a few polite sentences, but no one would keep up the conversation. The kitchen counter seemed to enclose us in a box from which we were observing the events in the living room as some new kind of theater in the raw. There was absolute silence in the house. In embarrassment we turned our backs on the living room and stared at one another. The kitchen tap was dripping. I tightened the faucet. Then I turned back to watch this frozen drama where nothing happened.

Marilyn, with pure genius, had spoken to the heart of the matter: "I don't know what I'm supposed to do." Neither did anybody else, apparently. Who could have foreseen that parents and children, after all these months, would be reunited in *silence?*

Darlene's lips began to move now. I could hear nothing, but apparently Marilyn could. Darlene whispered rapidly and steadily and soon she began to sniffle as she had in court. She never raised her eyes from the floor. Very slowly Marilyn began to walk toward Darlene. Her body seemed very stiff. She appeared to be moving in the greatest discomfort of reluctance or embarrassment. I thought if only she would look at me I could smile at her, I could try to reassure her, but she kept her eyes down also. In an agony of slow motion she got onto Darlene's lap, leaning as far back as possible. She held her body stiff, with her arms pressing against her sides. Her eyes were still down and she was trying to keep from crying. I could see her lips trembling and I could feel the sting of her tears in my eyes.

Darlene's ceaseless, inaudible whispering continued. My God, I can't stand this, I thought. How can anybody possibly ask this of children?

Suddenly Robbie gave the plastic truck a violent push straight at Roy, who caught it with his hand very skillfully. His face colored, but he said nothing. He looked at Robbie and Robbie had become a cat.

Tears were now sliding silently down Marilyn's cheeks. I turned and looked at Hugh Crane, all the outrage I could muster in a silent question. Crane looked at Othel Travis. Both the men had children of their own. "I've had enough of this," Crane said to Travis. "How about you?"

"I think it's enough, too," Travis said, blushing. He went into the living room and the rest of us turned our backs on the theater. It will be over now, I thought. Over, over, over. Let it be over.

"What you building out here, King?" the sheriff said.

"We're making a room out of the carport," King said. "Come on out and I'll show you." The two of them went through the kitchen door, around to the side of the house, where the new room had a separate entrance from outside. That left Hugh Crane and me in the kitchen. We could hear Othel Travis speaking in a low voice to Roy and Darlene, and now Robbie came running in and stood behind me. I leaned down so that my head would be hidden by the counter and gave him a wink. He gave me one of his marvelous smiles and kept silent. I was afraid to touch him. From the very first news of this visit I had been fearful of getting either child in a position where two people might be pulling on them at the same time, and I didn't want to provoke any such thing.

What Roy and Darlene said to Marilyn or if they tried to kiss her goodbye I don't know, for I had my back turned, but soon they walked out the back door, followed by Othel Travis, who bade us goodbye.

Then I was free to turn to Marilyn, who ran into the bathroom. I heard no sound of vomiting and decided to leave her alone to urinate or cry or simply hide. Suddenly Robbie dashed back into the living room. Picking up the present Roy had brought him, he dashed out onto the back porch. "Hey, Roy," he said, "you forgot your truck."

"You keep it, Robbie," Roy said. "I bought it for you."

Robbie waited until all the cars had driven off (King had

gone back to work, too) and then he slammed the truck down on the cement porch again and again until he had beaten it to pieces. "Goddamn," he said. "Goddamn truck."

Marilyn came out on the back porch and now I was free to put my arms around her. "I want some lemonade," she said, "in one of our best glasses, the tall ones, and I want ice in it and I want to drink it with a straw and I'd like to have a cookie with it."

Old King-the-dog came up from wherever he had been keeping out of sight during the visit and both children fell on him and began to laugh and jump around until they got him wildly excited and running in circles, barking.

It seemed to me that he was handling the situation better than I could and I went into the house to make the lemonade.

The children never mentioned the visit. It had had such a quality of unreality that it sank into the background like the memory of a dream and within a few days it was as though it had never been.

Our lives were moving so fast in those days, for Marilyn was really excited with school. She was just eating it up. Each day when Miss Lillian brought her home she had all these new things to report. "Why," she said, "when you're counting and you get to one hundred, if you want to count more, it's the same thing all over again. One hundred and *one*, one hundred and *two*. . . ."

Most of the people we saw regularly assumed that we had been successful at the hearing or they took it for granted we would be. Hugh Crane had explained to us that the judge could take as long as sixty days to render a decision and each day that went by was reassuring to me, for it seemed such inhuman cruelty to allow the children to get more and more deeply entrenched in this life if it was not to continue. Miss Lillian was aware that we were still hanging in uncertainty. She often stopped in for a few minutes when she brought Marilyn home.

"You've not heard yet?" she said one day.

"No," I said. "I can't think why it is taking this long. King thinks I should be trying to prepare the children for possible bad news and they simply won't hear it. Marilyn just says, 'Don't talk about it. I don't want to hear,' whenever I try. And of course I can't believe it myself. I just really can't conceive of any responsible person uprooting these children now."

"I can't either," Miss Lillian said. "I'll go talk to him."

"*What?*"I said. "Why isn't that a crime or something, trying to influence a judge before a decision is made? I wouldn't dare. . . ."

"Oh, I taught him first grade," she said. "I'll talk to him anytime I want."

What I wished was that the judge would ask for the children to be brought to him and that he would talk to them alone and ask them what *they* wanted, and I was surprised that this didn't happen. In wild moments when King was pessimistic, I had fantasies of taking the children to Mexico, of not risking the outcome. But of course that was ridiculous. We could not afford to run two households and, even for these children, I did not want to live without King. Yet I was sorely tempted.

It was an agony trying to discuss possibilities with Marilyn. She had lived for so long in the present moment (whether it was enjoyed or just endured or suffered) that the idea of *plans*, of looking forward to things, was a new luxury. More and more she was enjoying the idea of planning: what we would do on the next Sunday when King would be off work, for example. And then there was the new one: *Christmas*. What would we do on Christmas?

"Oh, we'll have a tree," I started, "and. . . ." There I was, doing it again. I had been on the verge of talking of making gingerbread men and finding our own tree in the woods and making decorations for it, because I loved Christmas myself, and *this* year, with the children, would certainly be the greatest Christmas we had ever had.

I was lying on the bed and I said, "Come over here, Marilyn, and lie down beside me." Robbie was taking a nap and it was a rare opportunity to talk to Marilyn alone. "You know, we just have to talk about his." She left her play and came over to me, still holding something in her hand. "Now, darling, about Christmas," I said. "If we're all together, we'll have the grandest Christmas you can imagine, but it just isn't right for me to get us all excited until I know that Judge Ogalsbee is going to say that Daddy and I can keep you here. You know, darling, that's what we want more than anything, and we're doing everything we know how to do to make it happen, but it isn't up to us now. I can't *promise* you a certain kind of Christmas. I keep trying to explain to you about how Daddy and I were in the courthouse in Erin with Hugh Crane, and Roy and Darlene were there with—"

"I don't want to hear about it," she said. "Don't talk about it."

"Oh, darling, I know you don't want to, but we just *have* to. It's a good time, just you and me while Robbie's asleep. Let me try to explain it to you. I know how hard it must be for you to understand."

Tears were running down her face and she was fiddling with the thing in her hand, some piece of paper or cutout doll. "Don't talk about it," she said. "Please don't talk about it. I don't want to hear."

"Oh, honey," I said, "please stop fiddling with whatever that is. Come lie down with me. Let me hold you in my arms. Let's just be close together for a while."

She put her plaything under the pillow and lay down beside

me. I shifted the blanket so it would cover her and we lay quietly for a while. Lying on her side, she had her back to me, and I stroked it, trying to soothe her. "Roy and Darlene want you, too," I said. "You know things are different with them now. Roy has a good job and they live in a nice apartment. Don't you think it would be bad of me not to tell you the truth? Not to tell you that they want you, too, and that even though Daddy and I have done everything we can, still it's up to Judge Ogalsbee now. We'll have to do what he says."

She just lay there, crying silently, asking no questions. "Shh . . ." I said, holding her. "We won't talk about it any more for now. Let's go to sleep a few minutes. It's so nice and cozy here. Let's take a little nap before Daddy gets home. Here's a Kleenex for your nose."

I closed my eyes and lay quietly, listening to the sniffling, feeling the little warm body gradually relax against me. I thought she might really sleep. But in a few moments I felt the hand rustling around under the pillow and then she turned around, facing me. I opened my eyes and there, on the red, tear-stained, swollen face, was a big black false mustache. That was what she had been fiddling with, a part of a kit of disguises which she had seen advertised in a toy catalogue and had begged me to send for. *Astound your friends! Your own parents won't recognize you!*

Judge Ogalsbee took fifty-five of his sixty days to hand down his decision. Hugh Crane took the opinion over to King at work and there was no way King could delegate the job of bringing it to me.

"Well, it's come," he said. "It's against us. We've lost. Hugh Crane brought it over to me at work."

"Oh, no," I said. "No." I couldn't believe it. I really had believed all the time that the decision must go to us and because King hadn't, there was nothing he could say now that didn't sound like *I told you so,* so he said nothing.

I tried to read the opinion with its legal references and nothing much penetrated my brain. There was a lot about that Wolfenden case again. I turned to the end: "It results that the petition for adoption will be dismissed at the costs of the petitioners."

"Shall we appeal it?" I said to King. "Can we appeal it?"

"I don't know," King said. "I don't know what Crane thinks. He said he'd come out tonight and talk to us. Do you think you'll be all right now? I ought to go back to work if you're all right."

"You'll need some lunch," I said.

"Never mind," he said. "I'm not hungry. Just try to hold on. Get through the afternoon. I'll get home as early as I can."

"But when?" I said. "Roy and Darlene—they wouldn't come *today,* would they?

"I don't think so," he said. "Just try to keep in control. Oh, hell," he said. "I'm sorry."

"I'm stunned," I said. "I can't seem to take it in."

After King left I was consumed with a restless need to move about. Grateful that Marilyn was in school, I took Robbie to the woods with the goats and we sat on a big log for a while. The trees were all bare now and Robbie loved walking through the rattling oak leaves. I lay on the ground and looked up at the clouds. It seemed to me I had got into the wrong world by mistake. The clouds did not move and nothing was familiar.

"What's the matter, Mamma?" Robbie said.

"Oh, it's the petition for adoption, Robbie. Something's come up I have to think about. Something's wrong about it. We have to talk to Hugh Crane. We have to ask Hugh Crane about some things. I have to think about it."

We went back to the house and I got him some lunch. I read a story to him and when he was quiet I tried to straighten up the house, but I couldn't manage the simplest chore. I kept going back to the opinion.

Sentences would leap out at me from the summary of the testimony:

"Abandonment must be unequivocal. . . ."

"The Court feels that Roy Hackett has shown, by his conduct, a very indifferent attitude . . . that his inconsistencies make it clear that his conduct, if he were the only parent involved, would be that constituting abandonment. . . ."

"This court cannot find that Darlene Hackett willfully abandoned these children. That is, the evidence is not clear, convincing and unequivocal. . . ."

That phone call. That one, lousy phone call, I thought. And Darlene's mother had made her make that.

"I cannot escape the feeling that the children might be better off with the petitioners and that they would give the children a good home and provide well for them, but in Wolfenden, supra, the Court said: '. . . many children would be better off in other homes, but that is not and has never been a ground for adoption. This is an adoption proceeding; not a custody determination.'"

So let's *make* it a custody determination, then, I thought. Why isn't that possible? What do these legal distinctions have to do with *children*? What does it matter to a child if you call it adoption or custody or broccoli?

Surely somewhere there must be a country where the laws about children were for children, had something to do with children as children. Oh, if there were such a country, where children were not considered property, and we could go there. . . . Or if there were some community, even, some fortress, where we could enter and have a community of support behind us. . . .

I was trying not to be desolate, but to gather my forces to

fight, to organize the questions we would ask of Hugh Crane, to learn the nature of the battle, to get Hugh Crane's advice.

But Hugh, when he came that night, had no advice. King took the children for a ride in the car so that I could talk freely to the lawyer.

"Well," he said, "how are you? I know it's awful. I've been worried about you. My wife is giving me hell for getting so involved in this case. A good lawyer's not supposed to get his emotions involved the way I am about these kids. I can't sleep. If I'm this upset, I hate to think how upset *you* must be."

"I'll survive," I said. "Let's think what is best for the children and concentrate on that. Should we appeal?"

"I can't tell you," he said. "I'll do anything you want me to do. If you want to appeal, we'll appeal."

"Could we win an appeal?"

"I don't know," he said. "You realize there would only be the legal questions considered and the two attorneys present. We don't have any chance of bringing in the children or witnesses or you or King."

"I don't understand it," I said. "Right there in the opinion Judge Ogalsbee says the children would be better off with us. Then he denies the petition. Do you understand what happened?"

"No," Crane said. "He is proud of his record, though. He never has had a decision of his overruled by a higher court. Maybe he didn't want to risk that."

"Isn't there *any* court, *any* agency, where the children can be considered first? Not the petitioner. Not the respondents. But the children."

"We have to deal with the law the way it is here in Tennessee," he said. "You and King, you think it over and decide if you want to appeal or not. I'll do anything you want."

"I can't understand it," I said. "I was so sure. People like Annabelle Norfleet and Lillian Winters, and people who knew Darlene—they were positive we'd get the children. How about you? Didn't you expect to win?"

"You're never really sure until the opinion is handed down, but I got so involved with those kids. Yes, I guess I . . . I . . . Anyhow, I certainly was hoping we'd win."

"King thought we'd lose," I said. "As soon as we found out Darlene and Roy were back together, he began trying to prepare me for this, but I wouldn't listen. I don't know how you get prepared for a thing like this. I've tried to prepare Marilyn and I haven't made the slightest impression on her. What would you do if you were in our place? Would you appeal or not?"

"I don't know," he said.

"How long would an appeal take?" I said.

"Six months. Maybe longer."

"Tell me this, then. While the appeal was pending for this six months, is there any chance they could spend that six months with us?"

"It's not likely," he said.

That night after the children were asleep King and I talked it all over. It seemed to us that six months of uncertainty would be harmful to everyone, that the money spent on an appeal, which we could ill afford, would be wasted, and that the children might be subjected to very great pressure.

I, who had been so hopeful, so optimistic and so certain, was suddenly quite without any faith. I kept remembering a conversation I had had years before on the desert in California with a ten-year-old girl. The child was camped with her family in a trailer near my house. They had been there only a few days when she asked to hide in my house until her stepfather had slept off his drunk and left the trailer. She told me of how her stepfather had beaten her when they had lived in San Francisco.

"But, dear child," I said, "you should have gone to the police."

"Ha!" she said. "I did. They called up my stepfather and had him come get me. Then he took me home and beat me for going to the police."

I"ll never *be* as old as that ten-year-old face looked. "Why, Mrs. Baker," she said. "Children don't have no rights. Didn't you know *that?*"

We decided against an appeal and when we tried to explain the situation to the children we only succeeded in making Marilyn miserable. Once when my voice broke Robbie ran to me and grabbed me about the legs. "Don't cry, Mamma," he said, giving me a big smile. "I won't *let* them take us."

I thought of the frightened, disturbed child he had been seven months before and of how he could now be so full of confidence, ready to take on the world.

"Why don't we all try to have a good time while we're together?" King said.

Each morning I awakened to the awful question: Will it be today they'll come? And all day, moment by moment, I lived with this waiting. Then Marilyn would come home from school and King from work. We would have songs and supper and the children would beguile me into believing in our life and I would forget what was coming. Once we were in bed I could relax, thinking: they will not come now.

There was another day. And another. And another. And another. A week went by. I began to play with the idea that Roy and Darlene were not coming, that now they were faced with the responsibility they were not so eager to have it, or that as Grace Hickerson said they would, they had begun to fight again.

The children usually had their baths before supper and ate in their pajamas. These days especially it pleased me to see them so. It made me confident they were going to bed in our house. We were sitting at supper by candlelight. It was cool enough now in November to have a fire in the fireplace. I had let loose of today already. I wasn't even apprehensive when King answered a knock on the door.

Suddenly the house was full of people. Roy and Darlene and Roy's father and the sheriff were all standing around. King invited them to sit down. Everybody sat down except the sheriff.

"Go in the bathroom," I whispered to the children, and I left the table. They followed me. Marilyn was crying and I held her in my arms. Robbie, though, was still confident. "Don't cry, Mamma," he said. "I won't let them take us away."

"Marilyn," I said, "I can't help it. Daddy and I've done all we can. This is the law." I got a washcloth and bathed her face in cold water. "Roy and Darlene want you, you know, dear. They're going to be together. They're going to make a home for you."

Her tears continued. Her whole posture was one of abject defeat. "Listen, Marilyn," I said. "I tell you what. I'll come to Chicago. I'll find you. I'll keep track of you some way. I promise you. I'll keep track of you always, darling. I'll manage somehow. Whether you know it or not, I'll be watching over you. We'll love you always. Come on, now. We have to go out."

The children held my hands as we walked into the living room. Marilyn broke away suddenly and jumped into King's arms, her arms around his neck. Robbie simply climbed up my body and held on. I put my arms around him and looked into his beautiful violet eyes.

Roy's father stood up. "We'd better be going, I guess," he said.

The sheriff came over to me. "I hope you understand I'm not here by choice," he said, and then he walked into the kitchen, making it clear that he was not going to tear the children loose from us.

Roy came over to me. "I'm sorry there's been hard feeling,'" he said, "because I do appreciate you taking care of the kids when I didn't and my own family didn't. I know you took good care of them and I appreciate it. Come on now, Robbie," he said. "We got to go." He took hold of the child gently but firmly and began to pull him away. I shut my eyes and suffered it. It is a long journey down the collarbone by fingernail, a millimeter at a time.

Roy let loose. "We're just going to Maw's," he said, "for tonight. You want to see Maw, don't you, Robbie? We'll come back tomorrow and you can tell Mrs. Baker goodbye. We're just going over to see Maw now and we can stay there tonight."

"Could I have their clothes?" Darlene said. "We don't have any clothes for them."

"Of course," I said. "I'll have them ready in the morning when you come by on your way. I'm just not—not able to do it now."

Roy had Robbie in his arms now. "I'll carry Marilyn out to the car," King said.

"Wait," I said. "It's cold out." I grabbed up a blanket to put over Robbie and an afghan that had belonged to my mother for Marilyn. She was especially fond of having it over her for naps because of its softness. "There, darling," I said. "We'll see you in the morning."

"Roy," I said, "I must ask you: please take the children's dog.

We had such a time finding him again and the children love him so. Besides, I . . . really don't think I should have to see him the first thing every morning."

"Oh," he said, "sure. I understand. We'll take him. We can't keep him where we live, but we'll dump him out somewhere along the way."

"No!" I said. "Never mind. Leave him. We'll keep him. Don't worry," I said to the children. "We'll take good care of old King. Don't worry."

Even *yet* they were not through with dumping. Even now.

The children, quiet and supine, wrapped in their blankets, were carried out into the November rain.

The candles had burned themselves out, dribbling pools of wax all over the tablecloth.

"You want me to help you with this?" King said. "Before we go to bed?"

"Oh, no," I said, "never mind. You go on to bed. I'm too stupid to do it now. I'll just putter around until I wear down. I've got to pack all their clothes and have them ready for morning. I'll come out of this after a while. I've just got to sit."

He lit a cigarette and handed it to me. "They aren't coming, you know," he said. "They were lying. It was just too embarrassing for them to have to pry the children loose from us."

"I suppose so. But I'm going to pack the clothes anyhow, just in case." Because it had occurred to me that I could put toys and books under the clothes and in the books I could put self-addressed, stamped envelopes. Why in the world had I not had Marilyn practice mailing some letters? If only she had had that tiny bit more of school. If only. But how, if we had practiced, how could she possibly relate putting a letter in a rural mailbox and putting up the red flag to a Chicago street-corner mailbox?

King was sitting down on the bed, slowly pulling off his shoes and socks.

"Did you *hear?*" I said. "Did you hear what they said about the dog? *We'll dump him?*"

"I heard," King said. "He'll probably live to be a hundred and he's going to spend every one of his foul-smelling, reminding days with us."

While he slept or pretended to sleep, I puttered about the house, finding favorite toys, Robbie's alphabet book ("A is for apple"), clothes. I used up all the stamps in the house on self-addressed envelopes, which I tucked in every conceivable place. I put in the Chinese bowls out of which they ate their raisins and almonds. If Marilyn unpacked the box she would get message upon message, I knew. But did she have enough age yet to mark an X or draw a picture, or send an address in one of those envelopes?

All night long the cold November rain beat down. I might as well have been lying out in it.

Passing by the mirror, I noticed the long scratches on both collarbones, now beaded with drops of coagulated blood, as though two symmetrical decorations of miniature ball fringe had been pasted on me. I washed the scratches with soap and was grateful for the sting which opened up, for a moment, a big hole in the suffocating fog that enveloped me. Then for a while I knew what time it was and where I was and what had happened and I remembered how to start washing dishes.

In the morning after King had gone to work Roy came alone for the box of clothes. They hadn't brought the children, he said, because it was too hard on everybody.

"But I would have helped you," I said. "I would have gone out to the car. Don't you see that you haven't had them twenty-four hours and already you've lied to them? I beg you, *please* try to stop lying to them. These children have been lied to and lied to and lied to. For them to cry about the truth isn't as bad *for them* as to be lied to."

"Well, I wanted to say again," he said, "that I do appreciate the way you and Mr. Baker took care of them and I want you to know me and Darlene, we talked it over, and we aren't gonna fight in front of them any more. If we get into it, we're not gonna do it in front of them."

So they were really gone from us now and the last little hope of seeing them once again—that was gone, too. There was a high, moaning, cold wind rising and whining about outside. I stumbled to the barn and realized I had left the milk bucket back at the house. I was overwhelmed with a great clumsiness in everything I tried to do. The simplest task was inordinately difficult. Back from the barn, I managed to spill boiling water on my feet tying to sterilize the milk bottles. I could not remember if I had fastened the gate to the barnyard. I alternated sitting and staring with aimless pacing.

Just under the whining of the wind I kept hearing a sound as though there were an animal somewhere caught (or, as they say here, hung) in a fence. Could it be a goat? Or the dog? I put on a coat and ran outside. The noise did not get louder as it should have outside the house. I could not tell the direction of the cry and did not know which fence to check first. And then I stopped.

My God, I thought, *that sound is coming out of me.* I stumbled back into the house and walked about, still with my coat on. And still under the high whine of the wind there was that awful sound. I wasn't doing anything to make it happen. I couldn't even tell where, in me, it was coming from.

I know, I thought. I'll turn on the TV. I'll concentrate on a soap opera, on anything, until it goes away.

"We interrupt this program," a voice said. ". . . President Kennedy has been shot."

13

THAT.

That.

That changed the perspective. The children were gone, but they were not dead. They were alive.

President Kennedy was dead. And in a few days Lee Harvey Oswald was dead. The children were *not* dead. Yet the anatomy of grief ground on and on within me: two hot plates behind the eyes, a bellyful of rocks, feet of rubber, and a stupid, quixotic vulnerability. I would go to town on an errand, some perfect stranger or a casual acquaintance would walk up to me with a word of sympathy over the loss of the children, and without warning, I would be rendered helpless. I had an uncontrollable crying spell in Roby's Dry Goods Store and another in Cleghern's Market. I was at the mercy of any chance word, unable to predict or control my own behavior, and I couldn't bear to live like that. I retreated into my own house and stayed there.

Christmas was unspeakable.

King, being a man and having been brought up in a very different tradition, did not go around town bawling and embarrassing people and making a fool of himself. Once when he was a little boy convalescing from the flu, which he had found very impressive, a family friend of whom he was very fond asked, "How are you, King?" King, full of his news, began to tell the friend about his flu, whereupon his father called him into the library. "King," he said, "when people ask you how you are, they don't want to know how you are. The answer is 'Fine, thank you.'"

He bought it. He stuck with it right through his parents' divorce, when, a teen-ager, having an occasional visit with his father, he sat, full of unspoken love and longing, and silently smiled at his silent father as they silently ate ice cream together. And when his father asked, he answered, "Fine, thank you."

No, Mr. Finethankyou didn't go about town bawling in public. He went to work in the morning and tried not to make a mistake that would cost the company thousands of dollars in rejected parts. He was earning money to finance his orchard. In the evening he came home to an indifferent, unplanned and poorly cooked meal. At night he went to bed, where sleep betrayed Mr. Finethankyou into a land of horrendous nightmares.

Usually they were about Marilyn. She was being set upon, tortured, kidnapped, swept away by evil men, and King stood by, unable to help her or even to reach her, because he was tied or entangled in a web of ropes. The nightmares were followed by insomnia. It got to be a customary sight, his silhouette against the window, silently smoking a cigarette. We were never in absolute darkness because I could not bring myself to turn off the light in the closet, which had been Robbie's night light. I longed to reach out and touch King and yet, if I touched him my eyes would fill with tears, and if I spoke to him my voice would break. He was sick of my tears, I knew. He had taken over all manner of errands to protect me from public breakdowns. The private ones were tearing him apart. How had two people, who had loved each other for more than twenty years, got themselves into such a mess?

It would have been a great time for me to spend a month or so at the movies, hidden by darkness and wrapped up in somebody else's drama. Alas, Erin had no theater.

Hugh Crane saved the day by giving me something to focus on. Through a Chicago attorney who hired a detective at our expense, he came up with the children's address. And now I had something to do that I had a taste for. I could write a letter to

the children so that Marilyn could know I was keeping my
promise.

There were, of course, many problems. Darlene might not
show the children the letter. She might destroy the letter. Still,
there was a chance. Marilyn knew my stationery, had often
watched me writing letters. If I said nothing offensive, if I was
very diplomatic, perhaps Darlene would read the letter to them.
How much could Marilyn read now? In the few weeks she had
been gone had she learned new words? She could read *mamma*
and *daddy*, which it would be inappropriate for me to use. She
could read *kiss* and *love* and *Robbie* and *dog* and *King* and *goat*
and *cat*. And what else? What else?

Photographs! I could take pictures of King-the-dog and of
Eunice, Marilyn's favorite goat. But it would take time for them
to be developed.

First, a printed letter. Anything to test out the information—to see if the letter would be returned or not.

> Dear Marilyn and Robbie,
> We love you.
> We kiss you.
> King dog is OK.
> In the day and in the night, I love you all the time.
>   Rachel

Never before had I watched the mailbox for mail *not* to come.
A day went by, two days, three, a week. I went to Grace Hickerson.
"The letter didn't come back," I said. "It's been a week now and it
hasn't come back, so it must be the right address."

"I'd give anything," she said, "to know them younguns was
all right. I haven't heard a word."

"Would you go up and see?" I said. "Now that we have the
address?"

"I just might," she said. "I've got a friend who works on the
L & N who can get me a pass."

"How long would that take?"I said.

"Two weeks or so, I think," she said.

"Please don't wait for that," I said. "Let me get the ticket."

"Oh, no," she said. "I can get the pass. I just wonder what
would I do there if they wouldn't let me in."

"You could go to a hotel there nearby," I said. "At least you
could look in so the children see you. That's the main thing,
that they know we're still thinking about them."

"Oh, I never been in a hotel in my life," she said.

If she insisted on getting a pass on the railroad, I would just
have to wait. Meanwhile it was wonderful what having that
address to focus on was doing for me. I was not yet able to face
chance encounters in Erin, but I could go to the local grocery
and not stand in a daze, staring at the shelves. I could plan a
meal again and clean the house. I cleaned the goat barn and
took the goats for long grazing trips.

I ordered from Nashville the Russell Hoban book that
Marilyn had loved best of all books, *Bedtime for Frances,*
wrapped and mailed it. I imagined her coming home from
school (was she even *in* school?) and finding Frances there to enjoy.
She would remember going to the library in Waverly and King's
reading the book to her at night (*"Your* job is to sleep"). For Robbie
I got Dr Seuss's *One Fish, Two Fish, Red Fish, Blue Fish.*

I got film for the camera and went in search of King-the-
dog. We were on pretty good terms now. At first it had been
agony to see him standing by the road watching for the car
containing his children to come back. Tired of standing, he
would lie by the road, only to get to his feet at the sound of each
approaching vehicle. His head would move as the car disappeared in the distance and after a while he would lie down

again. I would call him into the house, but he was not long
distracted and soon he would be pacing around. We couldn't
both walk the floor in a one-room house. I would let him out and
he would go back to watching the road.

Of late he had taken to going with me to walk the goats. He
was quite good with them. He stayed at a distance and when we
stopped in the woods he would flop down, almost buried in the
deep piles of oak leaves, and get up when we moved on again. I
photographed him in our "playhouse," by the mailbox (would
Marilyn get the message?) and by the door to the new room. He
seemed to be enjoying all the attention and would sit at command, his mouth open, panting with eagerness to please.

It was one of those surprisingly warm days that come sometimes at the end of January. I had thought to get a picture of the
dog beside the children's footprints in the concrete of the back
porch, but it was too difficult. I decided to take the footprints
alone. By the time I had managed this, the dog had gone away. I
sat on the steps, aware of the pleasant warmth of the sun,
estimating how long it would be before I could get the film
developed and sent in a letter to Chicago. At some distance from
the house there was a washed-out place where we dumped our trash,
planning to cover it with dirt as it filled in. From this direction now
came King-the-dog with something in his mouth, which he proudly
dumped into my lap. It was not, this time, a rotting carcass. It was,
all covered with his saliva, Robbie's discarded yellow plastic duck,
one eye gouged out and the feet bitten off.

"Oh, King," I said. "King, King, King."

He was quite pleased with my reaction. Even if I was the
wrong size and couldn't leap about and laugh and run in circles
as Robbie and Marilyn had, at least I had noticed him in a
direct way. He stood close to me, panting and beating me across
the shoulders with his tail.

I ran into Grace Hickerson in the grocery. "Do you have your pass yet?" I asked her.

"No," she said. "I didn't get it. Maybe I can get Dixie Sugg to drive up there and take me. I wouldn't drive in a big city, but Dixie used to drive in Detroit. She wouldn't be afraid to drive in Chicago."

But nothing came of this plan, either. There was always some obstacle. In desperation I finally went to her and said, "Look. Please don't wait on anybody else. Here is the money. Please just take the train"—in those days one could still get a passenger train in Erin—"and go."

"Well," she said, "what would I do when I get off the train? I've never been alone in a big city before."

At last I began to understand why all the plans had fallen through. "Why," I said, "you just walk through the station. Outside will be a taxi stand. Give their address to the taxi driver. Tell him to take you to a respectable hotel as close as possible to the address. Get yourself a room in the hotel and then go to see them. If they're not polite to you, you'll have a room to go to. . . ."

"But I've never been in a hotel in my life," she said as she had before. "I wouldn't know what to do."

I realized at last that it was truly hopeless, that in all these weeks I had been waiting around there had never been the faintest chance that she would really go. And for me to go with her was far too dangerous. It would certainly be known if we left together and it might ruin whatever chance she might have in the future to be with the children or have them visit her.

That night in the kitchen I said to King, "Grace Hickerson will never go to Chicago on her own, I realize that now. I don't know how I could have been so stupid not to realize it before this. I'll have to go."

"Go?" he said. "You're *not* talking about going to Chicago yourself, are you?"

"Why, yes," I said. "I have to. I promised Marilyn that I would keep in touch somehow, that I would know where they were."

"You had no right to *make* such a promise," he shouted.

He was very angry, angrier than I remembered ever having seen him.

"But I did make the promise, King," I said. "And I've got to keep it. I made it the night the children were taken away. We were in the bathroom and Roy and Darlene and the sheriff were here. The children were holding on to me and crying and I promised. . . ."

King's face was very red. He began walking about the kitchen. I saw that he was trying to get his anger under control, that he did not want to yell at me. He wanted to *convince* me. Quieter now, he said, "Look. You should never have made such a promise. It's impossible. You have to admit that you can't keep it. It has to be over. Can't you get it through your head? It's over. We have to forget it. We can't go on living like this forever. *I can't stand it.*"

I stopped pretending to do the kitchen work and went in by the fireplace and sat down. If I start blubbering again, I thought, I'm going to slit my throat. "Well, anyhow," I said, "we know I'm not going to go tonight."

No doubt he regretted having shouted and no doubt he was aware that I was making a great anti-blubbering effort, for which he was grateful. He sat down, too, and lit a cigarette. After a while he said, very quietly, "You surely are not going to ask for a public humiliation? You're not going to get yourself physically thrown out of their place?"

"Oh, no, no," I said, "of course not. I know I can't do that. I just want to go and see where they live, see if they're all right, find somebody, maybe. . . . Really, I only realized today that

Grace Hickerson is not going to go. I haven't had time to work out any plan yet."

"I wish you would just *forget* it," he said. "The whole idea is ridiculous—going off half-cocked to—Why, you don't even know anybody in Chicago. What would you do when you got off the train?"

"Oh, I don't know," I said. "I don't have any plan yet. Maybe I'd ask the taxi driver for help."

"A *cabdriver?*" he said, shaking his head. "Listen. Cabdrivers do have a lot of useful information for a lot of people. But not about child care. You don't ask a cabdriver about child care." He began to laugh at the preposterousness of it.

"Oh, I don't know," I said. "I've always found cabdrivers to be very helpful."

"Tell me," he said. "I'm dying to hear."

"Well, a cabdriver found me that attic in Kansas City you thought was so great," I aid.

"A cabdriver found Sixteen West?" he said. "I didn't know that."

"I'm surprised I never told you. It was when I first came to Kansas City. I didn't know one street from another and so I thought it would be cheaper to hire a cab and go to all the places I had marked in the classified ads than it would be to do a few by bus and have to pay for a hotel. Besides, I'd left Fido with friends in Lawrence and I had to hurry on that account."

"Fido," he said, remembering.

Fido was this beloved brindle hundred-pound mutt who had participated in the first five years of our marriage. He was a great clown with a unique sense of humor who could ooze weight-lessly onto a bed so that King and I would awaken, each clinging to an edge, while Fido sprawled comfortably in the middle, deeply asleep.

"So I had this classified section of the paper with all the places marked that were five dollars a week and I'd have the cab wait while I went in and the place would be terrible and I'd come out and give the driver another address. The places were awfully close together, which surprised me. They were listed under 'apartments,' but most of them didn't have any kitchen, just a hot plate in a corner, and the buildings weren't what I expected apartment buildings to be. I realized something must be wrong. . . ."

King began to smile and I realized he was catching on.

"The last one, the manager's desk wasn't at the front. It was way at the back and I had to walk through a long lobby like a hotel lobby. All along one wall there were women sitting all dressed alike in black dresses, all with their knees crossed the same direction. It was like a chorus line sitting down.

"The manager was a woman and she and I got in a creaky old elevator and she began to tell me about the twenty-four-hour switchboard service. She showed me this ghastly room with a hole in the carpet and through that you could see another carpet with a hole in it. I told her about Fido and she said no, they just couldn't take dogs, unless maybe a teeny-tiny toy dog, and I told her Fido weighed one hundred pounds. . . ."

"Oh, God," King said. "Fido. . . ."

"So I went back to the cab for about the tenth time. I was so discouraged. The cabdriver turned around and said, 'Do you mind telling me what you're hunting for?' and I said, 'I'm looking for an apartment and these places are awful. They don't have any kitchens and they won't let me have my dog and—'

"'Do you know that you been in about every whorehouse in town?'" he said.

"'Oh, *that's* why they keep talking about twenty-four-hour switchboard service,' I said. 'I don't need twenty-four-hour switchboard service. I need a place where I can have my dog.'"

King began laughing. "Oh, rich," he said. "Fido in a whorehouse."

I started laughing, too. It had been years since I'd thought of that time. But now I could remember the look on that cabby's face. It was getting late and I'd wasted about the whole day. I handed him my newspaper and he looked at the places I'd marked. "I don't know how you managed it," he said, "but every single one you marked. . . ."

"He said," I told King, "that I should have told him in the beginning what I wanted. Then he turned the cab around and started away from town. 'I'll find you a place,' he said, and he went to Sixteen West. 'It may not be much, but it's respectable,' he said. The landlord wasn't there and he drove me to his house and we all came back and, sure enough, I had that wonderful attic with two great big rooms and a bath and a kitchen and a balcony overlooking the park, and the landlord put fresh wallpaper in all the rooms."

"Oh," King said, "I haven't laughed. . . . I thought I'd never laugh again. That's a great story. Even for somebody who didn't know Fido personally, it would still be a great story."

He began undressing for bed. We had both laughed. It *had* been good. And I hoped the laughter would kill his nightmares for that night. Suddenly I remembered Robbie and Marilyn in the woods laughing away the monsters and the devils. I turned my head away from the sharpness of the memory.

"Well, you'll admit now, surely, that a cabdriver can be very helpful."

"Aw, come off it," he said. "How old were you? Twenty? You remember what you looked like at twenty? The cabdriver, the butcher, the baker, the candlestick maker. Did you meet any man that didn't want to be helpful?"

"A few," I said. "You want to hear about those?"

"No, not tonight," he said. "No sad stories tonight. I just want to lie down and think about Fido barking all night in a whorehouse and laugh myself to sleep for a change."

What would have sounded even crazier to him than seeking help from a taxi driver was that I had the *feeling* that the children were a kind of magnet and I a lump of heavy metal which, if pointed in the direction of Chicago, would steadily be drawn to them. What I hoped for then was so vague I dared not even try to express it. I decided to go to the Quakers and see if there would be help there.

Quakers are few and far between in the South. The nearest Monthly Meeting of Friends was in Nashville. What a blessed relief it was to be in a roomful of people who I believed (whether it was true or not) would not think my emotions inappropriate. The great *rest* of the centered-down silence washed over me.

These were people who were accustomed to the contemplation of monstrous injustices with their cornflakes. Given the premise that the cause of world peace would be aided if a kitten were to eat an entire whale, they could believe the kitten could do it, would he be of good heart and take one bite at a time.

After the meeting, there was time for talk. No one gave me any advice. Especially, no one advised me on what we *should* have done. Best of all, the focus was, as seemed proper to me, on the children. How could they help? they asked.

Did anyone know Friends in Chicago, I asked, or have acquaintances who knew the city well? I was hunting for someone through whom I might get to know a person in the children's neighborhood. Nelson Fuson came up with the name of a Friend who had under his supervision a number of people working over the entire city.

Armed with this man's name, I hoped King would feel I was being less foolhardy about going to Chicago, but as he drove me to the railroad station in Erin, he did not seem to. He could hardly make me *walk* the fifteen miles to the station carrying a suitcase, but he still could not see what I thought I was going to accomplish.

"I keep saying the same thing over and over," I said to him. "I'm trying to keep my promise to Marilyn. I'm sorry you don't understand and don't approve. I just have to do this."

We were a little early, and we sat in the car by the station in an awkward silence. It was a very unusual situation for us, to be stubbornly at opposite poles. It had never before occurred when we were about to be separated. We had lived through the Second World War and had had many separations, but all of them had been with affection.

"We've never gone away from each other like this," I said. "I feel awful about it."

He came back from a great distance of restraint or irritation to smile at me. "What's the matter?" he said. "Are you afraid you'll be run over by a streetcar?"

"Exactly," I said, laughing. So I could touch him then and we got out of the car and he carried my bag into the station. I was so grateful to him for the question. My mother had based criteria for proper underwear and many other things on this possibility—that one might be run over by a streetcar—and my sister and I, growing up under the phrase, had developed it into a comedy routine, to which we had introduced King many years later. We would alternate the roles of Chief Surgeon Dr. Waternatzel and his nurse, Miss Picayune, in the emergency operating room of the hospital. Here we denied the lifesaving surgery to poor, helpless victims who had been run over by streetcars because their underpanties had frayed elastic, or the hems on their underpanties had not been turned with the proper stitch, or even, horror upon horrors, one victim had no underpants *at all*.

You, say, Dr. Waternatzel, this patient had no underpants *at all?*

That is right, Miss Picayune. No underpants *at all*.

She must die, then, Dr. Waternatzel.

You are correct, Miss Picayune. We cannot operate on people with no underpants *at all*.

My mother also felt one should not leave home with words of anger, or with unresolved quarrels. For after all, you never knew: you might be run over by a streetcar. Now that streetcars are gone, I don't know what mothers use to make their daughters wear proper underwear when they go out.

By invoking the streetcar, King had changed things so that I could get on the train not as a character in a tragic opera, but as a person getting on a train. "I didn't really mean to be such a shit," he said. "I'm not really angry. It's just that I don't see any sense in it."

I boarded the train about four in the afternoon and it lurched off before I was seated. At dusk we came to a small town in Kentucky where I had to change trains. Then the long ride to Chicago, clickety-click, dozing and waking as a crossing bell clanged or the train stopped at another station. Dawn came, and we were finally passing through the suburbs of Chicago. It was about nine the next morning when we reached the station.

As I had advised Grace Hickerson to do, I got a cab at the station and gave the driver the address. I asked him to cruise slowly by, told him that I was trying to locate the place, that I was trying to find two children, and that afterward I would like him to find me a respectable hotel within walking distance of this address if possible.

I couldn't believe the place. It was a dark basement with a bare light globe shining in a dark hall, off of which I supposed there were apartments. Above there was a business. We circled the block and checked the numbers again. The cabby said no, he didn't know anyone living in the neighborhood, he and his wife lived on the other side of town, and no, he didn't have any ideas about how to find someone who knew the neighborhood well. He said it all pleasantly, though, and he did know how to find a respectable hotel, all right.

As soon as I got in the room I called the man Nelson Fuson had recommended. I introduced myself and told him how I had got his name and that I had just arrived from Tennessee and was in a hotel. I asked for an appointment when he could conveniently see me.

"My husband and I took in two children, five and three, who were abandoned in our neighborhood," I said, "and at the children's request we started adoption proceedings. The parents, who live here, were reconciled and decided they wanted the children back and they contested our petition for adoption. They won. We lost. I understand that we lost the children. I am hoping through you to find a person who knows the neighborhood, a person I can talk to, perhaps write to, so that I can keep my promise to the little girl that I would somehow keep in touch and know where the children are.

"I understand that you would not want to be involved in a kidnapping. I also understand that middle-aged women sometimes go off their rockers over things like this. I will confess that while we were waiting for the judge's decision, I had fantasies about taking the children to Mexico and hiding them, but I know they're fantasies. We can't afford that. My husband has started an orchard in Tennessee and he has a job there and I don't want to live apart from him, even for these children.

"What I thought was that I would stay here in this hotel room until you call Nelson and check on me, which I would understand, and that you call me back after you've done that."

"Oh, well, I don't know as that would be necessary," he said. "Maybe we could save time if you wouldn't mind answering one question."

"Not at all," I said.

"Whose money did you use to get here?" he said.

"Our own," I said.

"In that case," he said, "I think I know someone who can help you much better than I could. There is a woman I know who works for a child-protective association. Let me see if I can get an appointment with her. That would save you a lot of time, because my office is a long way from your hotel. Give me the number there and I'll call you back after I talk to her."

The appointment was for the next morning, but by the time we'd made the arrangements it was too late for school closing time. So I had supper in the hotel coffee shop and then went out into the night. It was snowing. I walked to the address and stood across the street from that dark giant mouth of the basement entrance, its one dim light globe hanging there like a solitary tooth. Next door was a TV repair shop. Next to that a cocktail lounge and next a liquor store. The street was absolutely dreary. I could see no possible place for children to play. The building I leaned against was dark and had no windows, so there was no way I could stand out of the weather and be able to see the entrance. To think the children were just across the street from me and could not feel me out there longing to see them! If only they would run out to see the snow, just so that I could have a glimpse of them! I stayed as long as I could stand the cold and then walked back to the hotel. I fell into a deep sleep with all my clothes on and awoke in the night with the lights blazing.

It was still snowing when I took a cab to keep the appointment with Miss Christopher. I liked her at once. She was a young woman, tall, blond and blue-eyed, with a very direct and kind manner, and she listened carefully to the story of the children. How they had been when they first came to us, Robbie's nightmares, finding King-the-dog, the goats, the playhouse in the woods, how the children became less fearful and able to laugh.

"We even had our own songs," I said, and as I sang,

> The radar tower is working
> And supper's on the table.
> Light the candles. . . .

my voice broke and I started to cry. "Oh, I'm so sorry," I said. "I didn't mean to do this. You must have people crying all over your furniture all day long every day."

"That's all right," she said. "I see it must have been very hard for you."

I got myself under some degree of control and told her of the children's dread of the parental visit, of our hiding out at Monroe Allsbrooks', the court hearing of the petition, the theater-in-the-raw witnessing of the court-ordered visit, the long wait for the judge's decision, and then of having the children torn out of our arms. And I told her of my promise to try to keep in touch, to know if the children were all right.

"This is a legitimate request to make of our agency," she said. "The children apparently had been neglected or abandoned in Tennessee and it is reasonable to be concerned about how they are being treated now. This agency has a very good reputation. People trust me, you know. I've worked with the people in the schools before. Let me get to work now. Can you give me two days?"

I went back to my hotel and called King at work. He sounded relieved that my search was temporarily in the hands of trained, sane people, which meant that I was not just walking around in the snow asking questions of strange cabdrivers. Then I went out into the snow and wind again to take up my vigil across from the dreary basement apartment. The traffic on the street was very heavy and every time a truck passed, my view of the doorway was cut off.

Suddenly a little girl appeared (had she got off the bus?) and ran into the dark entrance. Was it Marilyn? Could it have been Marilyn? If only I could have had five seconds longer. It was wildly frustrating to have waited so long and then, my eyes tearing from the icy wind, to be given this dash, this blur of a child. Hoping she might reappear, I waited until the cold forced me to leave. I stood there freezing, trying to resist the urge to push with my hands the huge stopped trucks when they obscured the doorway. *Oh, go on,* I kept saying. *Move!*

Back in the hotel I tortured myself, trying to run that scene over again. I had the feeling the child was too small to be Marilyn. If it was Marilyn she had lost weight. How could I tell that about a child seen for two seconds in a snowstorm, wrapped up in a coat and stocking cap? Had there been any red hair shining under the stocking cap? No, there hadn't even been a face visible. There was no way I could make that little figure be Marilyn; there was no way I could make her not be for certain, either. I put in an early-wake call to the desk and tried to sleep.

Next morning there was sleet instead of snow. It was cutting and blinding. I crossed over and stood about twenty-five feet from the door on the same side of the street. I did not know what I would do if it was Marilyn. At last the child in the same stocking cap and coat came dashing straight toward me, schoolbooks under her arm.

"It's the wrong girl," I said the next morning to Miss Christopher.

She had just come in to her office and she put up one hand
to stop my talking until she could get her coat and cap off. Her
cheeks were very red and she sat down at her desk, reaching for
a Kleenex to wipe her nose.

"I know," she said. "I know."

I leaned back in my chair, trying to contain my impatience.

"It wouldn't happen again in a million years," she said, "but
there are two little girls with the same name in the same grade
at the same school. Can you believe it?"

"The same *name?*"

"Yes," she said. "Two Marilyn Hacketts. But yours has red
hair and came from Tennessee."

"You've seen her, then?"

"Yes," she said. "Did you know that she is very, very bright?"

"Of course I knew," I said. "The boy, too. He's just as bright.
Possibly brighter."

"They've given Marilyn some tests," Miss Christopher said.
"Her scores are very high."

There was a pause between us. She gave me a lovely smile.
"I'm sorry," she said. "There's nothing obvious that would allow
me to interfere. I had such a feeling for you; I couldn't help
hoping that I could maybe find justification for trying to get this
decision reversed. But there's nothing obvious like starvation or
bruises on the body or evidence of mistreatment. We do find
that pretty often, I'm sorry to say, evidence of mistreatment. But
it's not here."

"No," I said. "No one ever said the parents beat them. They
just went off and left them."

"Anyhow," Miss Christopher said, "you'll be glad to know
the right address is a much pleasanter-looking place than that
dreary basement apartment you saw."

"You were there?" I said.

"Oh, yes, I've been there. The father was not home, but I talked to the mother. I didn't mention you, of course. I simply gave the true name of this organization and said that we had heard there had been some difficulty in Tennessee."

"And Darlene talked to you?"

"Yes. She seemed eager to talk to somebody. She—she's such a child herself, you know, and she is very lonely. She talked about the court hearing. She feels people are all against her down there, that it's very unfair that people don't seem to blame her husband for going off and leaving the children, but that they blame her."

"She has a point," I said. "They do blame her more. I guess they would blame any mother more than any father for leaving children, but besides that, Roy has something likable about him that makes people not want to condemn him. They want to find some excuse for his behavior. Did you see Robbie?" I asked.

"Yes," she said. "He was playing in the room, quietly. He had some plastic cups he was playing with. He gave me a very fine smile and later brought a toy car over to show me. Marilyn had on a pumpkin-colored dress. The hem had been let down, but the dress was clean and not ragged."

"That means she has grown an inch or more," I said. "I know the dress. I remember the day we bought it."

"Now, Mrs. Baker," Miss Christopher said. "I'm sure you can understand that if I can gain Mrs. Hackett's confidence there is possibly a lot I can do for the children. But I have to be straight with her. I could not use her trust to report to you. I have to respect her confidence if I can get it."

"I can understand that," I said. "It would be a misuse of your agency here. It would demean your work. From *your* viewpoint, I can understand it immediately. But from mine. . . ."

"Yes," she said, very gently.

"I'm a threat to every good thing you could do for the children. I asked for your help and I'm very, very grateful for it. You can go where I can't. You have entrance where I don't. But it means now that I can't see them. I have to back off. It's awfully—awfully hard to accept."

She looked straight at me with those clear blue eyes, in which there was great concern. "Mrs. Baker," she said, "this is a situation that needs some healing time. You should go home now and let me see what I can do. You have to let some healing time go by."

Yes, it was perfectly clear in my mind, but it felt like the end of the world.

"I know there must be a roomful of people out there waiting for you," I said. "I do so very much appreciate what you have done, what you will do for the children."

"There is a lot I can do for them," she said, "if Mrs. Hackett will give me the chance." She made some notes on a piece of paper and handed it to me. "I know I can trust you not to misuse this," she said, "but I think you ought to have it. Here is the address and here is the location of the school."

"I can't understand why the letters or the presents never came back," I said.

"There's a whole world of people out there," she said, "Who just don't *feel* obligation, except the obligation to survive. I work with them all the time. It's something you have to learn to accept."

"Well, I'm sure the little girl in that dreary basement needs toys and *Bedtime for Frances*. For all I know in this crazy situation, she even has a little brother named Robbie."

I packed my bags and took a cab to the new address. It was a great improvement over the dreary basement I had been watching. Then I went to the school. It was a new, modern building with bright colors. While I watched, several lines of children came out of one building and crossed to another one. One of them had red hair and was the right size, with a walk I knew instantly. I leaned back in the cab so that my face would not show and said to the driver, "Please go on to the station now."

At home, after King had heard the whole story, he said he was glad I had gone, he was glad about Miss Christopher. "I have done the best I could possibly do for the children, Haven't I?" I said. "Haven't I?"

He shook his head back and forth a couple of times. Then he reached out and took me in his arms and held me awhile and then he walked out into the orchard.

The healing time that Miss Christopher spoke of—it's a matter of breathing in and breathing out. A certain number of inhalations and exhalations, and the black birds of time go stumbling by, dragging their broken wings. It helps if your companion in breathing in and breathing out is not trying to sell you the bluebird of happiness at a discount and does not expect a miracle overnight.

14

When Monroe Allsbrooks finished the cedar drawers, I stored bedding in the big toy drawer to fill up its emptiness, and that's as far as I got with decorating the new room. Actually the new room could have functioned as three room spaces, for by excavating at one end of the carport space, we had made a second area two steps lower than the rest of the floor and this allowed enough overhead space for a balcony. It should have been an interesting challenge to decorate, but now my mind was simply blank. Our plan had called for a spiral metal staircase to the balcony, but it was an expense we could postpone (who needs an expensive staircase to climb to a room he doesn't want to go to?).

"Well have to leave it unfinished for now," I said to Mr. Allsbrooks. "I can't seem to see it without the children." He had huge hands and he put one of them on my back, covering one whole shoulder blade, and gave me a pat. "Shame," he said. "Awful shame."

It was much easier when he finished the work on the new room and we closed the door on it and began work on the goat barn addition. This I *could* see clearly. Miss Dude had had triplets and the goats were very crowded. Besides, I wanted to try out a new system. On the other side of the feed room, connected to it by a covered walkway, I had planned two stalls, one for mothers and one for kids. The wall between the two stalls was to be largely of half-inch mesh, heavy-gauge woven wire so that the babies could see their mothers. They soon accepted being shut away from the mother at night so long as they could see her. Thus I was free to have the first milk in the morning before the kids could get to the mother, and the babies had access to her all day. In each stall there was a raised wooden platform so that the goats could stay dry even in heavy rainstorms. Kids dearly love, for some reason, to jump onto a low platform and huddle close together.

Now, that gave me a feeling of real accomplishment—to see the new barn addition taking shape, to have the milking problems solved and proper ventilation for the goats and the end of overcrowding.

A neighbor who owned a huge truck went to Crab Orchard, Tennessee, and brought back a load of the pink stone that is quarried there. Of this, Ed Stone (he of the handprint in the cement) built our patio, going carefully around the chestnut trees. This was the side of the house away from the road. Here we planned to have many meals in spring and autumn, and when the chestnut trees would be old enough to make a roof of shade, even in summer.

Also, we got the built-in oven and the countertop burners installed in the kitchen as we had originally planned.

In March King said, "Why don't you go with me to McMinnville to get the trees for the dwarf orchard?"

We asked a neighbor to come take care of the evening feeding of the animals and we took off in the truck right after the morning milking. One thing you never really anticipate correctly when you leave a city life for a farm is how difficult it is to leave the animals. We have neighbors who have not been out of the county for thirty years. Though it is understood by everyone that others will come to do chores or whatever is necessary in times of sickness and death, to ask just for pleasure is seldom done. Whether or not it is that animals often miss you and begin to hunt for you when you are gone, it does seem that if an animal is going to find a break in the fence or step in a rabbit hole or get its head caught between two upright boards or eat poison laurel or get bitten by a copperhead, it will happen on the day you are away. As King said about his trees one year when there was a prolonged drought, "Thank God they can't look up at me with big brown eyes and cry."

To be in that truck alone together, taking off on a trip—it was like being let out of school or playing hooky. There was the hint of something strange and foreign, something reminiscent of *fun*. It was still a winter landscape—the trees were bare—but it was a day of bright sunshine and a hint of spring was in the air.

Possibly there is some special quality to the soil around

McMinnville, for many nurseries are located in the area. One can go for miles past nursery after nursery. King dealt with Haley's of Smithville. Here we bought two-year-old dwarf trees, five to six feet tall, that had been cut back to three feet, all on Malling IX rootstalks: one hundred fifty Red Delicious, forty-three Yellow Delicious, forty Winesaps and thirty-five Lodi. The trees were tied in bunches, the roots covered with sphagnum moss, and the bundles tied with burlap and then loaded onto the truck.

We stopped for a light supper and the coffee afterward helped dispel the fatigue of the trip. Shut off from the world in the cab of the truck, lulled by the monotony of the motor, we were catapulted back in time to a former condition, of being two people, of being ourselves as we had once been before we had known the children. A dip in the road near a stream plummeted us into a sudden short-lived streak of fog.

"The white mists of Paola," I said, remembering an enchanted, floating ride we had once had in a landscape of nothing recognizable. Suddenly we were in touch with our own unique history before we had entered grim battles against hopeless odds. We brought out our special times and caressed them like jewels held to a light. A cave in Rocheport, Missouri, a perfect spider web beaded in dew, caught by our flashlight in Warsaw, Missouri. The perfect, veined ice leaves that had slipped all at once from a huge magnolia in Virginia and lay all over the ground like shining, unbroken leaves of glass. The smell of the air in Muscoy, California, when, in wartime, we had had an interlude of peace. Lying motionless by moonlight on the warm desert sand near the Salton Sea, watching kangaroo rats feasting on wild verbena. Climbing barefoot over the rocks at Portuguese Bend, exploring the tide pools. We had a

long history of high moments, as any couple has, I suppose. And
we were in touch with it all again. Our grief had not obliterated
our history of ourselves; it had only made it unavailable to us for
a time.

Next morning King dug a long trench in the dwarf orchard
and heeled in the trees so that their roots would not dry out
before he got them planted. He hired two men to help him dig
the holes, but most of the trees he planted himself. It's not just a
matter of digging a hole and sticking a tree in it. The hole is a
bowl two to four feet in diameter and about two feet deep. The
roots must be stretched out horizontally, all the fine threads of
them. On his knees, King would patiently crumble the hard
lumps of dirt into fine dust for the first layer over the roots and
then, as the bowl got filled up, he would trample and press out
the air.

The peach trees that spring were like pink sunset clouds
fallen to earth. We had not expected so many blossoms in such
young trees and a few weeks after the blossoms had gone King
said, "There are peaches on the trees. Real, tiny peaches. Come
and see." And there they were, covered with soft gray fur, pale-
green miniature peaches nestled under the slender, folded
pointed leaves. I could not resist touching them.

"We might as well take them seriously," King said. "I can
hardly believe we'll have many mature peaches. But anyhow, it
will be good training for next year, I guess."

The trees had already had their dormant spray of copper
sulfate against the peach leaf curl and now King began the
fungicide sprays of lime sulfur and sulfur every two weeks. This
was before we had the big spray tank, which puts out four jets of
spray from each side as it is pulled between rows of mature trees.
This first spraying was done with a hand gun connected to a

fifty-gallon tank mounted upright (and prone to slop over) on the rear of a small tractor.

Poor, dear peaches—the enemies they have! It is a wonder one ever reaches its glowing, beautiful maturity. There is the curculio beetle and there are stink bugs, which leave deforming scars called catfacing. There are the peach tree borer and the codling moth, and the Oriental fruit moth, which causes the end of leaf shoots to die. There are leaf rollers. There is brown rot disease and scab, and this was before the days of Benlate and Imidan. It is a constant war. Some days it rains and you have to rest.

Miraculously, there were twenty-four bushels of Red Haven peaches to sell. Word spread fast and the number of people who came showed us we were not likely ever to have any surplus of peaches to worry about. There was no other commercial orchard near and those peaches were the big event of the summer. They were as large as tennis balls (some were baseball-size) and each one was perfect. No peaches ever were spread so thin or so far. "Had me one of them peaches," one man said. "My wife's sister give it to her. She got it from their aunt." It would make an interesting study, I always thought. If you wanted to trace a network of how people show real love and regard, you could give a few people bushels of peaches and trace where they went and how far they got. But then, as in so much of the life here, it might only show the degrees of kinship.

We also sold two bushels of Lodi apples that year, the earliest green, tart apples. They are meant for cooking, especially for applesauce, but the earliest sales each year were to pregnant ladies who came with salt in their hands and ate theirs raw right off the trees. "Got me a terrible hunger for green apples and salt," they'd say.

And we had one bushel of Summer Champions. This is a huge red apple, which turned out to be a great and steadily increasing producer on alternate years.

I had written to Miss Christopher before Robbie's birthday, hoping she might be able to get a birthday cake for him. A long time went by before I finally heard.

> Dear Mrs. Baker,
>   I would have enjoyed taking Robbie a cake or a present, but it was not possible. The children and their parents have moved to Detroit and so I've lost track of them.

They were lost to me again, my darlings. And now the whole process of finding them. . . . Must I begin it all over again? I read on, my heart sinking.

> I visited Mrs. Hackett several times and found her very responsive and really quite eager to have someone to talk to. I felt quite hopeful that this was the beginning of a relationship in which I could, through her acceptance of me, help the children. So I was baffled when she suddenly stopped being home when I went nor did she answer notes I left in the mailbox. I finally did find her at home and found out why she had been avoiding me. She had been to visit her mother in Detroit and her mother told her the only reason I would keep coming to see her would be to get evidence to take her children away from her. She should have nothing to do with me or she would be sorry!

A better enemy than Bess Swoboda Darlene couldn't have, I thought.

> Mrs. Hackett did tell me that Roy's father had made the down payment on a house for them in Detroit and they would be moving after school was out. She seemed happy about this. I

think this tangible family support gives her some feeling of security she has never felt with Roy. Perhaps some responsible adults around will provide some safeguards against the kind of situation that developed in Tennessee.

The threatened loss of the children and the contact from our agency has had the effect, I believe, of making them aware that how they care for their children is not just their business but the concern of the whole community.

You and your husband must feel at times that what you tried to give the children was all lost when they left you. The effect, however, has been to bring about a better life for them with their own parents. I know you hoped this might be true. Besides, what one gives children is never lost. The kind of warm, trusting relationship the children had with you affects their feelings about people all the rest of their lives.

I became very interested in the children. I have to tell myself that I have done as much as was possible to do. I hope that you can do this also, and really believe it.

Sincerely,
Joan Christopher

My mind was full of Detroit. The children would certainly be easier to find there than in Chicago. There were so many people in Houston County who had kin in Detroit, the news would certainly filter back in time. In fact, it was surprising that Grace Hickerson had not already heard it. Before I could get to her to discuss it, though, King came home with the news that a woman had called his office from Chicago, leaving a telephone number for me to call.

"You're supposed to ask for Myrtle," he said. "Do you know anyone named Myrtle in Chicago?"

"No," I said, "but it must be about the children, don't you suppose? Maybe it's someone who knows where the children are."

I couldn't wait. We drove into Erin and called from Hugh Crane's office. A man answered, saying the name of a bar. I asked for Myrtle. I could hear him calling her name and finally a woman came on the line. I told her who I was.

"Are you the woman took care of them Hackett kids?" she said.

"Oh, yes," I said. "Yes, I am. Do you know where the children are? Is that why you're calling?"

"No," she said. "I don't know where they are."

"Oh," I said. "Then why did you call?"

"I want you to have my baby," she said. "I'm alone and I'm too sick to take care of it and if I ever get well enough to work I got no one to leave the baby with."

"Well, I—I don't know what to say," I said. "I'm absolutely flabbergasted. I . . . Do you know that I'm fifty years old?"

"I know," she said.

"Maybe I don't understand," I said. "Did you just want someone to take care of your baby while you're sick or are you talking about adopting?"

"Adoption," she said.

"But surely if you're willing to have your baby adopted, Myrtle, it would be best to go to an agency, wouldn't it? Then you'd be sure that the parents would be young and healthy and—"

"I would never do that," she said, "never."

"This is terribly unsatisfactory," I said, "trying to talk about something so important on the phone. I—I couldn't even think of such a thing without talking to my husband, you know. And—and right now I'm so concerned with your baby. Who is taking care of your baby right now?"

"The baby's in a nursery," she said. "They keep them for

thirty days and then after that they send them to a foster home if the mothers don't take them."

I made arrangements to call her back at certain hours on certain days at the same number. "I used to work here before I got sick," she said, "and if I get able, I'll help them out again when they're short-handed, so they let me use the phone."

I went into Hugh Crane's outer office, where he and King were talking. "That was some woman who had heard about the children," I said. "She wants us to adopt her baby. She's sick and can't take care of it."

"What did you tell her?" King said.

"I told her I'd talk to you and call her back in a day or two," I said.

"Is it a boy or a girl?" Hugh Crane said.

"Why, I don't even know," I said. "I was so stunned I didn't ask her. I spent most of the time trying to get her to go to an agency and do the best thing for the baby. I must have read a thousand articles on adoption and they *all* say that the best protection for a baby is to go through a regular agency, and of course an agency wouldn't even consider people of our age."

"What did she say to that?" Hugh Crane said.

"Absolutely not," I said. "Never. She was like a stone wall. It was as though I had asked her to do something contemptible."

On the way home I asked King how he felt about adopting a baby and he said, "Fine. If it could really be legally arranged."

Myself, I simply didn't believe it. Even after more telephone calls, when I came to know that the baby was a blue-eyed girl, only a few days old, that all Myrtle had to do was do nothing and the baby would go automatically into a foster home at the end of thirty days. And after a certain period into another foster home, and from then on possibly a series of foster homes. I kept

on thinking of her as a baby for whom, by a strange quirk of
fate, I had been given a chance to do the very best possible and
that if I kept on thinking and trying and offering to go with her,
I would be able to convince Myrtle that a legitimate agency
offered the best future.

At home I would have these imaginary conversations with
Myrtle and it would seem to me that I had an argument that
couldn't fail to convince her. I would get to a phone as fast as
possible and then I would hit that absolute wall of *no!* As the
days slipped by I stopped thinking of us in relation to the best
parents that an agency could find, and started thinking of us in
comparison to a series of foster homes. We looked very good all
of a sudden. The responsibility of a tiny, helpless infant, as I
began to accept it as something that might really happen, shot a
considerable amount of adrenaline into my system. I had never
had the care of an infant before.

Near the end of the thirty days Hugh Crane and King and I
were on an airplane flying to Chicago. Hugh went to set up the
hearing before a judge and to have an interview with him and
arrange for the preparation of all the necessary papers, while
King and I went to see the baby.

She had these dark, well-defined eyebrows, for which I had
not been prepared. Most babies have very faint eyebrows or
none at all. I guess that's what makes a baby's face look like a
baby. But Melissa had these strong eyebrows that somehow
made her, when she opened her violet eyes, appear to be very
wise. I wouldn't have been surprised if she had sat up and begun
a very serious conversation. What she did was go back to sleep.
She was incredibly tiny and fragile and beautiful and I wanted
her to be loved and cherished all the days of her life. While I
had it in me still to have one last glimmer of unselfish concern,
I gave the agency idea one more try with Myrtle. The anxiety

over having to appear at the hearing had quite worn her out. She looked very ill and tired.

She turned on me impatiently. "I don't know how you got all this faith in strangers," she said. "Strangers never did me nothing but harm."

"I won't say any more about it," I said. "I am very grateful you called me. King and I are going to give your baby all the love and care you want her to have. You can count on that. She's going to have a lovely life. Anyhow, she's going to have a lovely start."

Hugh Crane came to our hotel room to take us to the hearing. "Where's King?" he said.

"He just went out for a little while," I said. "He'll be right back." But by the time he did get back, carrying a package under his arm, we were a little nervous.

"It's about time for the hearing," I said. "We have to be in court. Where have you been?"

"Oh," he said, "such an important occasion . . . I just felt like I ought to have a new shirt. I'll just be a minute."

Melissa slept through the whole procedure in the judge's chamber. I held her in my arms and it seemed to me infinitely sad that such vital decisions could be made for one while one slept. That night in the hotel she slept in a dresser drawer. In the hotel kitchen's refrigerator we had enough formula made up to last through the next day. We ran hot water from the bathroom tap over the bottles. In the airplane going home we touched the edge of a tornado and for a while the plane was going up and down with considerable turbulence. She slept through it all.

We went straight to our doctor as soon as we got to Erin. He examined her carefully, said she had had a fractured clavicle, which had healed, and that otherwise she seemed quite perfect.

He thought her formula, furnished by the nursery, too high in sugar and changed it.

Later, coming out of Hugh Crane's office, where we had stopped to show Melissa to Hugh's wife, we ran into the owner of the local telephone company. "You mean," he said to me, "that you're going to be alone way out there with a baby that small while King's at work? I'm going to get you a phone if I have to string up those wires myself."

He got us one, too. It was an eight-party line and fortunately the dire emergencies for which we might have needed it never materialized. There was not even the 1 A.M. feeding we had expected, for from the beginning Melissa slept straight through the night and very soon woke up smiling. We couldn't believe it could all be so easy, such pure pleasure.

Early in the morning, while King stayed with Melissa, I went to the barn to do the milking. "Oh, Miss Dude," I said, putting my arms around her neck, "you wouldn't believe what I've got up there in the house." In time I got a baby harness called a Hike-A-Poose (there is no safe place to lay a baby down in a barn) and I carried Melissa on my back, knowing any door I could get through, any branch that cleared my head, would be safe for hers.

After a six-month probation period we all met in Hugh Crane's office with Judge Ogalsbee, who signed the final adoption papers. He said it was a real pleasure and to him it was understandable that a mother would want to know where her child went.

One child does not take the place of another, of course. But the one you are looking at has a right to your very best attention. And as you get in the habit of giving it, a certain order of priorities is established, except for those moments when one is overwhelmed by surprise and there is a temporary loss of control.

When Melissa was supposed to have teeth, teeth appeared. When she wanted to crawl, she crawled, and when she decided to walk, she walked. After *dada* and *mamma,* the first words she said were *apple* and *moon,* two very fine things to know the names of. We put a potty chair in the bathroom and when she was ready she tried it out with considerable pleasure. Over a period of time she decided she preferred it to its alternatives. She was remarkably sure-footed and graceful. She rarely stumbled or fell and the only accident she had was to drop a one-pound jar of peanut butter on her toe. She was truly outraged at the pain and the sight of the toe turning black.

There would come a day when, taking advantage of a friend's presence in the house, I said to Melissa, "I'm going down to the barn to check on the mamma goats; I'll be right back." She looked up from her toys. "OK," she said, and went back to playing. I was halfway to the barn before the impact of it hit me. When you say to a child, "I'll be right back," *and she believes you*—why, then your feet are on a different road. You're walking in another country altogether from the land where Marilyn and Robbie live.

Melissa had favorites among her blocks and at bedtime would pat them, saying, "Good night, T. Good night, W." She had no serious illnesses. She had a lovely, joyous laugh and, of course, she had those remarkable strongly defined eyebrows.

Shall we leave her there about this time, out on the patio in her oversized playpen, a day recorded in an old photograph? She is breathing the pure country air. Before her eyes a seemingly endless green vista stretches, without barriers. It is a lovely spring day with soft white clouds in a high blue sky. The apple trees are in blossom and old King-the-dog is fiercely guarding her against the danger of a pink-and-turquoise butterfly that is trying to light on her head. The young chestnut trees are about three feet high. In the sky a huge black bird appears, soaring. Melissa puts up her arms to the bird.

Oh, she will fly, all right. In a short while she will be over the side of that playpen. She will be running free and later on she will be riding a pony over the hills, her long blond hair streaming out behind her. Yes, she will be free, as free as her world will allow a loved and loving person who had a good start.

But I? Part of me will be forever chained to the light switch of Robbie's night light. I get my hand on the switch plate often enough, knowing it is silly to keep the light burning day and night, but I never can make myself deliberately flick the switch. And the times when the bulb burns out of itself, in that awful interval before I can get a new bulb in the socket, I can't breathe.

I can't breathe until the light comes on again.

Epilogue

The year that Melissa was first walking we sold 100 bushels of apples and 113 of peaches. People kept coming to the door to give me money and when the neat cigar box which I had prepared started to overflow, I began putting the bills into a gallon fruit jar which was handy. King came dashing into the house to get a drink of water for a customer and he saw the jar there. "A whole gallon of money?" he said.

When Melissa was two we sold 166 bushels of apples, but only 25 of peaches because of a hard freeze when the trees were in full bloom. Two years later we had 350 bushels of apples and 176 of peaches. Shelled corn was $3.05 per hundred pounds.

The year Melissa would start kindergarten all the varieties of apples were producing: Lodi, Summer Champion, Jonathan, Golden Delicious, Red Delicious and Winesap. We had 565 bushels of apples and 214 of peaches.

All the varieties of peaches were bearing by the time Melissa was seven: Red Haven, Belle of Georgia, Redskin and Madison. We had 740 bushels of them that year and 664 bushels of apples. And the chestnut trees put out a good crop, too.

When Melissa was nine King thought the orchard could at last make it. He retired from his job and devoted all his time to the orchard, which needed it, for each year the trees got bigger and the pruning, which must be done in the winter, got harder. The year that he retired a hard, late, killing freeze wiped out everything. The little peaches turned black in front of his eyes. Even the ends of the apple twigs turned black. He could snap them off with his fingers. He stood in the orchard in a state of shock while everything turned black around him, and his mind stayed more or less in shock for several months. The retirementplan payment was in a lump sum and it, with a bank loan, carried us into the next year, when the trees recovered and we had a crop again.

Last year Melissa was eleven. We sold 1,800 bushels of apples and about 800 bushels of peaches. The chestnut trees are taller than the house now and their foliage meets so as to make a solid shade roof over the patio, which is covered with chestnuts in the autumn. Corn was up to $6.00 for 100 pounds.

Roy and Darlene Hackett had many separations, and the year that Melissa started kindergarten they split up for good. Both of them made other associations, with whom they each had other children. Roy brought Marilyn and Robbie to Grace Hickerson again and left them. This time, though, Grace had a house of her own, her property settlement having been concluded. "I guess," she said, "I've got these children to raise." She said Roy told her it was too bad they hadn't left them with us in the first place.